A Necessary Distance

Also by Julie Salverson

Nonfiction
Community Engaged Theatre and Performance (editor)
Lines of Flight: An Atomic Memoir
Popular Political Theatre and Performance (editor)
When Words Sing: Seven Canadian Libretti (editor)

Plays
Beyond the End of Your Nose (with Patricia Henderson)
Boom (with Patricia Fraser)
The Pied Piper Returns
Thumbelina
Woyzeck on the Boulevard of Broken Dreams

A Necessary Distance

Confessions of a Scriptwriter's Daughter

Julie Salverson

WOLSAK & WYNN

© Julie Salverson, 2024

No part of this publication may be reproduced, stored in a retrieval system or transmitted, in any form or by any means, without the prior written consent of the publisher or a license from the Canadian Copyright Licensing Agency (Access Copyright). For an Access Copyright license, visit www.accesscopyright.ca or call toll free to 1-800-893-5777.

Published by Wolsak and Wynn Publishers
280 James Street North
Hamilton, ON L8R2L3
www.wolsakandwynn.ca

Editor: Noelle Allen | Copy editor: Megan Beadle
Cover and interior design: Marijke Friesen
Family photo on the cover of the book: George Salverson; daughter, Julie; and son, Scott. 1958, Toronto.
Author photograph: Bill Penner
Typeset in Minion Pro
Printed by Brant Service Press Ltd., Brantford, Canada

10 9 8 7 6 5 4 3 2 1

The publisher gratefully acknowledges the support of the Canada Council for the Arts and the Ontario Arts Council. We also acknowledge the financial support of the Government of Canada through the Canada Book Fund and the Government of Ontario through the Ontario Book Publishing Tax Credit and Ontario Creates.

Library and Archives Canada Cataloguing in Publication

Title: A necessary distance : confessions of a scriptwriter's daughter / Julie Salverson.
Names: Salverson, Julie, author.
Description: Includes bibliographical references.
Identifiers: Canadiana 20240460200 | ISBN 9781998408085 (softcover)
Subjects: LCSH: Salverson, George. | LCSH: Salverson, George—Travel. | LCSH: Salverson, Julie—Family. | LCSH: Radio writers—Canada—Biography. | LCSH: Television writers—Canada—Biography. | LCGFT: Biographies. | LCGFT: Autobiographies.
Classification: LCC PN1992.4.S35 S35 2024 | DDC 808.2/2092—dc23

For my brother, Scott.

Individual citizens are internally plural: they have within them the full range of behavioral possibilities. They are like complex musical scores from which certain melodies can be teased out and others ignored or suppressed, depending, at least in part, on who is doing the conducting.
– Zadie Smith, "On Optimism and Despair"

As a radio writer, I could do anything. You start nowhere and end up with everything.

Ok – away we go!
– George Salverson

FOREWORD

I find it hard to describe my first reading of *A Necessary Distance*. It is layered, full of deep inquiry and complex struggle. I was caught from the beginning and I shortly sent a note to the author saying I was experiencing "joy, worry, sadness, enlightenment, memories – glorious exhilarating times." I found it impossible not to think about the troubling questions the book was raising and I also often felt like I was among significant people, acquaintances I hadn't really known before.

There are now few people alive who knew her father, but I did, if only casually. My connection begins about forty years ago when my wife and I moved to a village where George and his wife, Sandra, had lived. By the time of our arrival they had moved away but fortunately for us they returned occasionally to visit friends, who were now our friends. I remember vigorous discussions about the arts, culture and, always, social and political concerns. We rarely, if ever, talked about George's career or Sandra's, that "glamorous actress in the silver blouse," a leading performer in CBC Radio's "golden age." My awareness from teaching "CanLit" years earlier didn't make a connection between George and Governor General's Award winner Laura Goodman Salverson. Other matters took focus. As a result, it was only from my Canadian theatre study that I learned about the man who had written many plays for CBC Radio by the late 1950s and whose documentary and extensive television credits continued to grow into the 1980s. I, like millions of others, had often seen his work without knowing he was the writer.

Their daughter, Julie, was not with them during these visits, and although our paths crossed coincidentally in the Toronto

/ ix

theatre scene, I was surprised when she showed up in a graduate class I offered at the University of Toronto. Her reputation as a creative professional outside the mainstream, a playwright/animator, founder of Second Look Community Arts Resource and Flying Blind Theatre, who was helping people deal with social and other disruptions through what was then called "Popular Theatre," preceded my meeting her. Needless to say, I was delighted when she came to Queen's and became my academic colleague and friend. Her exceptional breadth and depth of knowledge have fostered a wisdom that she shares readily and that has guided my thinking on countless occasions. Her publications and plays are rich in understanding and critical insight.

From its resonant title to the very end, *A Necessary Distance* explores the life process of learning to live with our inheritance, what we discover, what is strange, provokes fear, misunderstanding, the "things we don't have a language for." Julie's method is complex, much like that in *Lines of Flight*, her astonishing account of the journey she took, both literally and internally, following the path of the uranium mined in Northern Ontario on its way to the bombing of Japan in 1945. As she makes that journey, she examines the damages, the everyday fallout, if you will, the implications both at the time and since, and powerfully urges us to consider responsibility and the future of civilization. In a similar manner, in *A Necessary Distance* she traces and describes her father's actual journey and his internal one. She sensitively but critically considers his grappling with unfamiliar worlds and unfamiliar ways of living that challenge his values, his views of people, in fact, of whole cultures. And she shows us his courage – that he is willing to accept those challenges that leave him struggling with the profound question "How do I tell my friends and my wife what I now believe?"

A NECESSARY DISTANCE / *xi*

At the same time, Julie intensely examines her own life and values, her day-to-day understanding of her father, what he was and stood for, all of which shifts when she reads the notebooks, just as life shifted for him on his remarkable film trip. As readers, we are drawn into facing many of the same questions about our own life journeys and the values we carry with us. It is a profoundly unsettling but profoundly rewarding experience.

How does she do it? As her successful career as a playwright and animator shows, she possesses a true dramatist's control of a complex story. She has consummate skill in relating an incident, something her father saw or said, and then exploring it in relation to her own experience, values and (mis)understandings. It is a dramatic conflict that allows today's world, war-torn, chaotic and becoming aware of life and lives beyond boundaries, to look at itself in light of its inheritance from the "Freedom from Hunger" world of 1963, war-torn, chaotic and in need of compassion, understanding and action. The hunger that George's film was documenting has not gone away nor have the difficulties cultures and individuals face in forming an ameliorative awareness of the so-called "other," of life and lives beyond existing boundaries.

As readers, we will face some of that same dramatic conflict and struggle for answers at a personal and larger level, just as Julie and her father did. Her method and revelations will ask us, implicitly if not directly, how are we dealing with what we carry with us, what will we do with that inheritance in our day-to-day life and how will we carry all that into the future?

– Richard Plant

CHAPTER ONE

A Gentle Guy

In 1963, when I was seven and he was forty-six, my father left home to travel the world. It was probably his first time on an airplane. When he died in 2005, he left only a few boxes of possessions. Nine years later I got up the nerve to open them. Dad had thrown away most of his over one thousand radio and television scripts, but I found a large binder containing seven handwritten notebooks: his moment-by-moment account of the film shoot that took him to fifteen countries, including Japan, Kenya, Indonesia, India and Brazil.

George Salverson, an award-winning radio and documentary writer, was part of a team shooting a documentary in 1963 for the United Nations' Food and Agriculture Organization (FAO). The project was commissioned to accompany the Freedom from Hunger Campaign, a major international initiative launched in 1961. The notebooks are on delicate paper and the writing is deeply personal. My father is candid about his assumptions, his fears and his continually challenged expectations. He begins the trip believing all people are the same under the skin. He is a 1960s' journalist, committed to objectivity. He is a universalist and a liberal. At the end of the trip, he writes that people are profoundly different: "How do I tell my friends and my wife what I now believe?" I decipher the

/ 1

scratches of pencil marks. Already they tell me this is not the man I thought I knew. I hope they will lead me to my father.

How do we live with people? How do we escape them? Hard enough without bringing blood into it. I'm part Icelandic and Norwegian, my ancestors murdered each other for centuries. The smart ones sailed away, burned the letters, misplaced the photos. "I'm allergic to family," said novelist Patricia Highsmith, who wrote psychological thrillers. I recognize myself in these words. And yet.

My dad called himself a hack. He'd write for anybody if it paid the bills. He accomplished this well enough to marry, raise two children and leave a considerable legacy in Canadian television and radio. He understood this problem of living with people. He was an only child of difficult parents. Maybe there aren't any other kind. His mother, Laura Goodman Salverson, wrote an autobiography that won the Governor General's Award in 1939; in it, she makes only one reference to her son: "There is nothing to say of my baby, except that the prospect bored me." My father understood the attraction of solo flight. On this trip, however, he had two gregarious companions.

Gene Lawrence was a director and producer based in Vancouver. He worked with my dad a lot, but I can't find anything much about him. He was committed to justice and adventure and he produced the film. He made it happen.

Gene expended a considerable effort to get Grahame Woods as cinematographer and cameraman. Grahame was English born, had been in Toronto eight years and said he preferred Canada. From Dad's notebooks:

There had been some difficulty because of CBC's priority system for such assignments – rotation. But, said Gene, some of the people are such duds – so he insisted on Grahame.

A NECESSARY DISTANCE / 3

Grahame said he couldn't get the seventeen dollars per diem because of his union. Gene is annoyed. But anyone else can get it. Script girls, stenos. Afraid to set a precedent with the union. Cameraman's union? Find out. So Grahame travels on fifteen dollars per diem.

The first thing I remember of my father's trip around the world is mashed peas. Shortly after returning home he fell ill. There were mysterious conversations in the hallway outside my parents' room and an unprecedented home visit by Dr. Vale, our family doctor. Dad had contracted hepatitis in Jakarta. He was sentenced to bedrest and a diet of peas, which I would prepare by mixing the canned vegetables into a grey medicine. This all seemed very glamorous – the abrupt departure three months before, the colourful postcards with exotic stamps, now this mysterious illness. Nobody in our family, and nobody we spoke to during that time, had even heard of Jakarta.

If you think about it, the trip was an iconic colonial enterprise. A group of white men from the First World fly to the Third, with padded seats and per diems, to make a documentary about world hunger. To find out what's wrong over there. I suspect there was pretty much a complete lack of self-criticism about the level of consumption back home. But I might be wrong because I haven't read my father's journals yet.

Now in 2014, Dad's seven battered black-covered notebooks pulse in the corner of my study. I can't bring myself to read past the beginning and a few sporadic pages, glimpses of the trip. The cultural moment in which I open these pages is a murky surface that separates me from the water in which he swam. What is a first impression? An unexamined look before analysis. The brain is hasty, in a split second it recognizes and files away information that shocks or calms, provokes or reassures.

4 / JULIE SALVERSON

First responses:

1. The books vibrate with energy, movement. The man is present.

2. He is private, careful about the level of sharing with his colleagues. It is only with his notebooks that he shares his increasing discomfort as his perceptions of his fellow humans change. These are not the notes he would have been making about the script; those I presume are lost or, more likely, became the script and were discarded once editing was done.

3. What are my responsibilities to his privacy? Does blood lineage allow me a certain permission? The notebooks feel like an inheritance, an imperative – one that must be honoured. And I'm not looking *back*, tracing my ancestry, that has never interested me. The direction is different, the notebooks reach *forward* and make a claim. Do I seal them away, preserve them? Or do I break them open, seed them into a story?

It is already too late. I am a witness now.

I read a short section that Dad wrote in Nairobi. He has come from Jakarta and is in the capital a few days before flying to the Serengeti. I am impressed with his candour and honesty. He is distressed at his reactions as a foreigner. He observes how his Scandinavian background shapes his responses to this environment. He reflects astutely on what he brings to the process of steadying himself as he spins off-centre in his new surroundings. As I read, he comes into view across the years. Opening his veins and revealing himself. Thinking, of course, that nobody will read it. Although a few comments suggest that, well, somebody might. He is, after all, a professional writer. He is used to an audience.

On January 16, 1963, he sets out with Gene and Grahame. From then until a Saturday evening in 2005, when he turned to open a bottle of rum and fell dead to the floor of his downtown Toronto apartment, he kept the notebooks. He kept them despite a lifetime habit of economy, despite often throwing out what he was sure nobody would want and despite a habit of disregarding the past as surely as his Icelandic grandparents had turned their faces toward a new country. "We are Canadians," his aunt Dora told him in 1921. "This is our country now. We learn its ways and give it our labour."

Each time my family moved, each time my father emptied his files, he kept the notebooks. They held something he wasn't prepared to let go of. Something he didn't want to forget. Perhaps he wanted someone to know. Of the over one thousand scripts my father wrote, of all the projects of a lifetime, it was this story that he kept.

At this thought, I get a glimpse of what I want to offer him. I decide to write the story of encountering my father through reading his journals. What will I find? Can I present him as an honest man living in 1963, stumbling through the territory of newness, of his own disorientation, to show how he sees worlds he is meeting for the first time? The heart of my father's blind spots and vulnerability then, meeting the times I am living in now.

I would like to invite him into the future.

On a bright spring day, I sit in a coffee shop and count my father's age on my fingers. A life in numbers:

1916. Birth. A story in itself. It bears telling.

1926. Ten. Poverty in Western Canada, a railroader's son.

1936. Twenty. A young man at his mother's reading and political discussion salons in Edmonton. Four years later he is announcing the news over a radio microphone in Flin Flon, Manitoba. Hired because he was the only applicant who even *knew* someone who wrote (his mother).

1946. Thirty. Loses hearing in one ear on a ferry to the Toronto Islands. In pursuit of my mother, the glamorous actress in the silver blouse.

1956. Forty. The first story editor for CBC Television drama. With a six-month-old daughter, his first child. Me.

1966. Fifty. I don't know what signpost marked the fiftieth year, but my brother, mother and I surprised Dad on his birthday with a pogo stick. The solid weight of him rose and fell through fifty jumps, steady and sure on the steps of our newly rented Rosedale Toronto duplex. My parents could afford it for precisely one year until my mother's soap opera, *Moment of Truth*, was cancelled. They then fled, children and pets in tow, to a slightly cheaper neighbourhood across St. Clair Avenue; two years later, defeated by even those prices, they moved us to a country village.

1976. Sixty. I am twenty, already escaped to university, my father a swirl of scripts, college teaching, alcohol-infused fists through walls and the award-winning drama of all our lives, "Sandra." This is how he types her name in the journals I find from those years, the mid-'70s, when my father has purchased a new typewriter and begun a daily habit of learning the keys by typing the day's events. No longer by hand, as during his 1963 trip. Now neat rows defy the abrupt implosions of content.

1986. Seventy. No idea. I am long gone.

1996. Eighty. We – I, really – throw him a surprise birthday party at Free Times Cafe on College Street. He is delighted and gracious. His frame is still tall and solid. He and many friends of his vintage

A NECESSARY DISTANCE / 7

(Tom Harvey, Alfie Scopp) have energy, health. There is bulk on the frame that will shrink over the coming decade. Eighty to ninety is a long time. Perhaps the longest time. My dad almost makes it through. In this decade, my mother dies.

2006. A year after his death, the grieving is still sharp.

So go the decades of a man's life.

I am surprised to cry. In a noisy coffee shop. Behind the counter the café's young owner makes lattes; his hair is tied back with an elastic and he wears a black-and-white-striped T-shirt. A thin woman in a bulky coat cradles an infant as she sips her coffee. Several people sit alone, hunched over computers. At the next table, three young men are in earnest conversation.

I scribble these notes and there is something familiar about them. Their voices. They remind me of my father's. The tears stop. So. This is what it will be like.

Dad's Title: *Around the World, 1963*
My title: *A Necessary Distance*

A Radio Man

My father was my first competitor. He got the words down fast. Stories would spin from Dad's brain, dusting our dinner table with whimsy and adventure. The children of writers talk about the sanctity of the study, the private magical terrain of the parent's imagination. I guess I experienced some of that, but it also felt ordinary. Writing was Dad's occupation and he went to work like I supposed other parents did, except he was around. He found the job lonely, so when he carried his brown leather briefcase into the car and drove the hour to Toronto for rehearsals or meetings, those were good days.

I interviewed my father when he was eighty. The old cassette tape surfaces in a box in the basement as I'm writing this book. His voice, after almost twenty years:

My mother soaked into my head an instinct of what to do with words. She held salons to talk about ideas and writing and would sit up all night reading three books. I was six years old, learning about curtain lines. Live radio was exciting. Stimulating. You couldn't make a mistake. They drilled it into me that every word had to go on the air. For much of my life a producer would say, "Give me an idea and I'll give you a contract."

Dad often had to come up with projects in a day or two. Once he walked into a producer's office in Toronto. "I'd like a few days to develop this idea some more." The man looked at him for a moment. "Oh, come on, George. You know you just write it."

Radio dramas in Canada by the CBC (Canadian Broadcasting Corporation) had a one-week incubation period in the 1940s and '50s. Every Tuesday, Dad drove to the studio and pitched his idea to the producer. Wednesday through Friday he wrote the script. Saturday, he drove back for rehearsals, a read-through in the morning and rehearsal with full orchestra in the afternoon, conducted by Lucio Agostini or Morris Surdin. Sunday, they broadcast live. Monday was his "day off" when he puttered around the house musing story ideas, and Tuesday it began all over again. He would have been astonished at our astonishment at this level of achievement. To him it was a job. He said he was a journeyman not an artist, but I don't think semantics mattered to him. He was dismissive of notions like "writer's block" or "finding the muse." He had bills to pay and storytelling did the job. My father was the proverbial bum in the seat, words on the page kind of guy. I wish I had learned his talent for routine.

A NECESSARY DISTANCE / 9

Early television was also live. Dad was one of the first to write for the medium. It was a new art form; nobody in the world was ahead of them. My father told of an ACTRA (Alliance of Canadian Cinema, Television and Radio Artists) meeting where five members sat around a table and a writer from Halifax asked, "Shouldn't we wait until everyone is here?" The ACTRA rep replied, "You are."

My neighbour has lived in Canada most of her adult life and teaches renaissance drama at Queen's University. I send her a photo of my mother with actor Lorne Greene of the American western *Bonanza* fame; it's a publicity shot for *Othello* at CBC sometime in the forties. Greene is in "dark" makeup. It is shocking now but was normal then. My neighbour writes: "I don't know a thing about Canadian culture before the '70s except what my mother remembered. She used to talk about Christopher Plummer because he acted in Ottawa and Lorne Greene – one of them had a Queen's connection, right?"

I text back, "It was Greene who went to Queen's. He was born a Russian Jew in Canada and called Chaim at home in Ottawa." I tell her the books piled on my desk are full of people who were at our dining-room table. Lots of Scotch. Late nights after shows. "Mom . . . and the CBC *Stage* . . . did Shakespeare, Ibsen and adaptations of classics. In the '40s my mom played leads, usually opposite John Drainie. She had too much success too fast. That and other things undid her, but she was famous for a while. In that world and on the air."

In the 1920s Canadian radio was virtually indistinguishable from everything American, and the drama relied primarily on scripts from traditional theatre. Audiences listened to touring American and British companies. It took an ardent group of visionaries – in particular Graham Spry and Alan Plaunt – to rally for the establishment of the Canadian Radio Broadcasting Commission (1932), which four years later became the CBC. Immediately the

Corp, as people continue to call it, was caught between a philosophy of educating and uplifting. Lord Reith in Britain thought of audiences in terms of a church congregation, but others preferred fast-paced commercial entertainment, meaning American. In the 1996 book *A Dream Betrayed*, former CBC president Tony Manera writes: "For commercial broadcasting, audiences represent consumers to be delivered to advertisers; for public broadcasting, audiences are made up of citizens whose interests must be served."

The Drama department was established in 1938 and for three decades enjoyed an international reputation, winning rave reviews in the *New York Times* from critic Jack Gould and at home from the likes of Nathan Cohen and Herb Whittaker. With the Depression and then the outbreak of war in Europe, live theatres were closed or turned into movie houses, and radio became the main professional outlet for Canadian dramatists and actors. At one point CBC *Stage* was second in popularity only to *Hockey Night in Canada*.

My neighbour grew up in America, but Canadians don't know about this history either. Where would we learn it?

Scenes from a Marriage

When Scott and I were young we would climb onto our parents' bed, eat sardines and Cheezies and watch the *Academy Awards*. I don't remember them touching.

I once asked my mother why she married him. "I wanted children. He was reliable." We were entering an apartment building to visit someone. I stopped outside the front door, hoping for more. She went inside ahead of me and pressed the elevator button.

The confidences from my mother as I grew up were intermittent and had an intimate desperation. Raw glimpses that left most of the story hidden. A song they made up together and sang on their road trips through Quebec, trips that preceded us kids. An

A NECESSARY DISTANCE / 11

affair during the shoot of a film (Walt Disney's *The Incredible Journey*), in tears confessing to my father when she got home. "Is it important?" he asked. "Of course not," she sobbed. "Then it's fine," was all he said. Did he want to say more? Did she want more from him? Did his perceived calm bewilder her, infuriate her or was it reassuring?

I call Cheryl, partner of our life-long friend, actor Alfie Scopp. Alfie has moved into the veteran's home at Sunnybrook Hospital. He is one hundred and one. My mother would roll her eyes. "Alfie got away with hell and he's outliving us all." I love the story about how Mom and Alfie met. The young actor was hired for an early CBC *Stage* and everyone was sitting in the studio waiting for the director, Andrew Allan. A door at the back opened and Allan strode down the aisle, with my mother elegantly floating behind him. Alfie piped up from the back row, "Great legs!" After Mom and Andrew broke up, she and Alfie dated for a while. Mom's father, Bert, objected – Alfie was Jewish. That was the week Mom moved out of her parents' house.

When I was a teenager, Alfie took me to music clubs on the Danforth in Toronto and we'd sit for hours listening to bands of immigrants from all over the world. I didn't know the languages but would disappear into the dark mysterious harmonies. The world was bigger than my family. I sit listening now to the soft voice of his long-time Japanese Canadian partner on the phone.

"It's hard," Cheryl says. "But they look after him so well and he has adjusted. He likes it there." I tell her about the book I'm writing, that it's about Dad. "Oh my," she says.

"Could I ask you about him?" I'm hesitant, I haven't talked to her in years, and now after only five minutes I'm wanting something from her. But she doesn't seem to think I'm self-serving. Maybe she doesn't see everything in life as a transaction.

"I don't remember much. He was a quiet man."

12 / JULIE SALVERSON

"Yes," I say. "And with my mother, who wasn't."

Cheryl laughs quietly. "No, she wasn't quiet." Then, after a pause, "It must bring him back, talking to people about him, does it?"

"There aren't that many people left. There's my friend Brenda. She was the last person to see my mother alive. She visited her in the hospital, at St. Michael's. Dad was there, and then left. She saw my parents say goodbye to each other."

"Oh," says Cheryl. "Oh!"

"Brenda said Mom looked at him with so much love."

There's a pause. Cheryl sighs. "Yes. They had quite a bond. Despite . . ."

I help her out. "Despite the drama!"

"That's right. That's right, there was a lot of drama." She says it almost reluctantly, as if it's best left alone.

More notes from April 1974 to 1975. Lists of what to do. Money worries. Each venture into my dad's world causes shocks I don't expect. The mention of my name in an entry.

There is a photo of my father holding me on his lap. Tiny and wrapped in a white blanket. A black-and-white photo so maybe the blanket was colourful. Maybe it was pink, although that doesn't sound like my parents. On the other hand, my mom had so many ways she didn't fit in, perhaps she tried to make her baby daughter's clothes conform.

My father has a cigarette. The cigarette is burning because you can see so much ash. When and if it does fall, it will land on my small face. I am looking up, as if fascinated by the lengthening ash. If my father moves his arm, the ash will fall. If he adjusts the baby, the ash will fall. We wait there, me, my dad and his cigarette.

Who was my father when he wrote these journals? The man my mother begged to travel to Europe with her and wouldn't. Who once "punished" my brother and me with bread and water

A NECESSARY DISTANCE / *13*

but turned it into an adventure by taking us to the local bakery to slather butter over freshly baked loaves. Who cancelled boat tickets at the last minute for our family to go to Europe because he lost his nerve – probably money worries.

I have a small brass bird that used to hang by the door in Dad's apartment. He put every new bill there and paid it immediately. No debts, no obligations, no baggage.

In the last years of my parents' lives together they inhabited a two-bedroom apartment on the ninth floor of the newly built Performing Arts Lodges in Toronto. This is a home for old showbiz types without much money. My parents had their own bedrooms. Dad's was almost empty. He always joked he could move in twenty-four hours if he had to. The bags and boxes of accumulated emotions were my mother's. It's as if he married her to add weight to his thin frame. I find myself wondering what stuck to my father, what he carried. What did he have room for, in a life shared with the whirlwind that was Sandra?

Another entry:

January 6, 1965: "Sandra's Soap."
Today Sandra got job she didn't want (she said) on soap show "Moment of Truth." She was delighted by praise of American producer "Maxwell" and couldn't refuse. But it seems a good deal. Seven shows! Talk of a contract for two years. She wants to save the money to go to Europe and told them so. They think it will work out.

Mom is in her early forties. I try to imagine her girlish excitement, bursting with her dream of Europe. She never kept her cards near her chest, she never dissembled and she expected everyone to share her good will.

14 / JULIE SALVERSON

I read a bit further:

So we had a drinking party, all gaiety. To bed, S in elegant nightie and hair done up. Myself, blotted out with exhaustion.

All my dad's Christmas gifts need to be returned: a can opener that doesn't work, a chafing dish the wrong size. Then:

Thursday, January 7
We woke quarrelling. Resented cross-examination as to how I deal with Mitchell Investors, also big quarrel with Julie and Scott, over her missing glove and lunch box and new $4.50 hat from Holt Renfrew, which she refuses to wear. Only Scott got out the door unscathed and happy. The rest of us burning with unhappiness.

I sit back. Check the front of the notebook. The first two pages, *Please return to address* and address crossed out, replaced by Crescent Road, where we lived for one year in Rosedale. We moved there because of the money from the soap opera. Trip to Europe seems to have been replaced by upscale neighbourhood. Then names and phone numbers.

I look again at the date: January 7, 1965. I'm surprised, I'd thought I was a teenager refusing to wear a hat. From a store nobody in our family could afford – who was she hoping to impress, what dream made her buy something there for her daughter? And then I realize – I'm ten. No, nine. Not even ten. And she is enraged because I lost a glove, a lunch box, and won't wear a hat.

Mom was an emotional person with an enormous personality. She didn't do things halfway. I have few memories of them buying theatre tickets, but in February of 1962 she reserved two seats for her favourite singer, Judy Garland, and presented one to me. We

A NECESSARY DISTANCE / 15

left the suburbs in freezing rain, and Mom did not drive carefully. Sandra was late and she was excited. As we careened down Yonge Street a siren wailed and a police car pulled us over. When the young cop gestured to Mom to roll down her window, she did so frantically, yelling, "You can't give me a ticket! We're going to see *Judy*!" We got to the O'Keefe Centre in time and years later, listening to a recording of Garland's week in Toronto, I hear a raucous shout from somewhere in the balcony and I would swear it's my mother. She once recorded herself singing "Everything's Coming Up Roses" from the musical *Gypsy* and shared it around to friends. She absolutely could have played the part – she was Mama Rose and then some.

When this book is almost finished, I tell my husband how in high school we lived in the country and in terrible winter weather – freezing rain, snowstorms – Dad would not make the half-hour drive to get me to an evening play or choir rehearsal. My mother always did. "She'd have done anything for me," I say. And then I sit back. "I have to put that in the book."

The Story Guy

My father was an only child, a shy lonely boy. His mother was absorbed in her writing and the family moved numerous times with George Senior's successive railroad jobs. In my interview with him, he described the world around his mother: "She became a professional writer when I was six. Then she wrote a big novel and as a consequence the house was full of people who wanted to talk to her. Reporters who wanted tips about how to do it, and actors, professors, all sorts. Culture was interested in my mother. She would set up salons and I would listen."

He was thirteen when the stock market crashed. Imaginative, making up stories until his death, the last ones published in the newsletter at the Performing Arts Lodges where he lived. Where he wrote *Around the World in Eighty Limericks*.

In Vienna it's best to avoid
Too much attention to Freud:
If you blame your defects
On Mother and Sex
Your friends will get quickly annoyed.

The first stories Dad remembers learning to read were Camelot stories by Tennyson, "so I thought I'd try my own. I wrote a poem and wrapped it up and hung it on the Christmas tree for Mum." Laura must have respected his sensibilities. When Dad was eighteen, they walked together in a park in Port Arthur as his mother talked about her new book. "She needed a title to sell." Laura was amused by the prurient interests of the public to hear an author "tell all": "The trouble is, you have to have a selling title, and the things that sell today – you know, all the wicked things that people are confessing in a magazine, are called 'true confessions.' And the word 'immigrant' has a dirty connotation, it did in the old days in the West. Being the daughter of an immigrant, this must sound right. Particularly if I call it *Confessions of an Immigrant's Daughter*, I've got it about as dirty as I can. Everybody will want to know what terrible things happen in this book!"

Dad was a Depression-era kid. No jobs. In 1940, at the age of twenty-four, he began what would become his career at a radio station in Flin Flon, Manitoba, despite recording a terrible audition. "You must be wondering why we hired you? Because of your mother, you are the only person who applied who even *knows* a writer." He gamely worked the midnight shift and learned to write copy: commercials and, finally, news and drama. In later years, he told stories about how Duke McLeod, who ran the station, would have a stringer sitting at Maple Leaf Gardens in Toronto watching the hockey game. On the breaks the guy would get on the phone to Flin Flon and relay each play-by-play. The announcer in Flin Flon would pretend to be live in Toronto broadcasting the game. Dad called it Duke's "genius at faking the real."

Another story was about an ex-madam, "the boss's non-wife, part Indigenous and part Irish," Nehuska Collins. She was a good broadcaster and a "fearless leader of ladies of the night, the prostitutes being reputable members of Flin Flon society and patrons of the station." Her philosophy: "Pay the bootlegger, who takes the risks, before the butcher who won't be arrested for selling you meat." I have a file of notes Dad typed up about this in 1990. A sample:

Notes for a Play about A Remote Radio Station

Parties: Julie and George Salverson. **Discussion:** George, unable to write for present generation (a new society and language), could write for a period in his own past. Julie questioned and extracted stories about [radio station] CFAR, and persuaded George that the material could be valuable and would be willing to join a venture to create a play for stage, combining skills and talents. It was agreed with a handshake.

Ideas Mentioned:

- Horrible recorded audition: "You must wonder why we hired you?"
- Trying to teach writing: Failure to teach Tom Argue to write a commercial, despite the boss's orders.
- The girls on the hill: The prostitutes, rather reputable members of Flin Flon society, patrons of the radio station, good friends of the station's own ex-madam. Of course, also patrons of the station's own library and flower shop (good heavens, forgot to tell Julie about that – whole new scenes and situations!).

I look up Nehuska Collins. No luck, but something interesting turns up. In 2015, a cairn with a bronze plaque is unveiled at the Neighbours of the North Park in Flin Flon. It is adorned with a star blanket provided by Margaret Head-Steppan, great-great-granddaughter of David Collins, whose Cree name was Namekus. It is believed that in 1914 or 1915 this Métis trapper showed prospector Tom Creighton the outcropping of an ore body that led to the development of one of the richest mines in the country. When I look further, I find Tom Creighton credited as discoverer of the mine. I read in a story by Libby Stoker-Lavelle, "It is said that all [Creighton] ever gave Collins was $6.30 worth of flour, lard, and bulk tea."

Nehuska Collins. David Collins. The age would be right. Also the geography. Wouldn't Dad get a kick out of this!

My father left Flin Flon in 1942 after a rather embarrassing incident involving Duke McLeod, fraud and finances. He also wanted to see streetcars again. He got a job at CKRC Winnipeg running a theatre company on the air. The army wanted a series of plays about the armed forces. Then he was hired by Eaton's department store and for four years wrote, produced and directed eight hours of radio drama a week – about products! "The actors were also my researchers. Every word I wrote had to be on the air, no time for revision."

One day, CBC director Esse Ljungh was told by his girlfriend, actor Beth Lockerbie, "Guess what they've got over at CKRC. A playwright!" Ljungh commissioned Dad to write a show for New Year's Eve. Fletcher Markle from Vancouver was on his way to Toronto and stopped by to watch the live recording. He said to my father, "You're the first writer to have his first play performed in evening dress!"

Esse called my father into his office one morning. "You can stay here, but you won't get anywhere. Go to Toronto, buy yourself

A NECESSARY DISTANCE / 19

a thousand dollars worth of furniture and wait for the phone to ring." In 1948, he took the plunge to try his hand in the big leagues of national radio. His first show for producer Andrew Allan was an adaptation of *Dracula*.

"I was fresh from commercial drama," Dad says in an interview I found at the Library and Archives Canada. "You learn not to upset anybody. I wrote a draft and Andrew said, 'It's okay. But isn't it supposed to be a horror story, George?' 'Well, yes.' 'Then let's make it horrible!'"

Values

Any characterization of Canadians in those days will inevitably leave people out, but many of the listeners weren't wealthy. As far as radio reached, it gave its listeners a sense of belonging, whether they were isolated families on prairie farms or in coastal fishing villages. Dad was thrilled to be part of that.

One of the CBC dramas he was most proud of wasn't his. *The Investigator* starred John Drainie as Joseph McCarthy, the vicious and virulent senator from Wisconsin. It was denounced as communist propaganda by American television host Ed Sullivan and became an underground hit during the chilling days of the "Red Scare." To my father, speaking out against bullies was essential and radio had the means to do it.

One of his favourite films, *The Front*, is the story of a bookkeeper who fronts as a writer for a group of men prevented from working by McCarthy's purges. The screenwriter was formerly blacklisted Walter Bernstein and the film, starring Woody Allen, features several blacklisted actors, including the luminous Zero Mostel. Twisted comedy in a time of mass hysteria and finger-pointing. Dad despised people who went along with the crowd. The worst word in his vocabulary was "quisling," meaning someone who betrays his friends. Dad was part Norwegian, and the word comes

20 / JULIE SALVERSON

from the surname of a Norwegian World War II leader, Vidkun Quisling, who collaborated with the Nazis.

I don't remember which meltdown it was, over which boyfriend. I was sitting in the kitchen of a third-floor stifling Toronto apartment. I can see Dad across from me, cold cup of tea in front of him, worry on his face. Telling me the story of Quisling. Saying it was the most despicable thing a person could do, to betray a friend, or even a stranger. To not stand up for someone. His values were personal, face to face, not prescribed or inscribed in any document, oratory or, for that matter, screenplay. I think his integrity is present in his writing, but the measure of it, to him, was how you treated other people. He was capable of bitter condemnation and pitiless dismissal. In one of the Icelandic sagas, two families quarrel for two hundred years. Two hundred years wasn't long enough for some of my father's disdain. That August afternoon, where the humidity soaked our clothes and added to the perspiration on my father's forehead, he told me why the boy in question – he did not deign to call him a man – was not worth my tears. Or his time. It was a lesson it took me decades to learn.

A call from Stacey Stewart Curtis. Our mothers were actresses together. We met as small children and she is one of the few people living who knew my father. Did she remember anything about Dad? She is talking on speakerphone while driving back to her cottage a few hours north of Toronto.

She takes a breath. "I remember the lovely softness of his face." I sit back. What a thing to say. "And he had curious eyes. He was always interested. He was busy, with his writing, you didn't see him often, but when you did he was always open to you, not someone who ever shut you out. It's a nice quality," she says.

Stacey took my dad's writing class at Ryerson in the seventies before becoming a television and film director. "I never thought I'd be much of a writer. But I wanted to try, and he was . . . He

A NECESSARY DISTANCE / *21*

was always very generous and kind, but also clear about where my writing was good and where I had dropped the ball. I don't . . . [here she laughs] I don't take criticism very well and I don't remember being affronted or upset. I had an idea and a tone, and he told me I'd captured what I was chasing. But in that class I fell into the trap of coming up with an easy answer. I was looking at a difficult situation, and I skirted the issue and tried to come up with a fast way to end it. He didn't let me, he pushed me to keep looking for what I really wanted."

I tell her, "Because I'm living with these notebooks, I'm thinking so much about the dead. And aging – mine, my friends, the cats, my horse."

"We will be completely gone in thirty, forty years," she says. I tell her I'm reading Hilary Mantel's trilogy about Thomas Cromwell. England in the 1530s. "All these people living complicated lives; their fury, their delight, their passion, their desperation. Don't they know what's coming?"

And of course, everybody in Dad's journals is dead. The farmers and staff they meet in each country. The animals they see. And Dad, who lived for forty-two years after that journey.

April 2005. Newspapers piled up outside his door. He hadn't answered his phone. I'd meant to stop by on the Friday, when I got back from a trip. I'd meant to tell him then, in person, that Bill and I were going to get married. But I was tired when I landed at the Toronto airport, so I took a bus right to my fiancé's apartment. I called through the weekend, but no answer. It wasn't until Monday that I rang the buzzer of his apartment at the Performing Arts Lodges in Toronto. No answer.

CHAPTER TWO

Departure

January 1963:

- Japan airs its first televised manga series, *Astro Boy*.

- Thirty-two Soviet citizens from Siberia seek refuge in the US Embassy in Moscow, claiming political asylum as persecuted Christians. They are refused and the group, including fourteen children, are put on a bus and taken away by Moscow police.

- *Camelot* closes on Broadway. It is a musical starring Richard Burton as King Arthur, Julie Andrews as Guinevere and Robert Goulet as Lancelot. Goulet is Canadian and a friend of my parents. He greets me backstage with a kiss on the cheek. I don't wash my face for a week.

- In China, an eighteen-year-old fisherman and his seven-year-old brother are fatally injured after the man took home a piece of radioactive cobalt-60 that had somehow been dropped on farmland owned by the Anhui Agricultural University in Hefei.

- The Rolling Stones play together for the first time as a group at the Flamingo Club in London's West End.

A NECESSARY DISTANCE / *23*

- US attorney general Robert F. Kennedy makes his last appearance as a lawyer in a courtroom.

- A Boeing B-52C Stratofortress US Air Force bomber carrying two nuclear weapons loses its vertical stabilizer in turbulence. The plane breaks up in mid-air and crashes into the Elephant Mountain in Piscataquis County, Maine. Seven of the nine-man crew are killed. One of the unarmed nuclear bombs falls from the plane and breaks apart on impact on a farm. A part of that bomb, containing enriched uranium, is never located.

- Canadian prime minister Diefenbaker addresses the House of Commons as to whether Canada will accept nuclear weapons for its combat aircraft. The Canadian Press writes: "At no point in his two-hour speech did Mr. Diefenbaker say definitely whether Canada has rejected or accepted a nuclear role for Canadian forces."

- African American student Harvey Gantt enters Clemson University in South Carolina, the last US state to hold out against racial integration.

- American poet Robert Frost dies.

- Suzanne Farrell, muse of choreographer George Balanchine, dances her farewell performance, the waltz in *Vienna Waltzes* at Lincoln Centre.

- Soviet premier Nikita Khrushchev visits the Berlin Wall from the east side and delivers an address at a meeting of the Socialist Unity Party of Germany (SED). He states bluntly that the Wall had accomplished its purpose of stemming the exodus of citizens from the nation and stabilizing the East German economy. Further

Soviet economic assistance, he tells his audience, will not be forthcoming. "Neither God nor the devil will give you bread or butter if you do not manage it with your own hands." He adds that East Germany "must not expect alms from some rich uncle."

In Toronto, George Salverson, Gene Lawrence and Grahame Woods board an American Airlines Vanguard jet for Chicago, en route to Tokyo. Assignment: a thirty-minute documentary on world hunger. It is an icy winter day, but they have no problem getting to the airport. My father notes that he was "shocked and alarmed to see Sandra's face at the moment of goodbye, outside terminal building. Wouldn't let her and children come inside. Eyes upset me. Depth of emotion disturbing. Suddenly felt it was wrong, two people to be parted. Felt a new realization of lives in common, different from feelings about children, who are temporary comrades."

A Writer's Life

I have a handful of personal notebooks that are separate from Dad's trip in 1963. He titles them *Logs and Journals*. He wrote to keep track of, well, his preoccupations. How many men do that? Notes about Mum, money worries, script ideas, teaching exercises, all jumbled together. I open the first two pages:

Journal. Special notes, 1972.

"A call about the Corwin Series: he loves The Name of the Dog Is Murder. But is afraid of the dog. Will call in ten days to let me know."

"Doing accounts. Horrified by the money situation."

After a few lines about projects to "make money fast," he says: "'Held' a thousand dollars loaned to Sandra by Bert [her dad] over the Xmas season. We didn't use it. In red a few dollars one day but only in my own book."

A NECESSARY DISTANCE / 25

A thousand dollars. That's a lot of money now and was more in 1972. Then January 2. I glance up to the top of the yellowed page:

After a severe bout of illness, Sandra "quit drinking."

This will be fun. This I know something about.

Another notebook, 1968. Much of the writing is incomprehensible, a jumble of meetings, script ideas, phone calls peppered with family comments and budgets. Possible shows, invitations to shows. At one point, he commends director Paul Almond for being one of the few who doesn't leave him hanging; he returns calls and praises a good idea. Almond directed *Hatch's Mill*, a show Dad wrote episodes for in 1967. It was set in the 1830s and told the story of Noah Hatch (Robert Christie), who ran a mill and a general store and was the community's judge. It was a Canadian Centennial project, a series about settlers that ran ten episodes. I wonder how it would look now, through our emerging understanding of the colonial gaze. I think Dad may have created the show. I google "who created *Hatch's Mill*?" and up pops Dad's name and a photo. I love the photo. He looks like a gentle guy. He was a gentle guy.

The journal also mentions *The Littlest Hobo*, a hit about a wandering German shepherd dog and his adventures. Dad was on this one from the beginning too. It was our bread and butter while it ran. Not much butter. The show began in 1963, same year as this trip around the world. It ran until 1965 and was syndicated, which means it played simultaneously in several countries, including the UK, US, Australia and New Zealand. It was revived from 1979 to 1985 and had six seasons. I visited the set and was thrilled to pet the show's four-legged star and meet his trainer, Chuck Eisenmann. My dad is not mentioned as a writer when I google this, it takes some work to find him. He was never good at making sure his name went into history books.

Every few pages there is another budget, trying to juggle payments, make the bills. This reads as a chronicle of making a living as a writer in Canada in the seventies but, really, anytime. I find a thin typed sheet of paper dated in the early fifties. It is from my grandmother to the Writers' Union of Canada. She is asking for help to pay the rent. She apologizes for asking. She is not a part-time amateur writer, not even a vaguely published one. She was the first woman to win Canada's most prestigious literary award and she ran a boarding house to pay the bills.

Dad worried constantly. He was shy, but his livelihood depended on these lunches, scouting the next script, the next paycheque. This is part of the story. What must this trip have felt like, a job that paid him for three solid months and sent him around the world? With a per diem!

I imagine my father hanging up the phone. He has a decision to make. Through the small window of his office, he watches his wife rake leaves. A stray maple escapes and catches the wind, a flash of red in the dull day. He feels a sharpening in his bones, age knocking at the door.

His friend Gene's voice is urgent. "An opportunity, George! We can shoot something important; it could save lives. You'll only be gone two months."

He sighs. Gene exaggerates. But he's a terrific producer, he could be right. Maybe they could make something that matters.

Then there's his wife. He's only ever been away from Sandra for a few nights and he'd hated it. He was lonely. And the children are young. But lately the house has felt too small; the city, even the country, too provincial. Will his life never be more than the stories in his head, the tales he weaves from the lives of others?

I imagine my father leaning back in his chair. Beside his typewriter is the book he'd pulled off the shelf, one of his mother's cherished collections of old folktales, this one from Germany. It

A NECESSARY DISTANCE / 27

lies open to the page where he'd been reading and now he notices the next sentence. He straightens. Reads again. A jolt runs through him. It's faint but it's enough. He isn't a superstitious man, in most ways not a believer, but the words decide him.

"Think of the old saying: something better than death can be found everywhere."

> People who fly the Pacific
> Like things to be pretty specific
> If the plane is to crash
> It should make a big splash
> If it doesn't, the trip is terrific.
> – George Salverson, *Around the World in Eighty Limericks*

Departures Two

I head out of town to a motel in the woods and start working from the typed journals.

The Beginning. Notebook One.

Wednesday, January 16, 1963
1:35 p.m. to Malton. Ice cold. Two cars frozen up. Chev nursed on block heater. Sandra emotional.

Picked up Dodi – ran out carrying balloons! I fired new Olympus camera at her.

Dodi Scopp, Alfie's first wife, so long ago I'd almost forgotten her. Alfie was the ladies' man, the charmer who came to the alcoholic holiday dinners and saved us with his equilibrium, with how he treated my brother, Scott, and me as people. "Alfie rocks!" my brother pronounced a few years ago. And where are those photos?

I'll have to look up Olympus cameras. Dad and actor John Drainie were the first in their crowd to buy the latest technology. I wonder how they paid for it.

Some frantic picture-taking at house, first with camera, in cold, wind, staging over ice. Feared car would quit on 401. Sure something would go wrong. But no. Surprised to arrive at airport successfully and alive.

It would have been strange for our family not to have Dad at home over those months. He went to work every day in the little study off the living room. When I was in grade one, the teacher Mrs. Hammond asked the class a question about employment.

"Julie, please tell the class where your father works."

"At home," I replied nonchalantly. Didn't everyone's? Mrs. Hammond looked confused and the other kids snickered. I tried, tentative, "My mother goes to rehearsal," but the teacher had moved on and I trailed off. Nobody was asking about our mothers.

At recess, I was cornered by a tall skinny boy, "At home means no job, everyone knows that!" Always reactive, I rammed my head into his stomach. In the principal's office, I was reprimanded for unladylike behaviour and sent home with a note. Maybe this was why early in grade one I sprang up from my desk, screamed at the top of my lungs and dashed out to fresh air and freedom. I didn't stop running until I surprised my mother by banging on our front door. I don't remember being punished, only comforted, and I can't remember anything else about grade one.

"You yelled so loud it hurt my ears," said a pretty classmate named Marie. This incident fostered a passionate friendship that lasted until we moved three years later.

It was harder for Dad to leave my mother than to leave us, the children. I think he didn't really know us.

A NECESSARY DISTANCE / *29*

Departures 3

Notebook One.

Wednesday, January 16, 1963

Mechanics of getting on plane – confirm – baggage overweight because of little cloth-covered Olivetti. Must carry it. Gene is furious because of TCA [Trans-Canada Air Lines] conformity to the letter of the law. The same girl checker (very pretty) had forced him to pay for only three pounds overweight. He took this also as an argument against females in official positions.

We pottered down to Chicago, drinks before dinner $1.00 each. Two to a customer by international agreement.

Image: Chicago Airport, Gate K3. A Negro woman in fur-trimmed suit, high-crowned yellow straw hat. Beautiful arms seem carved out of some rich mahogany. Silver nail polish glitters under the lights.

I am now Mr. 11F. A window seat. Sit and listen to rush of wind. Stewardess returns suddenly, lowers table from centre seat, sets on it large oval glass like a wineglass with ice and lemon. The glass full of ice. Separately, two tiny bottles: "Heublein Extra Dry Martini – Bottled for American Airlines." 5:40 p.m. So, to my little airborne orgy.

Nothing to see outside. Murmur of voices sporadically raised and the rushing sound. Suspension in time and space. Should I try to save my white swizzle stick topped by the flying eagle with crossed wings for the kids? Save all such souvenirs? Bring them back in a basket? Declare them?

Over Lake Michigan. Water looks like black solid rubber with frozen ripples. Then, ice floes, white geometrical islands criss-crossed by a multitude of black veins.

30 / JULIE SALVERSON

Crossing USA to Southwest for first time. Nothing seen but a faint rim at the edge of the earth and a pale blue glow blending up to the black sky. Covered wagon better?

Martini is surprisingly good. Lemon flavour coming up too strong, but the ice has done less damage than I feared, despite two ice cubes! The man next to me is reading *The Ox-Bow Incident*. The damnedest books turn up on aircraft. Now he's asleep after a double Scotch and ginger ale (or was it all ginger ale?). I'm studying the camera manual again and getting hungry.

Can't sleep. Boredom sets in pretty heavily as the jet flies on. Better get a novel for the Pacific crossing.

San Francisco. We land at night. Lights on the hills.

Now the soft night air. "Like Vancouver," murmurs Gene.

The three filmmakers spend the night in San Francisco. Dad describes in detail the hotel, the complications of arrival. The profusion of concrete ramps above and below on the freeway remind him of Roman structures waiting to become ruins. He can't sleep and lies awake devising a prayer for a character he has invented to accompany him on the trip. Dad would do this, invent characters to make a trip more fun. The characters would narrate the scene. Maybe this started as substitutes for childhood friends. Companions for a boy whose father was away with the railroad and whose mother travelled with her typewriter. Or maybe it was just that the voices in his adventures carried themselves more lightly than those in the real-life dramas and documentaries he wrote for a living.

Elmer's Prayer
My Elmer in the Chinese Red Kitchen,
Fly over me;
Salt me and pepper me;

A NECESSARY DISTANCE / 31

Guard me well:
Cook me in Heaven
And fry me in Hell.

After a brief meeting about what they will purchase in Tokyo for filming, the men depart San Francisco on Thursday morning, January 17 with Japan Air Lines (JAL). There is bad weather, in Hawaii roofs are off houses. Dad enjoys drinking sake on the plane, loves the tiny blue cup with the white base and JAL insignia (a blue bird in the circle of its own wings). He is thrilled by the food.

Great God, I can't keep up with dinner! Elaborate tray – curried rice, yellow and delicate. Boned chicken, succulent. Roll. Two salads, meticulous-tiny tomatoes, whole asparagus. Olives. Eggs. Lettuce. Two sauces. Dessert with whipped cream and wafer. Some frappé. Shrimps, candied seaweed (black), a rice delicacy, a kind of cabbage roll dipped in mustard (dozens of choices). Japanese tea from a China pot.

10:20 PST on this day on which we began a flight from Frisco. Sun is high, about an hour above the horizon in west. We chase it with only a slight disadvantage in speed. Ocean now invisible except as a sort of colourless emptiness. A profusion of small puffs of clouds catch, now slanting light with a bit of pink, and the highlight convolutions appear thus: countless human brains drifting past in some colourless preservative. Seat-weary bones lead to many of us standing in the aisle; and refreshment with Kirin Ichiban beer. The hours pile up and the food keeps coming. "Help! I'm a prisoner in a Japanese restaurant!"

Wake Island

10:40 PST. Descending to Wake Island. We have just missed a seventy-five-miles-an-hour gale. One hundred thousand

32 / JULIE SALVERSON

Puna papayas lost, ruined many groves. A new crew for this leg to Japan. Capt's voice like a wartime movie villain. As we go down, I see the sun is lower than I thought: there is a startling effect of the sudden diving down, through a red sunset, below the horizon – but the sun didn't set: we did.

Wake Island a (coral?) U in the sea. Felt an Alamo mood, recalling war. As the plane tilted down to the tiny aisle, wondered "Where'll they put us?" The "U" surrounds a lagoon. Most of one arm is a runway. It's hot, humid, like a bad August night in Toronto. There is the Federal Agency Airport. Military aircraft. We are not allowed out, but they do let us go down the gangway to stretch. Chief thought: how strange to come here in a Japanese plane. The last time I thought of Wake was the wartime news and I also recall Brian Donlevy in a film about the last stand that took place here. Certainly no place (a few bushes) for embattled soldiers to take cover.

I had a few conversations with my father about the Second World War. I know he lost friends, but no specifics. He tried twice to enlist but was turned away because he had a crooked sinus passage. A doctor told him, "I could cut it – but I recommend you do it posthumously." He played his part in Winnipeg, writing scripts full of national pride and encouragement for the troops. He once showed me a box of thin blue typed pages that were instructions for patriotic messages to include in scripts. Propaganda, he said, but with an artistic flair.

I can't explain my own life-long fascination with that war except to surmise that all of us with parents from that generation ask questions. We wonder what we would have done if people around us started banning people from jobs, taking their homes and belongings. The last thing removed from the Jews, a historian tells me, was their pets. When, if at all, would I have spoken or

A NECESSARY DISTANCE / 33

written a pamphlet or hidden a family? And then there were the Japanese and Italian Canadians, of course, interned by "us."

Wake is one of three very small islands and is north of the Japanese-held Marshall Islands. It was annexed by the US in 1899 and in 1935, Pan American Airways built a town and hotel to service their trans-Pacific China clipper flights. In early 1941, as tensions increased between the US and Japan, the Americans began to develop an airfield and fortify their defences. Four hundred marines landed on August 19, joining 1,221 workers who were completing the island's facilities and the Pan Am staff. The Japanese attacked Pearl Harbor and Wake Island on December 8. There were many fatalities and the hospital was destroyed.

The Battle of Wake Island began on the morning of December 8, 1941, at the same moment as Japanese planes began to drop bombs on Hawaii's Pearl Harbor naval and air bases. It ended with the surrender of the American forces to Japan on December 23.

It is extraordinary that an airfield not yet fully functioning, with a squadron of twelve Wildcat planes that had only arrived four days earlier, was able to withstand the Japanese attack for fifteen days. The "last stand" that my dad refers to includes a relief battalion sent and then recalled when the US commander realized there were two Japanese carriers operating in the area. By dawn of December 23, over one thousand Japanese had come ashore. The Wake forces were outnumbered two to one but continued to fight. Many prisoners were taken from the island when they were captured, but ninety-eight were kept as forced labourers.

I have a photograph of my father sitting in a suit, hatless, by an old microphone, announcing the bombing of Pearl Harbor. That puts the photo's date December 8, 1941, which makes him twenty-five years old. He was in Winnipeg by the time of the October 5, 1943, US strike on Wake that resulted in the Japanese garrison commander, Rear Admiral Sakaibara, ordering the execution of all remaining prisoners. On June 18, 1947, Sakaibara was hung for war crimes committed on the island. After the war, extensive nuclear testing was carried out in the ocean surrounding Wake.

Brian Donlevy was an Irish-born American World War I veteran who served in the Canadian army. He re-enlisted after Pearl Harbor and starred in the 1942 American film *Wake Island*. The movie's co-star was Robert Preston (of *The Music Man* fame). This was the first realistic drama made about the war.

Dad, Gene and Grahame pass the international date line at 8:40 PST. Months later a certificate arrives in the mail from the captain of the airplane: "George Salverson has crossed the International Date Line, and thus has jumbled Yesterday, Today and Tomorrow from their mundane, time-worn order. Now, therefore, know ye, that the Seven Benign Deities of Good Fortune, Happiness and Longevity do hereby extend their eternal blessing to this esteemed individual."

Now a flight to Tokyo at 31,000 feet. The captain in his clipped Japanese voice tells us it is 4:07 in Tokyo. Just a little trip, as from Toronto to Vancouver. They've brought us hot towels, so here we go again. Filet mignon just came and most welcome. God pity the TCA [Trans-Canada Air Lines] traveller on a night like this.

Home Movies

When my father flew away on his adventure, we lived on Elynhill Drive in what was then the far reaches of northern Toronto. I look at a map. There it is, a small dead-end road, still not going anywhere. At its entrance is the gate to Willowdale Middle School, which I attended until grade six. My kindergarten teacher was Mrs. Long. My father walked me down that street. From the circle where

A NECESSARY DISTANCE / 35

we lived to the first day of school was a very long way. He held my hand. Mrs. Long had soft eyes. Her shoulder-length brown hair swung as she spoke. I watched her hair as my father let go of my hand. I see on the Google map that there is a Holocaust museum six blocks to the west of our house. I'm sure it wasn't there in 1963. We had a German friend who had left Europe shortly after the war. Carin babysat me and my brother. When she drove away I don't know where she went.

My husband, Bill, has been haunting Value Village, collecting old movie projectors. He sets one up on the round elm kitchen table. It's the only furniture I have from my childhood. The images flicker by as he turns the crank, slightly off-centre. Autumn leaves, sun through the flickering trees, my mother in a print dress.

"That's you," says Bill. What? "You're in there!" he repeats. I look again. It's my mother. My lovely thirty-one-year-old mother. Pregnant. With me.

Bill continues to turn the crank. Glimpses of this beautiful woman with thick auburn hair and lipstick, you can make out the lipstick even in the old print film. "It's autumn," I say. "She must be quite pregnant, I'm born soon. And it was after the typhoid."

My mother had typhoid during her sixth and seventh month of pregnancy. She and Dad told the story of how she was unconscious for all of August and the baby and the mom were supposed to die. And there we are, in the film. *Flicker, flicker*. Then there is a bassinet. And a baby, and they are getting into a car, the woman and the baby, and a man is taking the bundle, carefully, so carefully into his arms. Faces lean over, peering at the baby.

"It's my aunt!" I gasp, in the kitchen sixty-three years later. I lean forward, as she comes into the frame again, young, so young, and then they are getting out of the car, and there is a small black spaniel jumping around, jumping into my father's lap and onto the bundle – onto me – Smokey! "It's Smokey," I tell Bill. He is turning, turning the crank. And then there is a Christmas tree, like the one we just put up in our living room. It's Christmas again only it's before, Christmas before on Hillhurst Drive in Toronto. The expensive house they left to go to Elynhill, that years later Dad wished they had kept. "Imagine what it would be worth."

We watch. And then the film runs through the spool and out the other side.

"That's what it's like," I say to my husband. It's an hour later and we are laying in bed. "What?" "Life. It's going by frame by frame, flicker, flicker, and then out the other side. And then it's someone else's turn. Another baby coming home from the hospital."

Bill grunts. "There was somebody dying that day in the hospital when they brought you home." Yes, I think. Maybe I'll look up obituaries for October 14, 1955. But I don't.

I tell my friend Patti in Vancouver about the home movies, and she writes back, "Yeah, it's all so very strange this experience called life. I know it sounds like cliché but so true. The collapse of time or something like that."

I tell her, "Here I am reading this essay by Karen Barad, about time. About diffraction. Entanglements." It's only when I am going to bed, after Bill is asleep, that I read the rest of Patti's email:

The other day Jorah [her son] drove by me and I saw this man in a car and thought how strange I once breastfed that being? Gave birth to him and now he didn't even see me standing on the street. Could have been a stranger.

It's only when we recognize the moment that it has meaning. Otherwise all of it is rather random.

A day or so later I remember something and tell Bill, "My dad said I looked like a prize fighter when they brought me home."

Tokyo

Dad spends two days in Tokyo and makes extensive notes. They buy camera equipment and souvenirs. They visit a club or two in the area known as "the Ginza." Disoriented, fuelled by lack of sleep and alcohol, they are suddenly and sharply immersed in exoticism.

Became overpowered by scent of some incense. It's everywhere. No escape. Outside and in. Comes in waves as you walk. Seems to be in the food and even the coffee. Begin to hate it. Also, had adverse reaction to finding self in totally strange surroundings for first time in life. People, things, all seem unreal. An irrational, uncontrollable emotion. By uncontrollable I mean only that I can't force it to go away.

Impressions of a Tokyo Night

A narrow alley, crowded, lights.

Men jump at us, from their cars, very gracious. "Want a nice club? Have a nice car!"

A little threadbare man, hatless, comes out of crowd. Says "What you want?" Gene: (puts arm on his shoulder in comradely way) "Nothing. What do *you* want?" The man: "Some business!" (Laughter.) "We have a place."

Busboy in white jacket rides bike, with tray of some sort of hot food held on the palm of one hand. At every corner, old women in odd garments, with street stands, sell objects wrapped in red paper. A man cooking on street at tiny stand: something like sliced deviled eggs.

The three men try a club Gene has been to before – but it now only allows Japanese businessmen. They run into their "street solicitor" again. More receptive after rejection, Gene asks: "You got nice girls?"

38 / JULIE SALVERSON

Solicitor leads us into a Ginza area alley near the elevated railway. Here are clubs in profusion. We go down several flights, apparently into the bowels of Tokyo. Find a dimly lit room with small bar and a few tables. I'm so nervous I tear the pocket off my coat, stuffing gloves into it.

(Cold out.)

Three girls move in on us immediately, take us over, seating us in corner table, snuggling close. Mine and Gene's in low-necked sleeveless party dresses, western. Grahame's is a real westernized cheesecake item in short skirt exposing netted legs (good) exposed, when seated, to the buttocks. Mine, all in white, is perhaps more angelic. This is the "Ace Club." My girl's name is Toshiko, which she says means "Fast Thinker," which may well be true. Gene's is Mariko and Grahame's is Makiko.

I try not to recoil as Toshiko pulls my arm around her and clasps my hand, winding her fingers tightly into mine, nuzzles my cheek, kissing it and nibbling at it.

In my urgency for diversionary conversation, I provoke a discussion of her life. Trying to evade such comments as: "If I get hot, are you going to take care of me?" My answer: "No." Then: "Tell me some more about your family!" (Grahame smirks.) She tells a sad story about how dreadful her father was – deserted the family – and how awful if her family knew what she was doing and how she has been working here for eight months. Toshiko wants to go to the hotel with me: I'm so tired, she'll help me sleep (massage) and make sure I get up in the morning.

The dialogue switches to Grahame: "Is he married too?" "Yes." "He looks so young. You are older, you have more experience." "Yes, but I'm also more tired." (She falls back laughing.) "Oh! You make me blush!" The bill is thirty-three thousand yen,

A NECESSARY DISTANCE / 39

or ninety-eight US dollars. Gene and I had two beers each, Grahame had one. (Large bottles, however.) After much negotiation (mostly in Japanese) we get out with paying only forty-five dollars. This is because the girls are (they tell us) generously paying the rest (by giving up their commissions). They insist on going up to the street with us to kiss us goodbye. I get away with a fast peck, at which they all giggle.

On the street, a man questions us (Japanese) about the bill and expresses horror. "Gyp joint!" he says. Makes no effort to sell us anything. Don't know why he asked. Having escaped, we agree it was worth fifteen dollars each for the experience. Next (Saturday) morning I said, "Now every time I see a Japanese girl I flinch!" Hangover breakfast in European dining room of Imperial Hotel. How strange everyone Japanese is.

Finding it all too bewildering. Crazy, weird, different world. People are so not the same. A strong emotional desire to be somewhere else, identified with an ever-present smell which seems to be incense or some food spice.

A few bits I write down because something about them . . .

Asaka: A huge gate, through which one enters what appears to be ancient Japan. A bazaar.

Old men in smocks and wooden sandals; bald heads; like figures on sale at Lichee Garden Restaurant.

Girlie shows, right out of the CNE [Canadian National Exhibition]. Although it's morning, the ticket offices are open.

Familiar American actors look out at you from meaningless Japanese symbols.

(I'm a child again, I can't read.)

A weird trio passing. I think they're monks, in black cassocks, one is enormous, fat, gross. But they're wrestlers. I try to photograph them, but rather fearfully, pretending to shoot something beyond them. They all disappear into a movie theatre.

In midst of all this, down one cluttered alley, children with golf clubs seem to be playing hockey. We come upon a temple. Japanese everywhere with cameras, taking pictures, posing in front of the temple, doing what I'm doing, which makes me feel better about firing off the Olympus at sacred objects. We come out the gate, take refuge in a café, Spanish atmosphere. Waitresses in western tailored suits, gorgeous, with elaborate makeup; they aren't real to me. Gene appears to be delighted with them. I find I don't relate to any sexual form of admiration – they are so unreal. The coffee house booths are too small for us, designed for people a foot or more shorter.

There is a man having his shoes shined and smiling pleasantly at the tired old woman, who is obviously ten thousand years old, who shines his shoes. He says something polite. I wonder if it's about the weather. (Chilly.) She says nothing at all.

Noticed at the airport there was no automation, as in baggage delivery machinery; but many porters. Why? Preservation of jobs? The approach from the airport featured a mass of electric signs, including famous camera names, and I noted Victor, with that old dog and phonograph. Lots of three-wheeled trucks, one wheel in front. For some reason, this upsets my stomach, and blends with the scent I think I smell and which increasingly nauseates me. What is it? Emotional? Allergy to something? The malaria pills?

Some part of me hates it here, some resentful conservative. It wants to escape, this stupid protected provincial element of me. The rest is exhausted by the tempo of fascinations. It's a combination of "Get away at all costs" and "Hurry on, see more." What is there in this physical reaction? Is it shock at discovering something really not in the least like Portage Avenue?

A NECESSARY DISTANCE / 41

This is interesting because I have always sneered at details which cause so-called differences between people, as between Catholics and Baptists. But perhaps, even to me, enough details become powerful enough to become what is the important thing. I love new foods, but now I want unseasoned food. I want a piece of bread from Brown's dull old bakery. I want a steak with no sauce. Ridiculous.

Images? I give up. Too many, too much, too fast.

I imagine these little brown men running about as energetically on war jobs and can easily understand American and Canadian attitudes toward these so different people when they were doing their best to kill us. This is a strangeness and a degree of difference which not only makes for overpowering interest and charm, but can also excuse and make easy, under the right conditions, a violent dislike – as a hatred for the man on the moon, if met face to face.

People are not the same. I no longer believe it.

People need their own around them. At least, I can feel that I do. I'm happy because I know Canada, the US, Europe, in that order, are still there somewhere. This is my feeling in one day. I have no way of knowing what I would feel if posted here for months or years. And so surprised am I at my reactions that I no longer presume to guess.

Images: Too much, too fast, too outside normal references for a quick phrase to catch it.

Give up. Let's see Hong Kong in the a.m.

End Tokyo.

Swelling to a crescendo, the first long forty-eight-hour plus day of travel ends. And they are in Tokyo only to buy equipment! Dad's candour startles me. Who, if anyone, did he share this with? No cellphones, no internet, letters that would arrive weeks if not months later. Perhaps he talked to Mom when he got home. His final notes suggest he tried to speak to Alfie Scopp, pretty much a family member. That ended in conflict. Dad has been away two days. What's going on at home for Mom? Is she relieved? Does she pour her Scotch and relax without judgment, or is Julie there to roll her eyes and walk away?

On the shelf by my desk is the typed transcript. In my father's own large binder are the books themselves, seven soft black covers holding scribbles of pencil and ink. He made those marks, all those years ago, while my seven-year-old self read, daydreamed, attended grade three and sat on the back porch "talking with Jesus," as my dad reveals to my astonishment on his arrival home in book seven.

April 30, 2019. My father's birthday. He would be one hundred and three years old. I feel such love for this almost innocently candid man writing in hotel rooms in 1963. No idea that the future is looking at him.

Fathers and Daughters

As I moved into my early teenage years I wanted to find my own words, either on the page or to accompany the few chords I knew on the guitar. I hid what I wrote. I suspected there could only be one writer in the family. It was a tumultuous place, our house, my parents' employment uncertain and the alcohol plentiful. Joni Mitchell was my emotional rescue. Her lyrics sliced open the festering boils of inadequacy and torment, and provided what might be my first memory of the exquisite balm of shared psychic suffering. Her voice fluttered up the octaves, spiraling precariously higher, dissipating in the ether where less and less led to suspension, zero, the perfect balance of forces, the nothing place.

Her perfection was tarnished one summer morning by my father's discovery of another Canadian songstress, Buffy Sainte-Marie. How he found the album I don't know, possibly it

A NECESSARY DISTANCE / 43

was mine, but one day he took my brown box record player into his office and disappeared into her album *Little Wheel Spin and Spin*. An hour later he charged into the kitchen, face glistening with excitement, "Wow!" he gasped. "*This* is the real thing!"

I stirred my tea and pouted. I had played him a song by Joni the night before and he had been polite but noncommittal. Now he held forth with the fervour of the converted. "*This* is heart, blood, life, Julie. *This* is what it means to be *alive*! That other stuff, esoteric, in the head, *intellectual*!"

The word conveyed my father's ultimate disdain and condemnation. Years later I understood this rejection of anything "intellectual" was fallout from his mother's incisive brain striking at anything that crossed its path, most particularly the love of my father's life, a French-Canadian called Denise. Growing up I had heard allusions to a painful story about a brutal encounter between this mysterious old girlfriend of my father's and Laura. Years later I will learn how his mother lacerated Denise with words and how the actor John Scott, a close friend of the couple, threw up in the bathroom, sickened by Laura's venom. Now, aged twelve, my father's rapture stung and defeated me. My small efforts at poetry, at songwriting, were not pulsing with the driving rhythms of Buffy, they strove for the geometric designs of Joni. "All in your head" was an accusation I took to heart. Well, to hell with him because who wanted to be like my mother, whose heart exploded with rage at the tip of a Scotch glass.

It was Andrew Allan who rescued me.

Uncle Andrew

A few books tell the story of early Canadian radio drama. One is by Andrew Allan, the producer/director who created the first national theatre – a company on the air – and changed the landscape of radio in Canada.

The man I called Uncle Andrew, my godfather, spent pre-war years working in England, where he kept company with the likes of T.S. Eliot, Gracie Fields, Noël Coward and Sir Ralph Richardson. They were surrounded by news of Hitler's rise to power and British prime minister Neville Chamberlain's attempts at appeasement and conciliation. One day a letter arrived from the CBC asking when he might be available. On September 1, 1939, Andrew, his father and Andrew's fiancée, actor Judith Evelyn, boarded the Canadian bound SS *Athenia* in Glasgow. He was headed for a job in Vancouver. Two days later England declared war with Germany.

He describes what happened next in his autobiography, *A Self-Portrait*. On a Sunday morning, "the sky far and fresh with blueness, the crests of the blue waves blown to white in the wind," the *Athenia* was torpedoed and sunk by a German submarine. She was the first passenger casualty of the war. Andrew, his father and Judith escaped, but hours later their lifeboat was ripped in half by the propeller of a ship that failed to see them. Only a few managed to crawl onto the wreckage and cling to safety until dawn. Seven people were rescued and one died within hours. There had been eighty-five in the lifeboat. He and Judith never married but were friends until her death. Andrew never saw his father again.

Andrew spent a few years in Vancouver running radio drama. Writer and director Fletcher Markle, who later directed *The Incredible Journey*, was there: "The human imagination has an unlimited budget. No one was quite ready for the intelligence, humour and growing range of Andrew Allan." When Andrew moved to Toronto in 1943 to run radio drama nationally, Markle, Drainie and others followed. Writer Charles Israel moved from Hollywood to get away from narrow formulas and impossible taboos. "CBC was so far ahead of everyone. They were making the best radio drama in the English speaking world." Fellow-writer Lister Sinclair had said to him, "What are you doing there in Hollywood writing

A NECESSARY DISTANCE / 45

cop shows? Come to Toronto where you can write anything!"

The people I grew up with – Drainie, Ruth Springford, Budd Knapp, Alfie Scopp, writer Len Peterson – loved Andrew Allan's professionalism. Journalist Bronwyn Drainie, John's daughter, describes her parents' shock upon arriving in Toronto from Vancouver in February 1943: "Toronto in the forties was not a place that particularly valued innocent enthusiasm. It was a busy, dour, self-important town in which the artists who were streaming in from all over the country during the war never quite learned to feel at home. Fortunately, CBC Radio in Toronto was not a Torontonian artifact and that may well have been the secret of its success nation-wide."

It is hard to find numbers or demographics for the audiences of radio drama. Scholar Mary Vipond emails me: "The sad story is that CBC didn't even set up its own audience research department until 1953, relying before that on letters from listeners, reports from regional officials and . . . primitive data from private firms. They only polled cities, for a start, and only a few of them." Telephone polls were like cellphone polls today – they only reach the people who have them. (In 1946, a mere 16.3 percent of Canadians had phones and most of those were urban. In 1981, the percentage had only reached 69.6.) Vipond tells me that producers knew their task was to promote a kind of cultural democracy, meaning develop a higher literate culture. Again, from Bronwyn Drainie's *Living the Part: John Drainie and the Dilemma of Canadian Stardom*:

What struck listeners as new and exciting about the "Stage" series was not just its crisp, quickly paced professional sound, but also its subject matter, which seemed to have grown up overnight. Canadian writers were emerging from the war years with an agenda: we had fought and proved ourselves in Europe, now we must do the same at home. All that blood spilled to defeat Hitler would be wasted if the dark forces that had brought him to power – racial hatred, class injustice, fear, greed and hypocrisy – were allowed to grow unchecked here in Canada.

I love looking through Drainie's book. My parents and their friends eagerly awaited its 1988 publication. My mother rushed to pick up a copy and poured through it over our dining-room table. Her pencil marks are still there, and I remember hearing her on the phone lamenting and exclaiming about who and what was in the book and what terrible omissions Bronwyn had made. I can't imagine what it was like for the author, if the drama in our house was anything to go by. My father avoided it all by hiding in his office. A few years before the book was released, Michael Drainie and I had played the old radio dramas in his mother's living room in Rosedale. We called our evenings *Speakeasy Radio* and many of the original company came, full of curiosity. Because the CBC *Stage* had been broadcast live, the actors and writers – including my parents – had never heard their shows before.

Andrew Allan was the brilliant force behind all of it. Writer Len Peterson said he had "a broad receptivity (and) best of all, some devilment in him." Despite Allan's quirks, he ran a tight ship and he kept people employed. Accused of elitism, he replied that the only way actors and writers could stay in the profession was to hire them regularly. All were paid the same. His company were, he said, "the ones who kept the standard of performance high." Not only that, he gave writers their heads. "It was to be a writer's theatre . . . to let them write what they wanted to write, and in the way they wanted to write it . . . In twelve seasons we found over seventy of them – all, I think, but two of them Canadian."

When I was a teenager, Andrew would visit us in our village east of Toronto. He discovered the key to my interest – a good

A NECESSARY DISTANCE / 47

intellectual argument. We were quite a pair, the brilliant mind and the Pygmalion teenager, going at each other on the back deck. I was strident with conviction, while Andrew was erudite and precise. He had ruthless diction. I was desperate in my seriousness and I'm sure he had a twinkle in his eye.

I remember the play *Antigone*. I was reading it in my English class, the Anouilh version that puts the king and his rebellious daughter into the context of the World War II French resistance. Who was right, the girl or the patriarch (said the patriarch to the girl on the porch!)? Andrew championed Antigone, who I dismissed as a headstrong ideologue. Creon, burdened by a father's responsibilities, stood for *the real world*. The arguments went on well past a late dinner and, according to my father, Andrew walked into the kitchen at the end of it, shaking his head. "She makes me look like a bush leaguer." It was the first compliment I ever had about my mind. It may have been the first time I wondered what it was to have one.

On Saturday, September 22, 1973, Dad wrote in his diary:

Andrew Allan ill: Chris Wiggins [actor] on telephone to tell us of Andrew's stroke. Sandra went to hospital but Andrew not conscious. She had them change the spelling of his name in their records – "He hates to have his name misspelled!"

Allan had an assistant for most of his years at CBC. Her name was Alice Frick, a crusty straight-lipped woman with a quiet wit who graduated from the University of Alberta in 1941. She helped with script selection, editing and various production tasks. She also helped find writers. In her biography *Image in the Mind*, Frick describes an afternoon in 1944 when she was on a cross-country search for talent:

A meeting of Winnipeg members of the Canadian Authors Association had been convened at the house of the president, Laura Goodman Salverson. I spoke my piece, answered questions, and the meeting closed with coffee and cake. During the proceedings I noticed a tall, blond young man – the only man present, as I recall – seated half-way down the stairs leading to the rear of the house. When the women had departed, he came to join us and to ask if I'd like a drink of something else. Mrs. Salverson introduced him: her son George. Years later, on September 20, 1950, [director Esse] Ljungh produced on *CBC Wednesday Night* George Salverson's adaptation of his mother's Canadian classic, *Confessions of an Immigrant's Daughter*, a chronicle of the Icelander's settlement in the Gimli area of Manitoba.

Alice Frick had the foresight to interview some people from the early days of CBC Radio, including my parents. The recordings are housed in the National Archives in Ottawa. Lorne Greene says those years prepared him for everything that was to follow: "My whole career in Canada was a huge learning process and I learned from the best. The people I worked with were all giving people, we all gave of ourselves. There was a great spirit. Those were the formative days, the exciting days, the days of learning."

The words that touch me the most are from Charles Israel. Frick asks him to describe the qualities of the best writers: "Lister Sinclair wrote the most brilliant, cool intellectual dramas . . . Len Peterson had great passion and a sense of the absurd . . . George Salverson had warmth, feeling and sensitivity for human relations."

Hong Kong Stopover

Sunday, January 20, 1963. The team are on their way to Indonesia. Hong Kong is a stopping off point, one night in the Miramar Hotel.

A NECESSARY DISTANCE / 49

Dad finds the city beautiful and notes details of street vendors and rickshaws. Small children carrying shoe polish and brushes want to shine their shoes.

The alleys:

A nightmare of claustrophobia, I saw no customers. Woman in black carrying two large boxes. One has printing on it: "Canada's finest apples." (Apple served on the Garuda plane. Is it one of Canada's finest?)

I follow his trip online. The Miramar was the first Hong Kong hotel built after World War II. It opened in 1948 and was demolished in 1990. It stood next to a large park and was near the Hong Kong China Ferry Terminal. I am interested in this stopover because I have Chinese students, some from the mainland and some from Hong Kong. In 2019, protests over China's attempt to gain more control were growing in intensity. Chinese students in my classes came to my office to share their increasing worry. They held competing views. One knew a journalist in Hong Kong and understood the resistance and the politics of dissent; another complained about the manipulation of the western media and how China was demonized in the press. This same young man told me he could not borrow my DVD of Ai Weiwei, the dissident artist; it would be too dangerous: "It would change me. I would be changed if I see it," he said. I felt sad when he left my office. "You are already changed," I thought.

The Covid-19 pandemic led to increased anti-Asian racism fuelled by what Trump continues to call "The Chinese Virus, the foreign enemy." The writer Fang Fang's *Wuhan Diary* is its own viral phenomenon and China is divided between condemnation and praise for her bravery. Another student tells me that those who have left China to study abroad are being blamed at home for "bringing the virus back."

50 / JULIE SALVERSON

"It is not like Canada where the government tries to bring their people home." Instead, my student implies, Chinese young people are encouraged to stay away.

What was Hong Kong like in 1963? I look at photos of the city from that time, skyscrapers climbing the mountain just as Dad describes it. He goes through Kowloon so I look at photos of that suburb of Hong Kong. My father's notes are brief. He slept at the Miramar only one night.

Sun 8:00 a.m. Up and bathed. Laundry last night a success.
8:30 Breck. Miramar Hotel. Coffee good.
9:00 Kowloon and ferry to Hong Kong Inland.
Mountains (brown rock) and the sea blue, sparkling sun, temperature ideal, no humidity, the city with beautiful tall buildings climbing the mountains. Off the big main streets, the harrowing honeycomb alleys teeming with merchants and stands and coolies and all this crowded poverty on the beautiful hill.

At the Hong Kong airport the three men check their luggage and pull out Lucky Strike cigarettes purchased in a side alley that morning. Dad nudges Grahame who is admiring the shiny new camera he purchased in Tokyo.

"Have a look at that! Our bearded captain!" The pilot and seven officers stride through the waiting room. "A smiley sultan on a mission, a man of consequence, bestowing a special sword on one of his subjects!" my father exclaims with glee.

"As long as it isn't me," murmurs Gene. "I'm not as romantic about history as you, George. I wasn't born a moment too soon."

"But where's the fun in our own time? Or, more like it, swashbucklers and sultans dress differently but act the same. No difference between a Hannibal and a Kennedy."

"Would Hannibal fund our film?" asks Grahame.

A NECESSARY DISTANCE / 51

"He'd fund it and pay you the full per diem!"
My dad loves the idea of this regal gentleman in the cockpit.

The captain passes through the cabin to go to the can, beard and dignity and all. I can see his grandpa swashbuckling grandly on the deck of a private junk in the Java Sea. He makes his uniform look like royal robes.

Mothers 1

Dad posts a letter to Mum in Hong Kong, possibly the first he has ever written to her. The separation is unfamiliar, they were never apart. Summer trips are the four of us, sometimes camping or at friend's cottages. What intimacies might have been in that letter? What did my mother feel reading it?

Mom was more adventurous and less thrifty than my father. Sometime in the early 1970s she decided to move to Los Angeles. My brother surprises me with this story. "Don't you remember? She wanted to become a movie star like Michael Learned." (Learned was an American actress who starred in Mom's favourite TV show, *The Waltons*.) Mom and Scott stayed with Canadian friends Joan and Perce Curtis and their children, Michael and Stacey. "Mike and I had a famous babysitter, we used to hang out at her pool. Raquel Welch!"

Mom once took me to Nassau for a week, a beach holiday. We took a tour on a glass-bottom boat. Mom spent the rest of the week sick in her room, while I read Erle Stanley Gardner mysteries by the pool. I suspect she paid for the trip from a show or a residual for a rerun. Dad looked after the bills; Mom's work was gravy. But maybe that's not fair, maybe for her it was independence. She took me aside once during my teenage years to show me a small brown cardboard bank book, the pencilled notations her deposits.

"This is my private account. If anything happens to me, it's for you." She insisted I write down the number and put it somewhere safe. Years later when she died I wondered about it. I didn't find any record of that account among her things and for all I know the bank book went to landfill or Goodwill. Or maybe it sits inside a file I haven't opened.

Mothers 2

On the wall by my desk is a photo of a small boy standing in a field. He is perhaps five, arms at his side and head slightly tilted back. He looks into the distance with a wrinkle of curiosity along his brow. White saddle shoes and socks that come halfway up his calves; bare legs sticking out from baggy shorts that end above the knee and a sailor suit top – I want to put my arms around him. A floppy hat sits back on short hair bright in sunlight. Half of his face is lit, the other in shadow. It's a black-and-white photo taken in 1921. Someone has coloured in the background with chalk: greens and yellows for the ground, swirls of blues for the sky. It's a place-less location, no detail. What does the child see? The curve of his mother's back? A dog in the distance? The life ahead?

I would like to summon my father back from the dead. "Was your mother down the path from you that day? What did she call out?"

Laura named her son after her husband; perhaps it was easy and allowed her to get on with things. His mother avoided the realities of child raising even before my father's birth. She was one of a small group of Canadian women brought to St. Catharines, Ontario, in 1916 to take a new sleeping drug that allowed the mothers to bypass childbirth. Twilight sleep was induced by morphine and scopolamine. The drug gained popularity in Germany and spread rapidly to other countries. The lucky mothers woke up with an infant and no memory whatsoever.

A NECESSARY DISTANCE / 53

I have a handwritten letter, the only one of its kind by my grandfather George Senior, written from his St. Catharines' hotel room to his sister describing the experience:

54 Ontario Street, St. Catharines, Ont.
April 30, 1916

Dear Sister,
It's 10 p.m. Sunday and you should have my telegram by now. When I went back to the hospital at 8:30 the nurse said Laura was just beginning to come out of it. They wouldn't let me see her, so I hollered for the kid. They were pretty busy, but I kept right on the job bothering them with questions about it until at 9:30 they brought it into me. Ain't a newborn kid a funny looking thing? Its hands were blue, everything else red . . . It's only given a little peep so far and when I asked the nurse why in thunder it didn't yell and if it was dumb, she just laughed.

Scholars call my grandmother a major chronicler of poverty in North America at the turn of the twentieth century. When still in her teens she helped pregnant women in unforgiving circumstances at her aunt's maternity hospital in Duluth, Minnesota. She described the flies, dirty drinking water and contaminated milk that killed almost a dozen of her infant brothers and sisters, and the lack of medical care and nutrition during pregnancy that led to death in childbirth. She seldom revealed incidents of sexual harassment in her low-paying and back-breaking work as a domestic servant in Duluth and Winnipeg. She wrote of the Winnipeg saddlery sweatshop where her father worked fourteen-hour days with little light and few breaks.

54 / JULIE SALVERSON

In a letter to her friend J.S. Woodsworth, the first leader of the Co-operative Commonwealth Federation (later the New Democratic Party), she wrote:

> There is in me a great bitterness that with every new invention difficulties increase for the poor. I remember very well how Great West Saddlery worked her wage slaves in her dirty shed – how their hands which lend her fortune sweated and starved and how no man might even dream of a workers' union – we lived to see the end of such things sooner but, alas, who of us is free?
>
> I may not even write of it – editors are afraid. One must not be bitter if speaking for polite readers.

A maid, a seamstress, a retail clerk, a nurse's aide, a rooming-house landlady and, eventually somehow, a writer. My father's diaries are an archive of the financial reality of life in Canada as a writer. But they are nothing compared to what I unearth about his mother. From a document written by George Senior just after his wife's death:

> At age four she became the victim of a diphtheria epidemic. At times, it seemed she would not survive. She was saved by a Dr. Chown in Winnipeg who she said drove wildly through the snowy streets to fetch a young surgeon who performed a brutal tracheotomy on the child.
>
> When she finally recovered, she had lost her voice. Six years passed before the first little peep came out and two years more before she could talk almost, not quite, normally. Telling me about this years later she shuddered, the memory as strong as if it had happened only yesterday.

A NECESSARY DISTANCE / 55

Probably, her uncle, her mother's brother, was as responsible as anyone for the arousing of Laura's imagination. A deep-sea sailor for many years, he had been to all the ports of the sea-faring world. Coming to see Laura and entertain her during her illness, he moved about the room, telling her they were sailing the high seas. A chair was a port in Spain, in the corner was the British Isles, over there was Norway and all this stuff hanging against the wall were mountains rising straight up in the fjords.

Her father read to her nightly from the classics. Rome became her first love. It remained her chief historical interest for the rest of her life. By the time she recovered her voice, a library had opened in an empty store building. Approaching the librarian one day she was asked what she wanted. "A book about Caesar," replied the child. "Oh, my dear, that is much too heavy reading for a little girl. Come and I'll show you where the children's books are." "No," replied this unusual child. "I want a book about Caesar."

When first in graduate school I wandered into a national academic conference in Calgary. In a large hall were rows of tables with literature from each society. One had a sign about Iceland. I noticed the name Laura Goodman Salverson. I crashed the talk and afterwards introduced myself to the speaker, Daisy Neijmann, and discovered the world of scholarship on my grandmother. Most of the quotes in the rest of this section are either from *Confessions of an Immigrant's Daughter* or from Neijmann, who is a primary source for helping me understand the woman who died in July 1970, just short of eighty. I was fourteen.

Laura's father, Larus, wrote and told stories despite working endless days in the saddlery. Laura called him "a scholar at heart."

She admired her mother's ability to tell traditional stories and folktales but was horrified by the drudgery of women's lives: "For girls like us the dice were loaded from the start. The ensign of the mop and the dustbin hung over our cradles." She dedicated her novel *When Sparrows Fall* to her suffragette and politician friend Nellie McClung. Laura particularly respected her aunt Halldora Olson, who worked hard and didn't indulge in chatter: "For gossip and small talk she had no taste, and this indifference to insignificant details was extended to all those unimportant matters that clutter up people's lives."

Laura's dilemma as a sharp-thinking poor immigrant writing in a period of conservative nation-building captured the attention of scholars. I read their articles and wonder if I ever knew my grandmother at all – or if my mother did. To my mum, L.G., as she was called by family and friends, was a hypochondriac buried in her books. On weekend afternoons when she would look after me at her home, we would turn pages of a large scrapbook and paste in photos of faraway lands and peoples. It was my first introduction to a bigger world. I've no doubt this was deliberate on her part. No granddaughter of hers was going to end up thinking about boys and babies. She was not indifferent to her grandchildren as she had been to her son. In the National Archives in Ottawa I was surprised to find greeting cards written to "little Julie." Possibly I was special because I was a girl.

After some success with poetry and a published short story, she was told by an English teacher in Regina, Austin Bothwell, that when she had a few chapters of her first novel she should send it to McClelland and Stewart in Toronto. Laura sent off the chapters and one day a telegram arrived. Her husband yelled, "It's from the publisher!" The reply came instantly from upstairs: "For heaven's sake, read it!" "Viking Heart accepted. Your next five books also."

A NECESSARY DISTANCE / 57

Laura gained instant popularity with her first novel, *The Viking Heart* (1923). By the time her autobiography came out in 1939, she had written eight novels, one serial novel and one volume of poetry, together with more than thirty short stories published in newspapers and magazines. Neijmann calls her one of the most popular Canadian writers of that time. This period of success came to an end and gained her little financially. It is a familiar tale of circumstance that includes geography, colonialism, a religious suspicion of fiction and book publishing politics. The condensed version is painfully simple. She wrote as an Icelander and a Norse woman in a time that Canada was defining itself as distinct from its origins beyond its borders.

Laura did not fit in the ongoing debate between popular Canadian literature and experimental cosmopolitan intellectualism. Despite encouragement from the recently formed Canadian Authors Association, she was "not uncritically proud of Canada. Coming from an immigrant worker's family that had been reduced to the lowest rungs of society that had been regarded with suspicion by many middle-class Anglo-Canadians, she hardly endorsed the bourgeois WASP ideology so blatantly espoused . . . and often denounced the genteel, sentimental fiction poured out at so much per word. She grew up on literary and philosophical debates and craved the same from her colleagues, who, as it often turned out, preferred to shun controversy."

Laura grew up in different immigrant slums in Canada and the United States and was poor all her life. She married her husband, George, "a breezy young man from Montana, who thought he could put up with me for better or worse." The couple moved sixty-five times during their marriage looking for economic stability as George was in and out of work for the national railroad. Barbara Powell writes that Salverson "is especially reticent in her writing about her own sad story" and in letters to her friends and to long-time editor Lorne Pierce she refers to keeping her "tragedy" out of it. Nevertheless, although she refused to write as a victim, she was bitterly clear about what she had lived and what she wanted to write.

It was a popularly held belief after World War I that worker unrest (for example, the Winnipeg General Strike in 1919) was due to the "imported radical views of foreigners."

In numerous speeches and talks – live and on the radio – Laura stated her belief that nothing could really change Canada without a complete overhaul of the social system. "She was appalled by Canada's lack of support systems, by the general suspicion of people not of British descent, and by the traditional views on morality, especially as they pertained to the role of women."

Laura ran into challenges about style as well as content. Technique, to my grandmother, should be guided by a social or philosophical vision rather than an aesthetic. Literature in colonial Iceland had been a central part of advocacy for independence from Denmark. The idea that art could promote change was more than metaphor. She had no interest in "highbrow skepticism and irony" or in experiments in formal representation that showed "little interest in using literature to effect concrete social reforms."

In a letter to politician J.S. Woodsworth: "Of course my heart goes out to your work . . . in my own way I have been trying to interpret some of the New Canadians . . . alas, one meets with little support from editors and publishers if the truth is told too well!"

And to writer Morley Callaghan:

Anyone is lucky dead who tries to write truthfully in this country . . . your Grove, Knister, whatnots – all wrote of the foreigner from a grandstand seat. *I am one of the animals!* I've suffered all the small humiliations and cruelties which were the lot of those who could not speak English in the

A NECESSARY DISTANCE / 59

dear pioneer days [Laura learned to write and speak English at age ten]. Most of the stuff these nice letter men digging for realism imagine to be truth is just sheer bunk. Almost as sentimental as the Green Gables and all that crew of cheery songbirds pour out so much per word . . . I feel like raising hell whenever I see that lie about editors wanting, welcoming, individualism and reality. For fifteen years kicked hither and yon and sick most of the time I've been trying to make my Norse contribution and got kicked in the pants so often it's a wonder I'm alive!

Laura turned to historical "yarns" to give her more freedom to write truthfully. If it was set in the past it might not offend. She often wrote to Pierce about her struggle for the right form (something Canadian writers had been worrying at for decades) and she begged for constructive criticism and editorial help. Pierce gave little back, supportive but unwilling or unable to provide the rigorous editing she needed. He "tacitly contributed to her eventual conviction that she should leave the contemporary scene and stick to historical novels. By doing so, Pierce must have realized, especially during the later years of Salverson's career, that he was helping to relegate her work and her reputation to an outmoded realm of literature in Canada, along with other women writers he worked with, such as Marjorie Pickthall and Audrey Alexandra Brown."

My father grew up an only child in the bubble of his father's desperation about employment and his mother's growing bitterness and frustration. During these years, L.G. did much to contribute to literary and political culture in the west, mainly Winnipeg but also Edmonton. She was the Winnipeg president of PEN Canada and raised awareness about writers in repressive regimes around the world. She must have found this somewhat ironic, the enthusiasm for fights against governments beyond our shores, while Canadians, for the most part, ignored the plight of their own writers, homemakers and factory workers.

A major turning point came when she published her autobiography. She fervently hoped the book would earn her an income that could allow her to keep writing with regular stretches of time and focus. It was not to be. Although *Confessions of an Immigrant's Daughter* received good reviews in Britain and Australia (and middling in Canada), it was published in 1939 just as the Second World War began. The war "killed its potential for the commercial success that she badly needed at the time." Her first royalties were three dollars and some cents. "It seemed a shoddy estimate of my life! Well, that put me in a nosedive . . . I tried so hard to keep self-pity out of the book, and we could have done with a life of some kind, the shock of that experience almost finished me as a writer."

People who appreciated Laura's writing, she said, could not afford to buy it. They got the books from the library. She was also disheartened by pushback from the Icelandic Canadian community for revealing hardships a proud people would rather keep private. Instead they wanted her to write more about their strength and resilience.

In 1943, Pierce writes that they need a "bell wringer, . . . a gripping tale" that will make money because publishers also need to eat. She finishes "Salute to Life." The novel exposed anti-Semitism and racial prejudice through the story of a Jewish community on the British Columbia coast. At the time, she worked with the Winnipeg Council of Allied Victory helping different groups (Jews, Ukrainians, Russians and Hungarians) raise money for Europe. "In her letters, she mentions how she herself was regularly under suspicion of being 'Jewish,' 'Red,' etc., because of her charity work." She tells Pierce she feels strongly about the novel. "Just between ourselves [it] nearly killed me. I have not been so affected by anything

A NECESSARY DISTANCE / 61

for a long time so I know it is a good job – even if it takes years to place the damn thing."

"Salute to Life" was never placed, "apparently because reviewers were unwilling to believe the existence of such prejudices in Canada, because they felt the social tirades had taken over from the characters and plot, and because they considered the work to be lacking in structure." She was willing to revise, but protested "if I have to cut the Jewish motive all the social and political stuff goes with it – the one is enmeshed in the other, as everyone knows."

The manuscript can't be found, perhaps destroyed in a fire that claimed many of her records, manuscripts and research notes, as well as the home they were living in.

Laura's last years were difficult. After the war, Canadian literature "increasingly became the domain of an academically trained, artistically avant-garde elite that consisted largely of central Canadian, anglophone, white males, while the larger reading public continued its infatuation with American popular culture . . . The new establishment did not favour women's writing and appreciated ethnic writing even less." She continued to work on "Salute to Life" but nothing came of it. There is mention of a cranky critic: "To put it bluntly: I have spent all the money I dare on these wild efforts to please this critic and that . . . who cares. I realized very well when my autobiography hit the dust that no one gives a hoot about any Canadian who has not had the good sense to be born of French or English stock." Late in life, despite serious illness and with Pierce's unfailing support, she worked on a new manuscript, an expression of her often-noted "desire to write one thing really well." Her focus this time was the form of the Norse Saga – she was determined to put one into Canadian literature.

My grandmother was proud of *Immortal Rock*, her most experimental novel that we know of, proud that it was "so unusual, so Norse – so out of the blood and bone." The book won the Ryerson

Fiction Award but did not sell well. This was a crushing blow to Laura. She continued to write, including a second autobiography, which I found a few years ago in her archive in Ottawa. It is called "The Funny Side of Failure," and ends mid-paragraph around page eighty-two.

She talked with my grandfather about a last book called "The Stars Are Neutral." "She says that with such a title she can say anything she likes but that it will be humorous, so as not to hurt anyone's feelings," said George. For Neijmann, this was evidence that until her last days she felt a failure for not having written exactly what she had wanted. "She once wrote to Pierce: 'All I know is that in my dearest endeavours I have been defeated no matter how well I fought with blunt swords . . . you see, my dear friend, I am the only failure in an otherwise perfectly respectable family.'"

I'll close with a letter to Pierce where she talks about how many phone calls she received after *Confessions of an Immigrant's Daughter* came out: "'That's the way it is,' ran the tale, no matter what we do, we foreigners, it never is good enough – always damned with faint praise. So it dawned on me that in some small degree I *had* done what I set out to do. I had become a champion of the 'stranger,' of the little people society (to its peril) still presumes to despise."

Writer, poet, early feminist. Preoccupied, proud, brilliant, impatient, angry. That's who raised the boy who became my father.

Once upon a time a poet's son went around the world.

CHAPTER 3

Indonesia

Gene, Grahame and my father take window seats on the Garuda Indonesia airline flight to Jakarta, Indonesia. Dad copies down "Badju pelampling dieawah kursi" and adds, "an old Indonesian proverb meaning 'Life vest under your seat.'"

A "wild-looking hostess" hands out maps as they fly over what he calls "Our Viet Nam." It's the middle of the war and President Kennedy had recently said in his January State of the Union Address that "the spear point of aggression has been blunted in South Vietnam."

Then: "Things are different in Indonesia."

An international airport near midnight, the shock of steaming heat, confusion at customs as their passports change hands. Soldiers in "US-type uniforms at the door, women in Indonesian dress – very dignified, four-and-a-half feet tall. Brown eyes catch me staring. Polite shift of eyes."

They walk into pitch-dark to a private car. Their first contact, Mr. Song, sits "huddled upfront under my huge black suitcase. Children run and play outside the airport. Nightmare processing through the streets, all unlit. Lamps, some sort of gas, under the bottoms of hundreds of tricycles. Bare-legged drivers in the back. Clusters of them. Horrible roads, pitted by rain. Groups of weird humans dimly seen by headlights. A kind of fear in the

/ 63

dark procession through another planet. Huge floodlit building, extremely modern. Must be the Parliament."

Two days are spent in frustration, bureaucracy and traffic. They have trouble getting a vehicle to take them out of town. Plans are made, changed, made again. Dr. Ali Morad, an Egyptian, drives them to the FAO office. This is the arm of the World Health Organization that is sponsoring the film.

Mr. Tabor, the head of FAO Indonesia, greets them with news. "Indonesia is the most difficult government in Asia to deal with. Not enough time to negotiate with the various departments: Agriculture, National Film Board, the television people, customs (for equipment)." They get stuck in the street surrounded by Russian jeeps full of soldiers in American helmets, armed. "This country like another planet – another great blur of startling impressions. Unable to focus on detail. The emotional effect exhausting and stunning. Looking around, thinking revolution has begun." Dr. Morad explains, "It's President Sukarno's car." The car passes, escorted in front and behind. "A big black limousine. It is empty!"

They spend hours trying to arrange a car for tomorrow to take them to their first location. They run out of cigarettes, Lucky Strikes are fifty cents a pack, they can't use rupiahs, they need tourist cheques. They go to the Bank Negara Indonesia, buy ten dollars' worth, sign papers: "We figure the island is sinking under paper. At last get cigs. Has been more complicated than buying a car in Canada."

The first morning in Jakarta he is so drugged by humidity the phone can't wake him.

Tuesday, January 22, 1963
All the difficulties previously resolved so smoothly have become intensified and we have ranged today from optimism into adventure, through frustration and on down to utter boredom.

A NECESSARY DISTANCE / 65

After breakfast, micro bus comes okay. Off to FAO. Discussion and goodbyes as we are to take off into country. Over the humpy streets, past the teeming millions not necessarily yearning to be free. A jam of traffic, bicycles, old cars and trucks. An officer on duty directs all buses into a checkpoint.

Driver must report to group of officials at table outside rickety house. Woman with us speculates it's a check to see if everyone has paid their taxes. She seems uncertain about most things in her country. Driver returns, lots of talking in Indo. Much laughter. Great joke. Constantly laughing, woman explains: "They've taken his licence and commandeered all buses for a 'national emergency.'" Bus returns to FAO, then to hotel. This bus, by the way, is going to cost a thousand dollars for five days, but Tabor thinks he can negotiate. Try to get taxi. Have another, breakfast. Taxi will cost seventy-five dollars for the day. Refuse. Quit for the day.

Gene has been fighting hotel for two days to recover his laundry. Now appreciate our country where you can call a cab, phone Vancouver, all in moments, where the police don't dare and don't care about questioning your movements. If Prime Minister Diefenbaker's car received a shattering escort as we saw yesterday, we'd have him out of office overnight, as he knows, thank God.

So the day went. Time in pool, noticed no chlorine. A palace, grass cutters sit on boulevard with knife and slowly turn each blade of grass. Russian cosmonaut stopping at hotel. Place full of Russians. (Well, a dozen or so.) Wondered what would happen to Jakarta and this hotel if US and Russia became friends and stopped competing, as we agreed they will in face of China attitudes. Russian heartily choosing a pastry, as we do, by going up to counter in coffee shop. Wondered if a gift for going around the Earth.

This is Yuri Gagarin, the first person to travel to outer space on April 12, 1961. He toured the world after his flight and here he is in Jakarta. A statue will be erected of him in 2021, a gift of the Russian government to celebrate Indonesian-Russian relations.

Tasted the papaya – looks like a slice of carrot. In eighteen months tree produces and you can pick fruit all year. Same with bananas. Other fruits seasonal. Well fed, but imbalanced diet. Sixty million people on island of Java. Price shortages and import one million dollars a year. But no hunger except in flood.

Revolution here went on for three years, ended last year as authorities state last pocket of resistance controlled. But even yet some areas not cleared by them as secure. No real struggle but some harassment of officials. Sukarno Govt ambivalent about East–West struggle. And gets aid from both US and Russia. Damned if that isn't Paul Robeson record on radio. Does this mean that variations on the theme of discrimination is all-important here?

Dad spends the afternoon in the hotel and is bored by 5:00 p.m. When will they get on the road? He tries to call Gene's room but can't get through. The hotel's eight hundred rooms are mostly empty and staff outnumber guests.

Fascinating country could make millions out of tourists, but regulation would bar anyone. Who would want it as a holiday? Depression and boredom setting in as this sort of thing prevents us from doing our work. Further: FAO jealousies. Tabor could have gathered us a UN vehicle, but didn't because he's jealous of the UN rep, a charming Yugoslav. We are wondering if we have to play these men against each other just to go on about our business.

A NECESSARY DISTANCE / 67

The hotel has advertised a Hollywood movie, but it's cancelled for technical reasons: "Won't need tuxedo today."

They spend Wednesday morning sitting in traffic in a rented bus. "Pick up laundry damp from humidity. Mouth scorched from smoking too many Lucky Strikes. The Russian cosmonaut presented with a medal by President Sukarno. Grahame: 'Wonder what effect on economy would be if they didn't quit work at two in the afternoon?' A do about neo-colonialism. Want a navy, for some reason. Suggest they are Neo Democrats."

After several hours in traffic, Gene sits with his head in his hands. Turns out it's an accident, with people spilling into the streets to watch and splash in the mud from flooding waters. They eat lunch in the car. Eventually they reach the airport to do paperwork and drive south out of the city to Bogor to interview a rice farmer. Instead, they find an old man who gives no details about the farm, and "talks like a chicken. But rather sophisticated. Been photographed before and been to Mecca. A gap-toothed primitive, very quick. Luxuriant setting of mud, water, palms, foliage, ponds, valley and a huge mountain beyond, normally covered by clouds. Outhouses of bamboo with space for the classic squatting position, over the fish ponds to feed the black-and-white carp."

They return to the city and arrange transportation for the next day. The agriculture representative, Mr. Rajid, has joined them. Gene says, "We'll leave at five a.m." Rajid and the driver don't react. Dad looks at them, smoking and leaning against the side of the bus. "I won't expect them at five."

End of Notebook One. Start of Notebook Two.

Dad, Gene and Grahame find the farmer. Hajii Monsura has people working for him and the crops are divided among the farmhands at the end of the season. The team pay Hajii a thousand rupiah a day to play himself in the film. It's what the Agricultural Rep makes in a month.

Thursday, January 24, 1963
4:40 a.m. Up for bus at 5:00.

Bus two hours late. Arrives 7:00 after we sit all this time in lobby. No one to phone. Then off to railway station. Agricultural Rep, Mr. Rajid, waited since 5:00.

Up to Hajii Monsura's. He is in plowing clothes – baggy knee-length Bermudas and shirt. Everyone sleeping about in the mud. Gene eating a banana whilst slouching across the road. Grahame calls: "Gene, this is going to be long lens stuff?" Gene nods and chews. All the kids stare in fascination at exchange in this strange tongue. Beautiful day, good shooting until 2:00 p.m. Eight-hundred-foot shot. Good for this type of shooting in organized dramatic sequence. Couldn't make up minds about story so put in some possible useful details:

Sitting in rain under little temple, Grahame half-hour under paper umbrella protecting camera. Me under banana leaves. Urchins haunt us. Adults soon lose interest as spectators. Women ask me for American cigarettes, chatty but slight language barrier. Said "Gracias." Terribly thirsty work. Steaming heat down in the lush valley.

Sent drivers for native beer and cigarettes. Ate hated sandwiches in silver paper. They cost nine dollars.

Gene gave Rajid twenty dollars US. Twenty months' salary. He'll cash it in black market.

4:00 p.m. gave up in rain and returned hotel 6:15. Mud all over us. All sunburned. I'm not too bad as kept out of rice paddy. But we all have a rosy glow.

A NECESSARY DISTANCE / 69

Friday, January 25

4:30 a.m. Up ahead of time, ordered brek. "No food yet, sir. No orange crush, bar not open."

5:20 Downstairs and saw micro bus. Shock. But not ours. Taking bets bus will come at 7:00.

6:15 Still waiting in lobby. No bus. Betting on whether girl in leotard is French. She calls to someone. Gene triumphant. She's Fr. American. In elevator gives me a "Good morning" with a fellow-American glance. Gene hopes to finish shooting today, both of farmer and viewpoint shots of the valley. Thinking of taking Hajii to the Hotel Indonesia. Wonder if they'll let him in?

6:20 Bus coming!

8:30 On location. No Hajii and no light. Dark and cloudy. The paddies were plowed yesterday – all mud and most are now smooth square pools of the shit-coloured water. A light cooling breeze ripples it.

Hajii gone to nearby field to pick vegetables, returned 8:40. Ag Rep is telling him about going to Jakarta. The child is crying [Hajii and his wife have a three-year-old]. Hajii's house is woven straw on a wood frame. Wood door and glass windows with ornaments. Roosters run through yard. Hajii says, "I'm going on a spending spree!"

Beduk = Clappers – hang on porch. Five times a day he prays. Anybody who knows it's praying time sounds the *beduk*. Hit with a stick. To summon to prayer. Not everybody has a watch.

Custom of leaving shoes on step (Hajii leaves his sandals) must have a practical origin – these people live in mud all rainy season.

Since 2019 I have been part of a small Zen community led by Karen Maezen Miller. When we do *kinhin*, walking meditation, the leader indicates stopping and starting with wooden sticks. Clappers. They summon us not to prayer but to attention.

A Careful Democracy

It is the second day of shooting in Indonesia. In my mind's eye, Dad sits on the stone steps of the temple trying to ignore bad smells he can't identify. Sewage? Rotting vegetation? Mr. Rajid appears from behind the bus and joins him. There are bananas in the yard, avocado, papaya shaped like cucumbers and something oddly shaped Dad doesn't recognize. It is yellow and prickly. "Breadfruit," says Rajid.

The two men watch the filming. Dad will have ideas about what to shoot, but for the most part he constructs the story after the fact – the footage suggests a script, then the script determines the edit. The men will know they are looking for personal elements, characters the audience can make a connection to so the documentary isn't just blunt information. This would be one of the reasons they hired Dad, he is a dramatist. He is also a bit of a philosopher. He thinks in the big picture and is fascinated by myth, by history, by the forces that change lives and cultures. Maybe he kept notes on these things somewhere else, but it's just as likely he trusted what was building in his head.

At Gene's request, Hajii walks up the hill for the camera. Grahame perches among bamboo trees on a ledge trying for the best angle. Hajii's baggy Bermuda shorts splash colour that contrasts with the white shirt. Does he always wear white, wonders George. Has he put it on for the film? Should he mention it? White is terrible on camera.

"Stop, I'm changing something. Wait please," Grahame calls.

Hajii strolls back down to the steps and points at my father's cigarettes. "Of course," says George, handing him one. My father gestures toward the leather pack Hajii wears on his hips. "Very nice. What is it for?"

A NECESSARY DISTANCE / 71

"Tobacco! But empty!"

George nods. He wishes he had one, he is carrying the passports and his money in a briefcase.

Grahame is ready with the camera. "Once more please, sir," he calls out from his perch. Hajii nods and walks again up the hill. Not for the first time reading these notes I notice the cameraman's courtesy.

My father, most at ease when only talking to one person, asks about the Indonesian government. "How would you describe the way things work in this country? Anything like Portugal?"

Mr. Rajid gives an explosive snort. "Here is not like anything! Certainly, the hardest place to do business."

Dad shrugs. He is thinking about the bus that never comes. "We make things hard for you, perhaps," says my father.

"Not at all. Excellent project. I love the movies!" proclaims Mr. Rajid.

"Do you have a favorite?"

"Now, *Lawrence of Arabia*," he declares. "The blue-eyed actor was magnificent."

"Yes, Peter O'Toole, marvellous!" Dad agrees.

Mr. Rajid cracks his knuckles. "But for all time? *Casablanca!*"

George offers Mr. Rajid a cigarette. Both men smoke, perhaps contemplating great drama as the farmer repeats his walk up the hill of mud. Filming can be a boring business.

"So," continues my father, "would you call Indonesia a democracy?"

Rajid nods vigorously. "Yes, yes. But a careful democracy. It is very dangerous to criticize the president. But things will be better. You see this" – he gestures his cigarette at the rice paddies, the fruit trees – "land reform, people work hard and things will be better."

Dad considers. "There are elections?"

Rajid laughs. "Of course. But it is not probable the president will not be elected. The army backs him up."

The shot is finished and Hajii calls to his wife, a wiry woman in glasses, "I'm going on a spree in Jakarta!"

"Have to take money with you," she tells him. Mrs. Monsura wears a thin blue blouse, a kebaya, covering a sarong woven with greens, blues and yellow. She stands by the small coffee tree in the yard, red buds almost ready for harvest. As she speaks with Hajii, George hears a mix of words with the odd English – he will later learn that she has Malay, Arabic and Dutch blood and draws on this heritage in her speech, a scattering of words that include Spanish although he can't make out any actual phrases.

They move to taking viewpoint shots in the valley, followed by a crew of local children fascinated by the exchanges in English. Gene slouches along the road eating a banana, the heat punishing as it nears noon. His light brown hair is flattened around his broad face.

"Can we borrow the kids?" he calls to Hajii.

"Of course!"

Gene smiles, gesturing to a handful between five and ten years of age who hurry down the lane after Grahame's camera. Dad talks more with Mr. Rajid, who tells him, "My job is mostly as an advisor to the government on land and rent reform, farming laws, soil research and conservation. I'm not usually out with the farmers."

Back in the hotel Dad jots down notes about the religion he is fascinated to see as a lived practice and not words in a book. As a young man, my father tried to make sense of what he ultimately considered the nonsense of Christian faith. He was desperate to understand Denise, the young Catholic from a devout family in Quebec who he planned to marry. My philosopher father studied for two years with Jesuits, certain he could make sense of the faith of this charming girl who he adored.

A NECESSARY DISTANCE / 73

One afternoon the engaged couple visited Niagara Falls with Dad's close friend Hugh. As the three tourists leaned over the rail admiring the view, Hugh and Dad got into an excited discussion about the geology, physics, time and evolution that had created this wonder of the world. Denise looked puzzled. "But God made it," she said. Dad told this story many times, how his body turned cold because he knew; it was impossible. Shortly after, he said goodbye to her at Toronto Union Station. He never saw her again.

Hugh and George

I'm trying to remember details about Dad's friendship with his best friend Hugh Horler, so I call Hugh's eldest daughter. When she was in her twenties, Aileen spent four years travelling through Africa and Northern Ireland. Dad thought Aileen was "marvellous" and full of courage. It's only as we talk on the phone that we realize that his fascination with her adventures was because he himself had been to some of these places. He may have been mostly remembering his own trip, and the idea of a young woman braving the unknown on her own impressed him.

"Of course, we wrote letters in those days. When something arrived from me, Daddy would invite George to come over and they would read them together."

"Because he'd been there!"

I ask her if she knows how they met. "My dad was living in your grandmother's boarding house in Winnipeg. George was an usher at Hugh's first marriage in 1942." This is news to me. But nothing compared to what she tells me next.

"When I came back from South Africa it was the summer of 1977 and I lived at home for a few months. Dad's second floor office was where they worked. When they were writing the book together." Book?

Aileen tells me that for several years our fathers wrote a novel – or tried to. "I don't know how much they wrote and how much they drank Scotch. They sold the movie rights."

"What? You're kidding."

"It was about Indigenous Peoples' rights."

I listen in astonishment as she describes what she remembers as the story. As trains run through the Ontario town of Parry Sound they cross a long trellis bridge. Just north of there is a town called Nobel. My dad and Hugh knew the town because the Horlers had a cottage on an island nearby and the family – and sometimes us – were in the area every summer. Nobel was built around a Canadian Industries Limited chemical plant that made fertilizer – and explosives. The hero of Hugh and Dad's book is an Indigenous guy from the area and he and his friends hijack a train full of explosives and park it on the bridge. They threaten to blow it up. To get attention to Indigenous Peoples' problems.

I hear myself say, "They were ahead of their time!"

"Way ahead of their time. Anyway, one day that summer when I was back I went into Dad's office and there was a pile of papers – a very big pile. Typed pages. It was the book."

She has no idea what happened to it. She thinks one of them put it in the trash.

"Every time I go to Parry Sound, and drive under that train trellis, I think about that book. Ask my sister about it, she was living at our Toronto house then. Maybe she remembers more."

A few weeks later I speak with two of her sisters, Georgia and Kate. They both remember. "They went to visit the reserve," says Georgia. "They sold the movie rights, or someone was interested. It was a crime novel. 'A Vision in Blood.'"

Offerings for the Dead

The first days in Jakarta are a frustrating mishmash of misinformation, traffic jams, obstacles and sensations. For the first time since leaving home he sleeps two nights in the same bed. Dad has a cup of coffee in the hotel, "in Java," and it's so awful he pours it down the drain. Does anyone still say "a cup of java"? If I made Dad coffee now I wouldn't know how he takes it.

Earlier today, overwhelmed by the pandemic, I told a friend, "I feel the dead are all around me."

"People all over the world are having huge dreams," she says. "A lot of energy is coming into the planet right now."

I don't know what to make of this, but I am dreaming in epic form.

My friend suggests I offer food or drink to my father. "Make a small plate, or pour a glass, you could play music. Leave the food for around twelve hours, then don't eat it, put it in the compost, the garden, dispose of it." Okay, why not. I go upstairs to write about Jakarta and pour him – obviously – a Scotch. Neat, but maybe that would be wrong. I think he and Mom put ice in, I didn't know anything about a drop of water to release the flavour until I grew up. I pour one for each of us, in two traditional whisky glasses, and set his underneath the picture of him as a boy.

It's odd to give whisky to a child, so I go into the spare room and look at the two awards that sit on a bookshelf. I pick the one he got for the show about the discovery of insulin, *The Discoverers*: "Max Rosenfeld & George Salverson, 1956." There is a drawing etched in metal, the happy/sad theatre faces set inside a map of Canada with a maple leaf and the initials CCAA. I've no idea what it stands for. The top of the award is missing, but I set it down by the whisky glass. *Salut. Skoal!*

The Jakarta Method

I find articles about Indonesian land reform and politics online and buy novels on Kindle. Most compelling is *House of Glass*, written in prison by Pramoedya Ananta Toer. It is the fourth of his series about Indonesian politics from the late 1890s to the mid-twentieth century. The first three books are from the point of view of a revolutionary intellectual; the fourth is told by a policeman who inadvertently climbs the ladders of corruption into high levels of government. The protagonist keeps adjusting to what is required, despite his admiration for the journalist whose imprisonment he engineers. The book excavates the process whereby a young Indonesian idealist, a policeman who wants to better himself and his community, becomes aligned with colonial brutality. Minor adjustments of behaviour – following small, seemingly inconsequential orders – accumulate over time until he narrates his horror at his actions. His wife no longer recognizes him and leaves with his child. He no longer recognizes himself. The novels chronicle a typical and yet unique colonial story – Dutch control over Indonesian islands, soon to be replaced by military control exercised by the well-taught pupils who replace one regime with another.

In 1948, an intelligent first-born son, twenty-five years old and educated in Dutch schools, helps to translate *The Communist Manifesto* into Indonesian. The Communist Party of Indonesia (PKI), declared illegal by the Dutch following uprisings in 1926, is re-established in October 1945. Dipa Nusantara Aidit joins with many young Indonesians and some foreign nationals who want to improve living conditions for peasants and farmers locked in rural poverty. D.N. (as he renames himself) is now a member of the Central Indonesian National Committee with a responsibility for labour and land issues. In 1951, he becomes General Secretary of the party in return for his support of Sukarno. By the time my

A NECESSARY DISTANCE / 77

father visits in 1963, the PKI is the third largest communist party in the world (next to the Soviet Union and China) with three and a half million members. Two years later, a million people are murdered in that country of islands, many party members and many small farmers. Possibly, even probably, including Hajii and his family. With the direct support of the American government. Again, I want to talk to my father. What did you think when the coup happened? Did you write about it in a journal I don't have or talk to Gene?

In his 2020 book *The Jakarta Method*, journalist Vincent Bevins uses recently declassified documents, archival research and eyewitness testimony to reveal a legacy across twelve countries that exposes the role of US-led capitalist governments in much of the developing world's not-so-peaceful "transitions." Central to this was the US military's involvement in the 1965 killings. What became known as the Jakarta Method was used in Argentina, Bolivia, Brazil, Chile, Paraguay and more. It was called Operation Condor and was used in Iraq, Mexico, the Philippines, Thailand, Sudan, East Timor, Nicaragua.

Could my father have imagined that in Indonesia in 2014, a former son-in-law of the dictator Sukarno, whose empty limousine stopped traffic in 1963, would be the main rival for president? Joko Widodo was a military strongman who called for a return to the "New Order" of 1966. He appeared at party rallies on horseback dressed like Mussolini and announced he would be happy with a "benign authoritarian regime." Widodo demanded of a foreign journalist, "Do I have the guts? Am I ready to be called a fascist dictator?"

This story of a country of islands on the other side of the world reaches out to me, sitting in Kingston, Ontario, during the Covid-19 pandemic in June 2020. It is eight days after a Black man named George Floyd died on a street in Minneapolis, Minnesota, with a knee pressed into his neck. At a memorial for Mr. Floyd on June 4, civil rights activist Reverend Al Sharpton tells mourners inside a university chapel that Floyd's fatal encounter with police and the protests ignited by his death mark a reckoning over race and justice. Floyd "died of a common American criminal justice malfunction," says Sharpton. "It's time for us to stand up in George's name and say, 'Get your knee off our necks.'"

What is the knee on the neck of people of colour in America? In Canada? There are knees on the necks of poor people, labourers and farmers in 1963, and now – people who sew my clothes in India and China and answer my irritated questions about my computer difficulties, whose ravaged forests provide my hamburger, whose occupied homelands supply my cellphone. I uncomfortably read old articles about Indonesian politics and history and wonder, as a young woman at the barn where I keep my horse said yesterday, "What is the point of doing anything else right now? Except facing all this."

Brittany does the books for a local entertainment venue. She looked at me despairingly, absent-mindedly stroking her ten-week-old terrier puppy, and took several inhales of breath. "What's the point of doing accounts right now? Who needs accounts?"

In 1953 D.N. Aidit launched his analysis of Indonesian agrarian society. He said land reform – what is grown and who owns it – must be the essence of people's democracy. A year later the PKI adopted his analysis as the core of their new agrarian program and called on the party to put its efforts into rural land reform, using the slogan "land to the peasants." Twelve years later, a wave of killings swept rural Indonesia. Aidit was murdered and the PKI destroyed. The military and their allies targeted teachers and activists and set in place policies aimed to depoliticize the countryside, permanently eliminate the left and forbid the independent organization of peasants. This was a success for the US military, who

A NECESSARY DISTANCE / 79

had been training Indonesian soldiers on American soil. My father flew over Vietnam in 1963 with little comment. Unlike in that war, where American casualties drew attention and protest at home, in Indonesia in 1965 no Americans died. According to journalist and author David Swanson, the overthrow in Indonesia "was critical in destroying the non-aligned movement of third-world governments, and in establishing a policy of quietly 'disappearing' and torturing and slaughtering huge numbers of left-leaning civilians all over the globe."

The Jakarta Method was also used in Nicaragua, the country I visited as a peace activist in 1985. I was in my thirties and desperate to stop what I recognized as injustice. I wept in helplessness just as my young white students weep today for George Floyd and the realization that the communities they love are not the communities where their peers of colour live. These young people navigate their growing understanding that they do not share a home city with these friends or strangers, or not entirely. "I want Kingston to be a refuge for them too, as it is for me," says my barn friend Brittany. "But how?"

Shards of Glass

Each day there are messages in my inbox – "you *must* watch this, you *have to* listen to this." And I do. Bill learns about a Spike Lee production from Chicago and we watch. *Pass Over* is Antoinette Nwandu's play about two Black men in America who try to leave the city block they live on but are hemmed in by history, by police violence, by the ignorance of "bystander" audience members who are shocked and complicit and empty-handed. The production is sharp. It cuts away complacency. *Bang, bang.* Down they go, over and over. As reviewer Nick Allen puts it, the play "turns a wounded culture into artistic aggression, throwing it all on the stage and daring you to look away." *Pass Over* was produced at the Steppenwolf

Theatre in Chicago and drips with poison like the moments of George Floyd's death. The audience in the film is Black, familiar, unsurprised; heads nod, mouths fix in grim attention.

I receive an email: "My friend has been muted." A Chinese student asked her Canadian friends what this hatred and racism in America means. She was rebuked, "You should be an international citizen, you should know!" My student thought, "But, do you know about Uyghurs in China? Do you know about Tiananmen Square? Hong Kong right now?" She said nothing. "She has been shut out by her white and Black friends," writes my student. "What do we do? We need guidance."

"There is so much misery, so much violence in the world," says my husband. Outside there is a spring thunderstorm and the skies are dark; the rain shakes the trees in the park. "That's what is bothering me," he says. "People are posting that they didn't realize what Black people's lives were like, that they are ashamed, that they have been *changed* by this moment . . . changed! But – what world do they think they have been living in?"

Bill tells me a story about his mother. The family lived in central India. Bill was born there as was his father. His parents were missionaries – his mother a nurse, his father a pastor who became a counsellor after retiring in Canada. In this story, Bill is twelve and his parents are home on furlough. They have rented a cottage on an Ontario lake and a neighbour has invited them over for the evening. "The neighbours had a TV and it was a big deal." A Canadian movie was premiering, *Goin' Down the Road* by Don Shebib. It was 1970. It's about two young men who leave their home in Nova Scotia and make their way to the excitement and chaos of downtown Toronto. There was lots of swearing, things happened and the neighbour kept covering her mouth, shocked, saying, "If I'd known, if I'd known, I wouldn't have watched . . ." Bill's mother just looked at the woman. "What planet have you been living on?"

she asked. "I was so proud of my mom for that," says Bill. We look out at the shuddering trees, listen as another crack of thunder rumbles. "That's it," I say. "What planet have we all been living on?"

Where Are the Nazis?

Yesterday I told my Argentinian friend Victor, "I am stuck in Indonesia." His reply: "You are stuck there because killing a million people is a big deal."

Indonesia, and all the countries my father will visit. Disappearances, genocide, the slaughter of villages, the burning of crops, organized systematic dispossession of small farmers, peasants. "It always comes down to the same thing," says Victor. "There is racism, yes, but always for exploitation. There are two sides, the oppressors and the oppressed. The ideological battle for greed and profit, or for compassion, solidarity and fairness."

I think about this. I always tell my playwriting students, no one is the villain of their own story. It takes seeing from outside to perceive one's own complicity. At the same time, he is right, my friend who lived through Argentina's dictatorship. I see the rumblings of the future in my father's notebooks. The brutality that Victor describes is evident everywhere. Why are people surprised?

Victor asks me, "Why do you think Indonesia has so much silence around it?" I ask Bill this question. "America has orchestrated coups in many countries over the years. But Indonesia – it's a primarily Muslim country."

My father went to Indonesia to film examples of land reform. He sat in traffic as President Sukarno's limousine shut down streets. In 1959, the man had established an autocratic system called "Guided Democracy . . . that successfully ended the instability and rebellions which were threatening the survival of the diverse and fractious country." By 1960, Sukarno had become more and more of a dictator and was taking the country further left, "to the irritation of the nationalists and the Islamists." The president supported the farmers and labourers and developed aggressive foreign policies in the name of anti-imperialism. It was no doubt Indonesia's increasing closeness to the Soviet Union and China that made America support the horrific events that unfolded.

Vincent Bevins quotes a memo to the Rand Corporation by an American policy advisor and CIA operative:

> Were the Communists to lose Sukarno as a protector, it seems doubtful that other national leaders, capable of rallying Indonesia's dispersed and demoralized anti-Communist forces, would emerge in the near future. Furthermore, these forces would probably lack the ruthlessness that made it possible for the Nazis to suppress the Communist Party of Germany a few weeks after the elections of March 5th, 1933 . . . The enemies of the PKI . . . are weaker than the Nazis, not only in numbers and in mass support, but also in unity, discipline and leadership.

This was the thinking of international capitalism: "Where are the Nazis when you need them?"

The Answer Is on the Dance Floor

Saturday morning, January 26. Dad and Gene go to the Qantas Empire Airways office in Jakarta to secure tickets for the next day to Bombay. The man on the desk asks if they have their visas. My father's notes help me to imagine this exchange.

"We don't need a visa for India," says Gene.

"Are you sure?" my dad whispers.

"Yes, yes absolutely!" says Gene pointedly in the clerk's direction. The man brings a large book to the counter, sets it down and leafs through pages.

A NECESSARY DISTANCE / 83

"Our papers say that customs have a right to search our out-going luggage, but not to charge duty," Gene says quietly.

"Ah," says George. "Not likely they will look then, is it?"

The clerk finally nods and gives them back their tickets. "All good."

As they leave the office, Gene has a last word on the subject. "Travellers usually know more about these things than the local officials. Sometimes they won't believe you and you have to fight battles with assistant managers and managers. We were lucky just now."

They meet the FAO's Mr. Tabor at his house for lunch. Two servants in white jackets escort them into a spacious enclosed veranda. A bamboo bar opens into a room filled with antique Chinese curiosities – paintings of luminous rice harvesters, an old carved wooden chest, bamboo armchairs, a Chinese painting of a horse. On the coffee table is a carved box with American cigarettes inside. Mr. Tabor greets them wearing a beige suit with a tie of pale yellow. My father wonders, how can people stay so cool in these suits? Linen?

They sit. While two servants explain the menu to Mr. Tabor, a tall thin gentleman – hairdresser? – rubs ointment into Tabor's thick hair. They eat a mild soup and several rice-based dishes. Each setting has different coloured plates: blue, maroon, grey. Tabor talks a great deal. About the Russians. The following conversation is my reconstruction from Dad's notes, a technique I use throughout the book:

"I have great friend Viktor, a Russian correspondent. He drinks a lot and has adopted Indonesia, he stays as long as he will be permitted. Which, well, who knows." Tabor sits back. Gene's blue eyes twinkle with mischief. Uh-oh, thinks George. Here we go.

"So, is it an affair of love or hate for your friend, Russia and America? And what for you, sir?" asks Gene.

"With this country of islands," says Tabor. "Of so many hidden peoples and places, no? So many possible allegiances?"

A servant offers them a sweet, unidentifiable fruit juice. Tabor's long fingers stroke his crystal glass, moist with condensation. Tabor teases but won't commit himself.

"What does your friend think?" probes Gene. Tabor smiles, enjoying the challenge. Who did he lunch with yesterday, thinks Dad. Emperors and businessmen?

"Viktor does, indeed, have a theory. It is that Indonesia needs a period of capitalism to accumulate skills and capital goods, before socialism can have material to work with. Of course, then *you* would hope they would continue with capitalism," says Tabor, "and Viktor would hope they'd turn to communism."

"And who would be right?" asks my father.

"Perhaps neither," says Gene. "Anything with an 'ism' at the end is by definition reduced. Systems are a shorthand, but not a solution."

Tabor shakes his head. "You are avoiding," he says. "The answer in Jakarta is on the dance floor. Dance by dance." Dad and Gene look obligingly curious.

"Well!" declares Tabor, opening both hands and shrugging. "When President Sukarno greets US Ambassador Jones, and dances first dance with Mrs. Jones, the Russian wires home, 'Send more money!' When the president dances first with the wife of the Russian Ambassador, it is certain he wants something from the Americans."

"Ah," says Dad. "Both great powers are blackmailed in these simple ways and let him get away with it! If Russia and the US become friends, bad business for the blackmailing countries."

The head of the FAO in Indonesia is trying to explain, with a diplomat's finesse, the politics boiling around him. "This is a very Indonesian situation. A very particular kind of dictator, if we will use that word for a moment."

Food arrives, plates piled high with noodles. George pokes his fork tentatively at what looks like a raging hot pepper. Gene digs in happily.

"Particular how?" ventures my father.

Tabor looks at him. "What is your background, Mr. Salverson? Are you a Swede?"

"Norwegian. Icelandic. But mostly Canadian," my father says. "The Icelanders keep their food but like to blend in, be part of their new country. We aren't isolationists."

"Hmm. And how would you describe the Icelandic character?"

Dad doesn't have to think long about this one. "Independent! And readers. Have you heard the joke about trying to find a library book in Iceland? You can't! The libraries are always empty!"

"Ah, good, very good," says Tabor. "Well, let me tell you about the Indonesian character because it is the basis of this dictatorship. Not cold or harsh, like a Nordic version. And very local. People want to look after their farms. Maybe their local community. But something broader? No. Keep things going well at home, that's enough. That's a lot."

"I would agree it is a lot," my father thinks, but says nothing. He waits.

"Sukarno sees himself as a man of destiny, like all dictators. But it is mixed: he has both self-aggrandizement and the glory of his country, the welfare of his people, in mind." Their host pauses to take a bite. "He has done very good work with schools." Gene leans back from his empty plate. "Let me offer a perspective your visitors hear. Some say, or say to us, that Sukarno is a bit of a Bonaparte. Living in his wealthy palace surrounded by great art. Pronouncing on freedom and liberty."

Tabor looks at Gene carefully. "Liberty. But not freedom. Or perhaps it is . . . freedom. But not liberty. Which would you choose, gentleman?" The servants enter and clear plates. Tabor smiles. "Our president was able to guess very well at what the Indonesian people would accept. He is, of course, Indo himself. So, in a way, there is a democracy. Telepathic democracy."

Rajid's wife wants to shop for American records and show Gene and Dad a popular restaurant. Minnie has been given money to pay for her own food and shows papers to prove she is Indonesian and can pay with rupiahs. They talk about America. "I have been twice," she says. "New Orleans, Arizona. Americans are informal and kind, but only to get something out of me as an Asian. They want me to love them."

"They want everyone to love them," says Gene.

Minnie frowns. "They are rich people, so it's sensible to like them, no?"

My father laughs at this pragmatic idea, responding with "I don't think it's necessary to take something from someone you dislike. Disrespect. I would rather look after myself."

Minnie looks at him with a smile that Dad describes later as a veiled sneer. "You love Vikings."

She pays the bill and pockets the change. As they walk to the door, she says, "I tried once to ski in Catskills. New York. Other Asians laughed at me. Also, angry at me for loving boyfriend and American music. But my boyfriend gave me books. *Lady Chatterley's Lover.*"

"Really?" says my father. "What else?"

"*Brave New World*. I discovered reading, and English. After that, my parents lost control of me."

Minnie tells them she read Marx at seventeen. She is proud of this – perhaps with reason, thinks George. She identifies emancipation from the Dutch with emancipation from her parents and the old ways. She is working for the UN because she won't work for the present government. Minnie "bounces away to the car like a schoolgirl, full of smugness," and the cab returns to the

A NECESSARY DISTANCE / 87

hotel. "Pamayou Room Restaurant is disgusting," she says. Gene and George look surprised. Haven't they all just eaten there quite happily? "But is a wonderful Jakarta night spot."

Dad writes in his journal:

Everyone hates America, despises her. Everyone of the present generation hates her and sings her songs, plays her music, wants to be like her, and believes her cash is theirs by natural right, "because we are poor." This showed nakedly in Hajii's wife. She wanted more for her husband and got it. She may think she made suckers of us all, but a Toronto actor would have been paid much more.

So Dad leaves Canada on January 16. He arrives in Jakarta, Sunday, January 20 after four days of disorientation and jet lag, and flies on to India seven days later. He is already homesick. When he spoke about the trip, he emphasized his hatred of Indonesia. I have peeked ahead at his time in Nairobi, in Brazil – later he is not so lethal in his condemnation. He doesn't know yet that he has already picked up hepatitis. In Indonesia, he talks about people's "brown skin." But he does the same with great admiration on his next stop, India.

My father had a horror of poverty. His judgment was harsh when he thought someone didn't fight hard enough to get out of it. In 1968, we moved to a small village east of Toronto. Across the street was a family from the east coast who were on welfare. We made no effort to get to know them. We looked down on them with a kind of snobbery that came from having money struggles but being hardworking, which was honourable, while being on welfare – that was not. I think for my father it was the residue of his parents' struggles and growing up in the 1930s' Depression, where poverty was everywhere and humiliation was scored into my father's skin. Dad was terrified of returning to that kind of life. He respected education, learning, the will to better yourself. He detested begging, which he associated with slipperiness, indirection and lack of character. In these ways, he was a true conservative, despite voting Liberal and later New Democrat.

What is it he is reacting to in Jakarta? My father – *my father* – writes this: "Three beggars on crutches in traffic among cars at intersection – hands stretched toward windows with sickening gesture, sick pitiful eyes seeking yours, altogether sickening, degraded, like vile animals. Feel no sense of pity. Only revulsion and hate. If one of them touched me I'd want to kill him." Yes, he is shocked by what he finds himself thinking and feeling. But he writes it.

Maybe his response was more out of fear than anything, with no time for his tired brain to process. Fear can turn into extreme self-protectiveness, a hostility toward perceived threat. These primal reactions he records faithfully. We are different people when we are afraid. And confronting extreme need in someone *is* frightening. It can rock your world if you've never seen it. To judge my father seems superficial. I suspect that this is more about wealth and poverty than white and non-white, or the Global North and South. As for my father – why would I know him any more than I don't know most people; the public faces they show, the private confusions.

I have a dream. I'm on a tour bus, and each segment of the trip I have to stand near the front and make a speech. The trip goes on, then I find myself at the back, so I look around, disoriented, and say, "I'll just stand back here." I attempt to speak but instead I start to cry. I say, "Everyone, look. These are my parents." I have a sense that my mother is here, but she isn't the important one. "Let me introduce you all," I say, pointing to the front of the bus, "to my father. This is my father, see?" I point. My father is driving the bus.

Dog Walking

On a cold spring day, I drive west to Burt's Greenhouses. It's a family business and worth the half-hour and the mileage. A young woman in a blue mask calls my name and wheels out a cart with three bags of cow manure, some potting soil and a tray of plants. She loads them into the back of my Subaru and I close the hatch. I drive across the highway and through the little town of Odessa. My friend Diana lives in the countryside nearby and is in her garden. The three dogs are thrilled to be out of their roomy outdoor pen.

We set off to the back fields. The two hounds, Chance and Bandit, float like gazelles through the large open acres that will so quickly, unimaginably, become tall grass. It's wet from yesterday's monsoon-like downpour. Diana leads me through the drier patches, my red boots stained from the damp. We "social distance," Diana ahead of me and just to one side so I don't lose her words in the wind.

When we reach the trees, she stops and points down. "Look. We did this on the weekend." She runs her finger through the delicate strands of a tiny white pine. Ahead of us run three long black lines where the machine cut into the soil. Wisps of what will be trees miraculously hang on, all six inches of them. "They planted six thousand and if three-quarters make it, that's a big success." It's part of an Ontario reseeding program. Social distance trees.

"Can I ask you something about my book?"

"Of course!" She stops and turns, a grin of expectation on her face. I notice, not for the first time, how open and willing she is. Whatever I want to ask, she will give it her best shot. "Okay, so I think this question will make sense in a minute." I hesitate. She raises her eyebrows. "Okay, um . . . What's a racist?"

She speaks immediately. "First, I think I'll be wrong. So many people have thought more . . ." She trails off.

I say, "It's that so many *not white* people have *had* to think . . ."

Diana nods. "A racist is someone who makes judgments about people based solely on where they were born. On skin colour."

Maya, the German shepherd, has stopped ahead of Diana. Why are we stopping? Her tongue hangs out and she pants patiently. I step forward and the dog turns quickly and trots ahead along the path. We follow.

"My dad went to different places on this trip. Some countries with brown people he loved, some he didn't. He said different kinds of things. He says how police in Canada never stop people for no reason, but well, he's white." I quicken my step and splash into a bog.

"You have to go quickly through here," Diana calls back. We speed up together, synchronized sloshing.

"He went to Nairobi. He loved it. He wrote, 'If self-government comes to Nairobi, in a few years it will be like Jakarta.' And, in a few years . . ."

"It was like Jakarta?"

"Yes. Meaning it wasn't efficient and orderly and what felt safe to Dad. This reminds me of a story from India. There used to be this swashbuckling crook of a chief minister in Bihar, Laloo Prasad Yadav. At one point, some Japanese politician said something like 'Give us five years and we can turn Bihar into Japan.' To which Laloo replied, 'Give me five years and I can turn Japan into Bihar.'"

Diana laughs. "So, your dad made judgments?"

"Well, he recorded his impressions. I have no idea how seriously he took his own notes, so how seriously I should. How do I evaluate them?"

"Why evaluate?" she asks. Then she tells me about the book she is reading, songwriter Garnet Rogers' biography of his years with Canadian icon brother Stan. "They were performing in the seventies, and they were such assholes. He says that straight out. They were *so* a product of their time, but Garnet doesn't excuse it, he describes it. They'd tell awful sexist jokes and they had feminists in the audience, more and more. It's hilarious, how he describes it. Because there's affection, and at the same time they were total jerks. You don't want a character to be a hero."

We walk into another open field. The highway is close – invisible, but a steady wall of noise. This protected little wood is not really protected at all. There are more cars than last week. People must be starting to go places again, or maybe the bare trees and the wind amplify the sound.

She stops suddenly, looking around. "We've lost the dogs." She's not concerned. "They are probably chasing the coyote." She puts her fingers in her mouth and deafens me with a whistle, then calls out, "Bandy, Bandy, Bandy, Bandy! Chasey poo poo, Chasey poo poo!" I don't laugh, this seems perfectly normal. I enjoy my serious doctor friend who treated prison inmates for years. She has a Herculean ability to compartmentalize her life, fiercely protecting her privacy and contained and professional at work. I watch her, at peace in this place, in this life.

As we walk forward there is a yodel-like howl and soon the two dogs appear, running a few yards, then circling and leaping into each other. Diana laughs so hard she stops and puts her hands on her knees. "Listen to that, do you hear that?" The dogs come up, "Good boy!" she tells them, "Good Bandy-Bandy, good Chase!" The slower German shepherd plods toward us. "Good girl, Maya!" Maya wags her tail and accepts the compliment, turning and leading us along the final stretch.

I go back to the end of Notebook One. Here is what I haven't mentioned yet:

92 / JULIE SALVERSON

- American music is triumphant everywhere. Elvis. The Art & Cultural Dept of the hotel is presenting a routine Hollywood movie. Dress required.
- Understand now why there are underdeveloped countries. Not because of colonizers. Because they are filled with underdeveloped people.
- To think that Canadians and Americans are so sentimental and idealistic that we love everyone, and really believe all humans are alike.
- It's a mistake to travel and learn differently.
- Do you suppose these people were any better or worse off under the Rajahs, etc.? How? The world has not been made smaller by the airplane. These people are 10,000 years away from the airport.
- Does it matter? To each his own. They would hate my life in Canada as much as I hate theirs. Then how are we humans ever to understand each other?
- At least, at last, the gear is at the airport.
- Hope we may leave by Qantas and enjoy new magazines and English voices.
- They say "Travel broadens one." Fear it will make me narrow.

My mind swims with all of this. Dad and his team were the beginning of a new wave of global connectivity, post–World War II and pre-internet. Radio, television, film, international NGOs – all were part of it. People around the globe have fast-forwarded through history – from no phone to cellphone, from village life to a job in the city, from bicycle to scooter to car. For many, in ten years or less.

When I started reading the journals at the end, with Dad's return to Canada, I thought he had come to his confrontation with his assumptions gradually. But he makes pronouncements

A NECESSARY DISTANCE / 93

after three days of travel. Is it jet lag and culture shock, is he "lost in translation" and never gets out? Can I accept him as a white, western male who brought everything he was to this encounter, including his childhood poverty, the provincial and arrogant nature of his culture's view of the non-white world, *and* his keen eye and his honesty?

I call Joy Kogawa. Her memoir *Gently to Nagasaki* is about the internment of her family in Canada during World War II and the bombings of Hiroshima and Nagasaki. From the book jacket: "Kogawa's memoir deeply explores how denial works with regards to racism . . . bravely detailing the intersection between mass global evils and those perpetuated intimately by members of one's own family."

Specific people were harmed by Kogawa's father, a father she continues to love and admire and whose gifts, strengths and good works stand together with his . . . I avoid the word. It is here, in my mind, resisted by my fingers on the keyboard. His sins. "It's hard to write about," says this tiny woman in her eighties who has become my friend. "But you do it for love. Why else?" Joy tells me that she had nightmares and panic attacks all her life. When she finished writing an earlier book about her father, his abuse and his love, all that stopped. "You have to go into the fire," she says.

CHAPTER FOUR

The Film

Interesting Bones

It is the pandemic. Today Ontario premier Doug Ford extended the state of emergency until June 2, for three more weeks. This morning, over the backyard fence, my neighbour is once again wrapping her new Japanese tree with a sheet. "If this tree dies I will destroy furniture," she says between clenched shivering teeth. We are all going mad because the earth will not let us have spring.

Noam Chomsky says America will either become green and renewed or fascist and brutal. Suddenly it's too much. I prefer to be back in 1963 Jakarta whose complexities aren't mine. I read in the comfort of my study. I dip into my father's personal documents, the Indonesian novels I am reading, the academic studies; chosen like chocolates from a box, communism and land reform this morning, later a lyric passage about village life.

"Have you dug up any interesting bones lately?" Cuban American Ruth Behar is repeatedly asked this question when she tells people she is an anthropologist. It's a field influenced by notions, she says, "which could only speak of natives in native lands, a concept of culture which was still inarticulate about borders . . . I think what we are seeing are efforts to map an intermediate space we can't

/ 94

A NECESSARY DISTANCE / 95

quite define yet, a borderland between passion and intellect, analysis and subjectivity, ethnography and autobiography, art and life."

Behar started writing as a *vulnerable observer* in the late 1980s. She was influenced by Renato Rosaldo whose essay "Grief and a Headhunter's Rage" blew open the constrictions of a field already challenged by the likes of Claude Lévi-Strauss. Rosaldo "gave us a new map. It was a map of our post-colonial, nostalgia-saturated world. And it was a map of our haunted global souls."

This image speaks to many of us today, nervously looking over our shoulders for ancestors we don't know if we can accept. More and more people join Ancestry.com, hungering to belong to something more than their social media accounts. We want to know our heritage, but we are caught in reductive traps that risk throwing us back into early anthropology, speaking only "about natives in native lands." We are inarticulate about borders, the fluid interplay of our relations to this planet now, as for the first time since the emergence of the atomic bomb we face global extinction and thus need, surely, a global identity.

Finding the Film

I spend months avoiding finding the film these men are making. Maybe it's a feeling I should only watch it after I've finished reading through the whole trip. Or maybe something else is going on.

One day Bill, fed up with my inertia, locates it in Ottawa. I send an inquiry, then forget about it. Months later an email arrives from Library and Archives Canada. Everything had closed because of Covid-19 but now my order can be processed. If I call and pay $141.68, they will upload the thirty-minute documentary and send it to me as an MP4 file. I speak on the phone to Dusty Langlois and give him my credit card number. "Should be tomorrow," he says.

I hang up. That was ridiculously easy. Thirty minutes. It's called *The Secret Hunger – Freedom from Hunger*. His trip is so alive in my mind, what will happen when it is translated into thirty minutes of scripted and edited material?

On the Library and Archives Canada website:

Canadian Broadcasting Corporation, Television
Release date:
1963-05-20
Production credit:
director/producer, Gene Lawrence; executive producer, Thom Benson; script, George Salverson; photography, Grahame Woods; editing, Michael Foytenyi; music, Ricky Hyslop
Description:
Documentary film about world hunger, prepared by the CBC in co-operation with the Food and Agriculture Organization (FAO) of the UN. It was filmed in India, Africa, Indonesia, and Latin America.

I hadn't realized the CBC connection. And I don't recognize the executive producer, Thom Benson. Dad doesn't mention him. The next morning, I find this email:

Material Protected by Third Party Copyright
Library and Archives Canada is not the copyright owner of the material identified below. However, we are pleased to provide you with the following contact information of the copyright owner so that you may obtain their permission for LAC to release copies.

I write to CBC. I say it is my father's film, and I would like a copy. I press send.

There are not many defenders of the CBC these days, but there are also few who know what it has meant to the making of a national

A NECESSARY DISTANCE / 97

culture. My father was the first drama story editor for English television. Here is what he told me about how he got the job:

> Sydney Newman was head of radio drama and Andrew was
> head of all drama. There was the old CBC Radio building
> and a new television building, and I was walking from one
> to the other when Andrew stuck his head out of the radio
> building and said, "Come up here." He told me, "Sydney
> wants to try out the idea of a story editor and I think you
> should do it." I thought, *Oh!* Here's a chance to learn tele-
> vision – by teaching it! Six months later it was going well
> so he thought we should have a second one. I said, "How
> about critic Nathan Cohen? He'd make a hell of a good
> one." So, I hired him, and after that everyone thought I was
> working for Nathan Cohen! Because he had a lot of prestige.
> He could be two completely different people. He'd come in
> raving about a script but then when he reviewed something,
> the actors hated him. He could be good, but he made the
> mistake, in order to catch the allure of readers, to do what
> lots of critics have done – be clever at the expense of the
> actors. I once told him Sandra would never do stage in
> Toronto because he might review it. He went beet red and
> I changed the subject. I learned a lot from him. Because he
> was so different from me.

In Dad's papers I find a typed document titled "ARSC CONFER-
ENCE." In pencil at the top, "Banquet Speech/NAC" May 1980. I
think the author is CBC's longtime archivist Ernie Dick:

> The CBC's accomplishments have not become part of Can-
> ada's collective historical consciousness in the way that one
> would expect. The CBC has fallen into the common Canadian

habit of re-justifying its rationale and re-inventing its purpose rather than building upon a tradition. Partly this is due to the ephemeral nature of broadcasting. Partly it is due to the CBC's peculiar and precarious life at the pleasure of Parliament.

But in great measure it is due to the fact that the CBC has not developed a greater commitment to its own history . . . To understand what it was like to live through a period of history one must have not only the facts but also be capable of imagination. And for stimulating the imagination radio has no peer.

The man who spoke these words wasn't interested until he started listening to old tapes. Then, "Nothing I heard on contemporary radio could be compared to it." Canadian radio drama, he says, "was the seed bed of the explosion in the Canadian theatre which has taken place in the last decade."

The impact of the CBC *Stage* series is told in a story from Andrew Allan's memoir. One day in the 1950s he got on a train with what he called a "lump of lead" in his briefcase. He had decided that the endless battle to keep the fully Canadian drama series on the air was pointless. "Several seasons of guerilla warfare had brought me, despite our reputed success, to the draft of a letter to the CBC management, recommending that the *Stage* be discontinued." He had decided to take a holiday in Vancouver, boarding in Toronto for a few days of incognito travel. He planned to make a good copy of his decision and mail it back east. He was relieved.

The train moved into the foothills: "light enough and free enough to lift the weight off any man." A horseman rode toward the train, stopped by the fence and waved his hat. Allan and the young woman in the seat beside him stood at the same time to wave back, then smiled at each other. "You're Andrew Allan, aren't you?" she said. He was. "You're the reason I'm here," she said.

This was enough to seize the attention . . . I made a suitable noise. "We live on a farm, away up north of Edmonton," said the girl. "We're just plain people, I guess. We haven't got any books to speak of, or music, or anything. But I have a little radio in my room. Every Sunday night I go up there to listen to your plays. All week I wait for that time. It's wonderful. It's a whole new world for me. I began to read books because of your plays – all kinds of books I never thought I'd be interested in. I'm on my way to Vancouver to stay with my aunt and in the fall I'm starting at the university. And it's all because of you and your plays. What do you think of that?"

What I thought about that was too deep to be said. But what I did about it was to go to my compartment and tear up the draft of the letter. We had seven more years of the *Stage* after that.

In January 2022, the British government announced it was freezing some BBC funding for two years. John Doyle responded in the *Globe and Mail*. He said that the "standing army of anti-CBC pundits in Canada [are] a noisy bunch, and any excuse to attack the CBC begets reams of prose about the CBC's irrelevance, bias or alleged incompetence." He gave a few examples and then added: "Most punditry about the CBC is drenched in naiveté. The majority of commentators know nothing about television or how the medium works."

Doyle acknowledges problems and successes – lots of them. He understands the complexity and diversity of people in this country. He understands that some people don't call it Canada at all. But he is saying, I think, that whether we like it or not, something binds us together that includes, and is greater than, the violence of our history.

The Cheery Side of Hunger

The film arrived by email as soon as I signed the papers. I downloaded it. The icon sits on my desktop like a tiny eye, watching me. I am afraid it will be terrible. I'm afraid it will feel cliché and shallow and politically incorrect, God help me. I can't bear if it's like that. Better it stays a mystery. Better I'd never found it.

"You're procrastinating," writes my friend and sister-in-law Vera. "You don't trust him. But Julie, think how amazing this thing was that they did. I mean, flying around the world in 1963 to get to those places, trying to get people on film talking about their lives, trying to get footage."

I am ashamed of myself. For not giving them more credit.

It's a very old film. The camera holds steady on the image of two middle-aged men leaning out from behind a sign: *Don Messer's Jubilee*. They are waving hats like old-fashioned vaudeville.

An announcer's voice that can only be from the sixties: "We wish to thank Colgate-Palmolive Limited, sponsors of *Don Messer's Jubilee*, for relinquishing their time tonight in order that we may bring you the following special program." Then a pause, and a bearded man in a dark suit and tie begins speaking. He sounds far away, and the film shakes slightly as old films do, as if the narrator is trembling. It is a very young Peter Ustinov: "I'm Peter Ustinov. I'd like to tell you a story about the cheery side of hunger."

The men have been immersed in hot humid smog. Family and Toronto winter are dreams from another life. Travel is always like this but surely it was even more so in 1963, when it took days and nights to get anywhere. The three filmmakers stopped mailing letters in Jakarta because the mail never left the hotel.

Three months later, this is the part of Indonesia that ends up in the film:

Minute 19 of 29 minutes.
Shot of a man bowing at entrance to a house.

Narrator:
It's useful to be at prayer when entering the
last chapter in the story of life. Hajii Monsura
looked into old age and found the day important.
He was going to Jakarta as he had done before on
his way to Mecca. Today he would see for the first
time his spanking new grandson. And the meaning
of his life seemed to gather about him as richly
as the bursting earth of Java.

Close-up of man's lined face, not old, not young.
white shirt and scarf, white round hat. He looks
out over the paddies, the hill in background,
palm trees.

Here was his life. Rice paddies. In the paddies
and ponds, fish ripe for harvest. Bananas and avo-
cados, papaya and breadfruit, a tropical downpour
of infinite fruits. If anyone had laboured to
defeat hunger it was Hajii Monsura, his helpers
and his neighbours.

Shot of woman planting rice in pools of water.
Shot of feet and hands pulling a long flat instrument through the muddy water. Shots of a cow
pulling the instrument.

Rice, of course, was the key to life, and life to
a rice farmer was work. There were occasions when

102 / JULIE SALVERSON

Hajii's bones and joints gave notice of his age, that the time was coming when all this would be too much for him. Then it was good to reflect that both his sons had gone up in the world and would never be farmers, would never grow a single grain of rice, would never grow anything but grandsons and perpetuate Hajii's line.

25:24 Shot of woman carrying child.

Hajii's wife came out with one of those beloved grandchildren, to warn him to get ready for the bus. It was certainly a satisfaction to have one son not only out of farming, but conducting his own business. Because his mind was on the escape from rice, Hajii thought of the government men who said there wasn't enough rice. Some idiot. And they wanted to teach the rice farmers, oh yes, new methods to increase the yield. What for?

Man washing his feet from water in a bucket.

There had always been plenty of rice for Hajii Monsura. Java was up to its knees in rice. Idiots.

Man puts woven hat on his head, picks up a cup and walks away. Shot of bananas.

Hajii waited for the bus with his son Dajat, the tailor, and Dajat's beautiful wife and children. Hajii could see that things were better not worse.

A NECESSARY DISTANCE / *103*

Shot of Hajii and his wife.

He could see it in the children. Now they had science and child welfare centres and nurses advising mothers. The children looked much better than they used to. In ten years, children were a head taller with good teeth. On other islands the people ate no rice at all, only sago (a starch like tapioca) and their children were strange and out of proportion — well, not his grandson in Jakarta.

Hajii waves as he walks down the path from the house, the small bus stops. Looks like it has four seats, perhaps seats twelve and one in the passenger seat. His family wave as Hajii gets on and bus drives away. Shot of back of driver's head.

27:04 Shot of Hajii looking out bus window, outside fields, palms.

So Hajii rode to Jakarta, looking out at the earth bursting with foods, thinking his life had been quite a success. And worthily renewed by a new grandchild.

Shot of city from bus window.

There was plenty to see in the city, particularly people. Unlike the lonely country road where you could travel a couple of hundred yards without seeing a soul, there was a bonanza of company.

Shot of more people, bicycles, vehicles.

It crossed his mind, there were rather a large amount of people for a farmer to feed. But he made no further interpretation of the evidence now before his eyes. Indonesia, at one time, exported a million dollars' worth of rice a year.

27:40 Shot of Hajii getting off bus, walking barefoot amongst crowd.

There are ninety million people. One and a half million babies born each year. Indonesia now imports a million dollars' worth of rice a year. The human race has become a desperate race, between production and reproduction.

Hajii walking, solo guitar.

So Hajii Monsura, who knew that Java was up to its knees in rice, walked into the crowd to see the renewal of life, the new grandchild. He didn't hurry, he was beginning to feel his age. But there was no hurry, the new child was born a week ago, it was no longer a novelty. In that week, a whole new Indonesian city of twenty-five thousand souls had come into existence. And in the world, an additional seven hundred thousand, all younger, and screaming to be fed.

28:25 Shot of one Indonesian man in hat, holding
stick.

One life. The cycle begins again. All man is one,
in living and in need.

CHAPTER FIVE

Quebec

May 2019. Yesterday I drove to a village in the Laurentides, Quebec. I will join four other women, all here for a writing retreat. Rose is an old friend from South Africa and works on violence and stigma. When she invited me, she said that it would be "a few women writing" but now she confesses that this is her research team and she wants me to join their project. "I tricked you, I'm sorry!" I'm surprised but not concerned. I have my own space to write and they seem like good people, two former graduate students of Rose's who have recently been appointed to university jobs: Hyunji from Korea and Molly from the US. Also, Rose's sister, Ann, a scientist from Ottawa.

Molly has dark-blond hair in a short blunt cut, vivid eyes and a rolling spring to her step. Her research is on the disappeared in Argentina. She is translating the poems of assault survivors. She sings as she moves around the house and has a beautiful fluting voice. Hyunji is thoughtful, does arts education and is trying to figure out how to live in the American South. We sit comfortably on the veranda in the early evening sun, the village of Saint-Donat below. We are high up, suspended.

As the light shifts Molly says, "In a lot of writing, wounds and scars are talked about the same way. But they are different. A scar suggests something has healed."

/ 106

A NECESSARY DISTANCE / *107*

"Or is hidden," I say.

I wake the next morning thinking about this. She is right. A scar is not an open wound, is not recent. It is a sign of buried pain. Is it old hurt that continues to fester and infect the present, as victim culture suggests? I think it is the marking of a life lived, with it's inevitable hurts and accidents and losses.

The next morning I'm the first up. I grab a coffee and find wet plastic chairs under a gazebo. Crisp and chilly, but with my down vest I can be outside. I wipe a chair and sit near some tall pines with *The Larger Conversation* by Canadian poet and essayist Tim Lilburn. I notice this: "The renovation of Western philosophy required to imagine a post-imperial world is a work that is substantial and, while dislocating, delightful. This re-making cannot be achieved by invention, but only by a retrieval, exact as possible, of lost cultural parts."

Retrieval. Isn't that what Indigenous people are doing? Reclaiming. Resurging. Isn't this what the rest of us – settlers, arrivants, everyone else here – need to do? Retrieve. Dig, listen, seek out anything in our own traditions, the wandering paths of our ancestors, any glimpse of help that reminds us how to listen and look and be. Nonbinary, non-Cartesian. This is what I am doing through this encounter with my father and my history: attempting to shape a story from the pieces.

Lilburn is my instructor in learning to look. He writes about being in a forest and looking at a deer, and knowing that he doesn't know *how* to see the deer. Here in these Quebec woods where I am a visitor, what does it mean to listen *here*? And how can I learn who *I am* as I listen? Lilla Watson, an Aboriginal woman from the Dawson River in Australia, warned people, "If you have come here to help me you are wasting your time. If you have come because your liberation is bound up with mine, then let's work together."

My father set out to learn, help, make a film. End world hunger! He is also a kind of first responder of an artistic order. Like a first responder, he did not have the luxury of time to really look and listen. Nor did he have the space required for what Lilburn calls the "collapse of confidence" that precedes real learning. George, Gene and Grahame had been assigned to a professional task. All three had families they supported through their contract work, something that had its particular challenges in 1960s' North America with its *Mad Men* class of new professionals. The team would have had some idea of their profound inability to understand what they were seeing, but they had to behave competently; shoot footage, write a script, finish the film.

I walk down the steep gravel driveway, criss-crossing to ease the angle of descent. Around me are dense pines punctuated by glimpses of sky. Just to my right in a clearing is a tall metal cross draped in lightbulbs. It is visible for miles around. I proceed with stops and starts and at angles. The view changes every few steps. Like how I am writing now. It is unstable, unpredictable, any straight-ahead orientation is confounded. There are breaks in the tree line, I see the village below. I step quickly past, preferring the illusion that I am the only one here. Alone, not the best way to think about being in the woods learning aliveness. And yet the openings mark a beyond, waiting for when I am ready.

I don't yet know how to see a tree, or feel the field I am standing in. Can I learn to see my father? Or my culture?

They're All Alive

Peter van Wyck calls from Montreal. He teaches at Concordia University and is my collaborator in atomic stories; we have travelled together for almost two decades. I talk to him from the deck outside my Quebec bedroom. Undulating hills curve along the edge

A NECESSARY DISTANCE / *109*

of the village below. Smudges of dark orange and black dot the hills. God's thumbprints.

Peter has been talking with a graduate student who is writing about auras. Seances, telekinisis, and inevitably the question comes up, "Is it real?" "Her problem," says Peter, "is does she remain agnostic, or say 'yes' or 'no'? Does she look for an answer, or look for a route for how to tackle the problem?" Then he tells me about Alfred Irving Hallowell.

The anthropologist from Pennsylvania was originally a social worker. He worked in the 1930s and '40s and spent a lot of time with Northern Ojibwa in the US and Canada. Hallowell respected "the intelligence and clarity of thinking of his informants" and championed an approach that emphasized the significance of their cultural world view. As Hallowell wrote in a mid-twentieth century essay:

> If, in the world view of a people, "persons" as a class include entities other than human beings, then our objective approach is not adequate for presenting an accurate description of "the way a man, in a particular society, sees himself in relation to all else." A different perspective is required for this purpose. It may be argued, in fact, that a thoroughgoing "objective" approach to the study of cultures cannot be achieved solely by projecting upon those cultures categorical abstractions derived from Western thought. For, in a broad sense, the latter are a reflection of *our* cultural subjectivity. A higher order of objectivity may be sought by adopting a perspective which includes an analysis of the outlook of the people themselves.

Somewhere in this anthropologist's writing he is confounded by the settler's dilemma. For my father in 1963 this took the form of acute disorientation, what he thought of then as non-overlapping world views. A representative of his times – not ahead of them – he was not yet able to conceive of himself as part of an intersecting and interconnected world.

I glance back through the glass sliding door into my room. I study the granite wall beside my bed. On the phone, Peter continues: "At some point in his research with the Ojibwa, Alfred Hallowell is sitting there in the Ontario woods with his *'interlocutor'* and his frustration gets the better of him. 'So,' Hallowell exclaims, looking around at the stones on the ground where the two men are sitting. 'What you're saying is, they're all *alive*! Right?' The Ojibwa laughs and replies, 'No, no, of course not. Of course not. No!' There is a pause. The man adds, 'But some of them are.'"

Huh? Some of them? Peter sighs. "Everything that shapes how I know, the traditions I've been trained in, the arguments and logic and sense-making I've taken for granted most of my life, does not help with this," he says. "In the face of 'some of them are,' we run aground. We are confounded by things that don't let themselves get contorted into these ways of being – of *this* or *that*. What is the logic, or the story, or the experience, of 'not all of them'?"

My dad had no vocabulary for any of what this trip exposed him to – or perhaps for only one layer of it: the story of food sustenance that he had been tasked with researching and recording. My father – the wordsmith, the storyteller – had little language for the worlds he passed through. He could only register how they impacted the worlds living inside him.

Scholars say we are shaped by our cultures: family, social and political surroundings, ancestry. Edward Sapir writes about "the unconscious patterning of behavior in society . . . essentially arbitrary modes of interpretation that social tradition is constantly suggesting to us from the very moment of our birth." Nothing is simple about meeting people who aren't like us. The difference

A NECESSARY DISTANCE / *111*

between now and my father's time is how surrounded we are with discussions about this challenge. And still, we expect ourselves to understand, and that we will *be* understood.

Eduardo Viveiros de Castro tells the story of a European and an Aboriginal person standing together in front of a sacred rock in Uluru-Kata Tjuta National Park. As the sun sets over the endless outback desert, the mountain Uluru changes colour. The two men stare at the monument. An epistemological account would say they are seeing the same thing but have different beliefs and thus different things to say, or they are seeing the same thing, but they tell different stories about it. But Viveiros de Castro says no! They may have even the same words, but they are *not* seeing the same thing. The two men, and the two men *with* the rock, are in entirely different worlds. This shared encounter, as they contemplate and perhaps talk together, he calls "a controlled equivocation."

Moments of encounter have preoccupied me for a long time. I have wondered what allows a point of contact between – well, now I can't just say "people," or even "subjects" – all sentient beings, perhaps? Living things? The language is inadequate – "things" – and the moment of encounter is also animate, in motion.

This notion of utterly different worlds coexisting feels right to me. But what animates my sense of "right"? It strikes me that I am not only trained in enlightenment sensibilities, the age of reason, the building of arguments, I have inherited other ways of knowing. Old Icelandic and Norwegian stories. What can I remember and retrieve?

I am trying to figure out *how* to read my father's journals. They are animate and carry a story, one that lives as a current passed between me, now, and him, then. As Dad took each breath, writing his notes, and as I take each breath reading them, something is alive and moving.

Until now I have been wondering who my dad met on his trip. But now I ask another question. What does it take for someone to be *capable* of meeting? Of hearing? I have had this presumption that reading the notebooks will let me know my father better. But now I feel the thinness of my encounters with him, with his parents, with obligations to those who came before me and those who come after. What do I know at all of listening, or of being *here*, or *there*, at all? To revisit Lilburn: What do I know of seeing the deer?

Oral Autopsy

I walk down the gravel road, plugging my earphones into my phone to talk to Bill. "I really have to read this whole manuscript from beginning to end soon."

"Why?"

I stop in front of a tall birch surrounded by yellow dandelions. "Oh. I don't know . . . I guess . . . because it's my plan?"

"Why not just keep doing what you are doing. Is it working?"

"Well, yes. I think so."

He changes the subject and I feel released from the pressure to accomplish things. I walk back up to the house, splash my face with cold water and lie on the bed. I flip through more of the journals. A mention of the Serengeti. I flip ahead. They are in Lima. Then I look at the end.

He and Mom arrive at Malton Airport, March 25. Bill Scott picks them up – people keep appearing, like the cast from a play I read a long time ago. Bill is Mom's cousin on her father's side. I remember him as a tall good-natured man with an easy smile and reddish hair.

Rose taps on my door and comes in, tentative. "Can I talk to you, I'm not freaking out and I don't want to bother you . . ." She looks so vulnerable and concerned.

"Yes, come sit on the couch, what is it?"

She folds her hands on her lap. "Is writing fiction always this hard? I have so much *feeling*!"

A NECESSARY DISTANCE / *113*

I smile, relieved. "Yes," I say. Yes.

When she leaves, I read a few pages of her latest book. She stands square in front of the startling relationship between a dying child, a petal falling from a bud, an accidentally murdered frog and a tortured chicken. She writes us through the staggering truth of all life scraping us raw. She must be in this territory with her fiction. Yes, I think. "Yes," I tell her later, "it *is* this hard. Why do you think so few people do it?"

My phone pings, it's Peter's reply to my note about the journals: "Jesus. You must be feeling pretty fortified to be doing this work."

I type back, "Say more."

"Well, I'm just trying to imagine being in your situation. Reading my father's journals. I think it would rip me apart. Particularly trying to work with them."

Indeed.

I hear Rose in the kitchen saying, "That's when you ask for an oral autopsy."

"What's that?" asks Molly.

"That's when you go to a traditional healer in South Africa and ask, was it TB or HIV that killed her?"

My last full day on this mountain in Quebec. Leaving is hard. Already the house is less solid, the trees down the hillsides more faded, the washes of light across the valley and lake less startling. Who wants to leave a good writing retreat? The mountain air, the solitude, the companionship, the cooking. Most of all, the quiet. I want to take this chrysalis I have woven and go safely back to my study. Nothing demanded except to follow my mind's investigation unhindered.

Our last evening. I make mushroom risotto for supper. The others have gone into town for massages and a hot tub. The black Lab and I enjoy our solitude. Hyunji, Molly, Rose and Ann return as I am stirring rice. "How was it?" I ask. "We are nicely mind muddled," says Molly with a sigh. Suddenly Rose is at my elbow.

"I've been thinking. You shouldn't go to the Serengeti."

Rose is not one to mince words. She is, after all, South African. And has opinions. I have told her that if I go anywhere that Dad went on this trip it will be Africa. I probably am ready to hear this, but I don't turn around. I notice my breathing has changed.

"Okay. Tell me."

Her arms are folded and her soft blue dress doesn't mute her determined look. "One of your anxieties comes from driving situations." It's true, I get carsick and my back isn't great. But I have managed on several occasions to spend hours winding up a two thousand metre mountain road to visit family in India. I feel my resistance.

"And?"

"This is a trauma trigger for you." This is Rose's expertise, so you don't mess with her when she brings up trauma. "On the continuum, at one end is your trauma about bad driving. On the other, terrible roads, potholes, accidents. The rate of accident fatalities there is enormous. It's a no-brainer, darling."

I glance at her over my shoulder as I ladle up a steaming spoon of chicken broth and pour it into the pot. Her reddish-blond hair casts a glow over her face. I make an instant decision, cutting my losses and moving on. This is a mildly invigorating feeling, and a new one. My zodiac sign is Libra – I weigh everything.

"Okay, no Serengeti. What could I do instead."

A wide grin. "South Africa, of course. With us!"

CHAPTER SIX

India

Dr. Livingstone

Sunday, January 27, 1963. Dad, Gene and Grahame at Jakarta airport. The incoming Comet aircraft is a wonderful sight, British Overseas Airways Corporation on charter to Air India, with a British Union Jack on the tail. The hostesses speak English.

Cheered it is our plane. Girls are human and unafraid. Making astonishing difference. If effect of colonizer's policies, shows astounding contrast between Britain and the God-damned Dutch. Sense of total release at atmosphere of plane. We are back in the Commonwealth. It never meant so much. I'll return home not only prejudiced (or more properly post-judiced) but an insufferable patriot. Have found the way to make modest Canadians rabid patriots. Send them around the world. What's wrong with Indonesia? Many good qualities seen, excellent one described by Tabor – the principle of saving face, which here means saving the other fellow's face as well. But they have been ruined by something. Poverty? Rajahs? The Dutch? The inflexible Bible-reading, stubborn, unimaginative God-damned Dutch. Even Minnie's horrible Commodore cigarettes (British-American manufacturers, Indonesia Ltd.) taste good in the new return to Life.

/ 115

116 / JULIE SALVERSON

Dad enjoys the open cockpit (because of the heat, the doors are open) and the interplay with passengers. Three white-clad nuns are across the aisle, cooling themselves with decorative fans. The crew is Australian. "God that homely genial man looks good coming down the aisle from the cockpit. I feel we should be having a sort of 'Dr. Livingstone, I presume' reunion with him."

A crowd comes on in Singapore, mostly Indian, lots of families. A new crew of Australians: "Right, do you know your spot? Good show!" The first seat in Dad's row is occupied by an infant, all alone. The hostess, in a blue sari with a bare midriff and gold trim draped over her shoulder asks, "Whose baby is this?" Passengers laugh. Another family comes down the aisle. "Is this your baby?" she asks them. No. My father pipes up, "Perhaps he's running away from home." The hostess takes the baby down the aisle, more questions, until Dad hears her say, "Oh, it's *your* baby!" Another Australian steward goes by and noisily kisses at the child. "A couple of Aussie uncles."

Time zone indicates we are now as far from home as possible and, from now on, are on our way back to the other side.

They eat a meal, comforting in its familiarity: roast chicken, tomato soup, spears of roast potato and, best of all, fresh fruit. "Pineapple, orange, cherry, all clean, wholesome chunks in own juice and two red pieces of papaya, which I refused to taste except very gingerly in Indonesia. It's very good (mild watermelon) but was flat and dull in hotel in Jakarta." They are served champagne. "By G.H. Mumm of Reims!" Gene: I think I'm going to like India. Dad notices that the Indian woman near him has eaten none of this dinner, just the fruit and tomato soup. Same with her five-year-old boy who also ate his butter with a spoon. He's very quiet and doesn't squirm. Mother doesn't eat her butter. He just wiggled

A NECESSARY DISTANCE / *117*

his legs a little. She put her hand on the child's arm, a rich intricate-looking bracelet on her wrist – looks like gold.

I come across an article by Jennifer Gonnerman in the *New Yorker*. She says that in the sixties, flight attendants were called stewardesses, and could barely see down the aisles of planes because of the cigarette smoke. "'We actually put little packets of cigarettes on the trays when we served people,' says Diane Tucker, who has worked for United since 1968." There were virtually no female passengers in first class, stewardesses had to be a certain weight, agree to quit at age thirty-two and not marry. They often took diet pills, had to wear girdles and could be fired for not complying. I wonder if any of this crossed my father's mind or occurred to any of the team. It would have been a great topic for a documentary.

The plane lands at Madras. "Marvellous lands below in first sight of India. Crowds of faces in building watch us come in. Terribly interested in what Indians will be like," writes Dad. Their papers, a "yellow book," is checked by a helpful official. "Says 'Good!' in a cheerful practical tone, returns it with courtesy and casualness. Find this hopeful. Sun is blazing hot." They take off in another plane. "I am over mountain badlands and there's the Arabian Sea and Bombay. Custom officials seem rather like our own. Danish chap to meet us – a miracle."

My husband was a missionary kid. His father was born in Andhra Pradesh and Bill's first language was pidgin Telugu. He had a few trips to Canada growing up and two years in school there – five years apart – when his parents were on furlough. At sixteen, faced with his parents' retirement and a final year of high school with strangers in Hamilton, Ontario, he wrote privately to the head of his parents' missionary society in Toronto, insisting he be allowed to return to India to complete his schooling in Kodaikanal, an idyllic village in the mountains of Tamil Nadu. Bill surprised his parents with the letter granting permission and a few months later turned seventeen in the only home he had ever known.

In the summer of 2004, I walked into a kitchen in Parkdale, Toronto, and saw a tall man with dusky white skin and silvery black hair. He was chopping garlic and onions for a curry and cheerfully taking the teasing of his elder brother George. One of the first conversations Bill and I had was about what it felt like to be a Third Culture Kid. Bill lived in between two "homes," India and Canada – and belonged in neither. I have been to India five times. Will I recognize anything in Dad's account of the country?

Bootleggers

He is thrilled with the efficiency at customs in Bombay. A safari of men carry their luggage to the FAO bus.

While they loaded, a fierce, almost Black soldier in black shorts and shirt and large socks, stood motionless, legs apart, watching us, not moving. He looked terribly impressive. Armed only with a pistol, only armed man so far, unlike Jakarta. They drive along a narrow road busy with buffalo and rickshaws and pass a sign: "Remembering our brave boys on the icy battlefront." What can that mean? [Note: War with China or maybe Kashmir.]

Streetlights and ads reassuring. Realize advertisements a sure sign there's something in a country to live for. Gorgeous, rusty red light across evening sky, dramatic. A narrow ally – huts and shacks. Wonder what dive FAO has sent us to. Sudden blaze of coloured lights suspended like Xmas, a glamorous modern hotel with a rajah for a doorman. Friendly, joking clerks. Everything seems comfortable and relaxing. To bed with nerves let down, great exhaustion, but anxiety over. Sandra and the Indonesian mail gap. I manage a letter and some postcards to mail in morning.

A NECESSARY DISTANCE / *119*

Monday, January 28
On the go all day. Into Bombay to FAO offices. An Indian the boss. Practical man, turns out to be a humorist. They all do. A Dutchman and a New Zealander, all very friendly. We set out to study milk in Bombay. Fantastic enterprise at Aarey.

The Aarey Milk Colony was established in 1949, two years after the subcontinent became independent from Britain, forming East and West Pakistan (later Pakistan and Bangladesh) and India. The new national boundaries had been hastily drawn and the division of mainly Muslim Pakistan from mainly Hindu India unleashed a frenzy of killing as Hindus were driven from Pakistan and Muslims from India. Many families retain scars from that time. A different kind of hysteria is being kindled today, with Prime Minister Narendra Modi and the Hindu right fomenting an at-times murderous communalism expressly aimed at Indian Muslims.

India's first prime minister, Nehru, inaugurated the Aarey Milk Colony in 1951 by planting a small sapling. In 1963, Dad describes the sumptuous guest house, the sterilizing milk that keeps three months in a sort of pop bottle with various flavours including saffron and rose leaf. The men relax in wicker armchairs on the porch overlooking a beautiful view. The jokes. The casual friendships among Indians, the Dutchman and the New Zealander; the Dane (they joke that his wife is always in his Volkswagen keeping an eye on him). The student residence, the man in charge who describes how they train dairymen here in tropical agriculture – and grads are given a year of further training in Denmark – the signs of UNICEF on machines, and the gifts of New Zealand (including the handsome school).

They tour the "gigantic new dairy plant in Bombay." Dad describes Mr. Mahoni, the general manager, as "sophisticated, easy, joking. The workers saluting him as we came by, but nothing more than the feeling of deference or unease a Canadian employer would show." They pass a shack near a boiler house and notice an interesting smell. Gene and my father look at each other, not sure whether to say something, but Grahame pipes up. "Bootleggers?"

"Yes," says Mahoni, laughing.

"But I thought Bombay had prohibition?" asks Gene.

Where there's a will, thinks Dad. Mahoni reads his mind. "Visitors may get licences somewhere," he says.

There were approximately sixteen thousand cows raised for milk here in 2021. Under India's current Bharatiya Janata Party (BJP) government, cow slaughter has been banned in many states and in most of these the alleged perpetrator can be arrested without a warrant. In some states, bail is denied. Even so, India is the world's third-largest exporter of beef, the second-largest exporter of leather garments, the third-largest exporter of saddlery and harnesses and the fourth-largest exporter of leather goods. These officially derive from water buffaloes, which are common everywhere and currently produce almost half of the country's milk. Old cows walk the streets eating out of garbage bins, often ingesting plastic, which can become fatal. A small percentage are taken into "gau sadan" or "goshalas" (cow shelters) where they are fed and cared for, but these facilities are overwhelmed.

The trees in the forest around Aarey have multiplied. I find a review on Tripadvisor from 2017: "I discovered this place accidentally and was shocked to see a green stretch in midst of tall towers of Mumbai. People visit here for morning jogs. It has a boating point as well. I like it."

Forty-Six-Year Gap

The men's tour of the dairy ends on the roof, and they stand looking out at a marvellous sunset. There is a breeze, the first stars and a crescent moon over the water. It is the Arabian Sea and I will land

A NECESSARY DISTANCE / *121*

there, in that city, forty-six years later almost to the day. But I don't stay, I take a small plane up the coast to Goa where I meet Vera, my friend and the wife of Bill's brother George. Two years later, I will return to the country, this time with my husband, seeing it through his eyes and hearing his memories.

The Arabian Sea is many things. To a visitor with no demands it is soft, like velvet. This has something to do with the quality of the light on the water at dusk and dawn. I walked the beach in Goa and then, later, saw that softness in the early morning light glancing off the shoulder of Mumbai herself.

Bill and I landed at 4:30 a.m. from Toronto and had a six-hour layover before flying south. We checked our luggage and took a rickshaw from the airport to the Taj Mahal Palace Hotel. We chose it because it was right on the water and easy to find. The drive took almost an hour, the rickshaw twisting through the mix of goats, cows, motorbikes and cars, the sides of the streets lined with early morning chai and shops whose metal rolling doors were still pulled shut. When we stepped out of the rickshaw and looked up at the vast Indo-Gothic hotel with its painted decor, archways and domes, we remembered the terrorist attack of the previous year.

In 2008, a jihadi group based in Pakistan attacked strategic locations in Mumbai including "the Taj." It went on for sixty hours and 174 people were killed, thirty-one at the hotel. Head Chef Hemant Oberoi and all of his seventy staff did not try to escape but stayed in the hotel trying to help the guests to safety: "To protect each guest was our foremost duty. The guests came to our house. Their lives were at stake." Many of those who died at the hotel were staff. Ten years later, in 2018, Oberoi tells the *New York Post*: "Everybody in the world should pray for peace. Everybody."

I am nervous entering the spacious dining room, and after a breakfast that cost more than a hotel room on the beach, I visit the marble-countered washroom and wonder who might have hidden there. Or walked out to discover gunmen. We leave the hotel and stand beneath the Gateway of India, built in the early twentieth century to commemorate the 1911 landing of King-Emperor George V and Queen-Empress Mary. George was the first British monarch to visit India. The welcome arch had not yet been built. A cardboard structure stood for what would come. It is considered a mark of colonialism and was also the spot where the last British troops left India in 1948. Today it is a prime tourist attraction, and since 2003 it has been the site of annual Hanukkah celebrations. The terrorists also attacked the Mumbai Jewish community, targeting a synagogue and a rabbi's family. India is as complicated as anywhere.

So, there was me in 2009. And there, forty-six years earlier, is my father. Standing on a roof. He is so relaxed already in India that he leaves his briefcase and valuables in safekeeping at the local bus station.

Do Indians Meditate?

I try to figure out the day they spend outside Bombay looking for "Aborigines." They are looking for Indigenous people – what else can it mean? It is Tuesday, January 29, they take a "wild ride in Volks bus driven by dashing little man in white uniform. Nago, of the Aarey Dairy or FAO." Here's what they find:

Desert mountains. Aborigine shacks. Stunted and also large but twisted trees. Rice paddies walled out in all this desert. Nago hits a sad little white house. Boy stroking sides of shaking animal as we drive away. Meeting with head man at dusty dreary village. Local types follow in a jeep as we tour into banana belt farms crowded together. One house with Radio India blaring from loudspeaker hung in rafters and a large modern amplifier. In this house live twenty persons of one family. Large blackened

A NECESSARY DISTANCE / *123*

unpainted building – ox carts everywhere. Buffalo in blindfold treading in circle turning wooden gears which drive bucket system bringing water from well. The men dig. The women carry the mud on their heads in baskets. Same system as highway construction near airport in Bombay.

Down to seashore.

Odd shape of Portuguese fishing vessels. Island with a fort. I think thirty thousand people live on the little island. Fish drying racks in endless vista.

Then lunch at wealthy farmer's patio. We washed at his well but didn't drink. The patio, cement-like, made of cow dung. Farmer in white Nehru cap, one of party guiding us. All discuss in English dairy problems with much talk of butter percent in buffalo milk and compare with Danish methods, with Dane in party. He refused all food, water, tea. Until we got in car. There he discovered bananas and Gene's bottled tea. Grahame and I took a sip each.

I don't know anything about Indigenous people in India. Bill remembers that the earliest inhabitants of the country, now officially referred to as Scheduled Tribes, were called "tribals." This includes 750 ethnic groups and in Central India – where Dad is – the Tribes are referred to as "Adivasis," which means "original people." I read that they make up 8.6 percent of the population of the country, approximately 104 million people, but I can't find what year this statistic comes from. Closer to now than 1963, certainly. The website where I find this statistic is International Work Group for Indigenous Affairs (IWGIA), a global organization working with Indigenous peoples' rights since 1968. The page "Indigenous Peoples in India" says there are many other ethnic groups not recognized. Adivasis assert their own beliefs and traditions but are classified as Hindu.

124 / JULIE SALVERSON

I read a section on crime. There are statistics for the number of "atrocities committed by Indigenous people against Indigenous people" but not for "cases of human rights violations by the security forces." These cases, it says, are numerous. Then there is a paragraph about sexual violence, trafficking, killing/branding and state violence against tribal women and girls. Then:

> Another struggle for Indigenous peoples in India is their right to the land. There are a plethora of laws that prohibit the sale or transfer of tribal lands to non-Indians and the restoration of alienated lands to tribal landowners. However, these laws are still ineffective, are not invoked or are intended to weaken them. In addition, a large number of tribes that lived in the forests were denied their rights and the tribes continued to live under the threat of an eviction in the name of forest and animal conservation.

Dad, Grahame and Gene drive back to Bombay in the bus. Their guide is a tall bony man with large ears who runs the school at Aarey. They offer him some of their snacks. "What do you think so far?" the man asks, delicately peeling a banana.

"There is so much it is impossible to know," says Grahame. "We film what we look for, but what would you film?"

My father looks at the cameraman with curiosity. He is enjoying getting to know this Englishman.

The school director closes his eyes for a moment, and before he can respond Gene pipes up. "Do all Indians meditate? This is what we think in North America, but is it true? Are Indians more spiritual?" Dad sighs, not delighted with this question, but Gene is tired and he likes to provoke.

The school director nods rapidly. "Religion is a profession which compels a man to shut his eyes and ears to the cries for food

A NECESSARY DISTANCE / *125*

and clothes of his wife and children, close his eyes so visitors find him in meditation. But what is he really doing? He is shutting out the cries of his family."

"You are a Marxist?" asks Dad.

"I am a pragmatist," says the guide, wiggling his head in the yes/ no motion the visitors are starting to recognize and enjoy. "What does a religious man do? His family cry out, but he leaves them anyway, and so lets in by the back door the necessities which his religion won't allow by the front door!"

There is a loud groan and the bus coasts to a halt. Unfortunately, so does the conversation, the most interesting of the day and recorded later in Dad's journal. While they wait for a part to be replaced, the Danish farmer shares his restricted beer ration and the school director retreats into grumpily staring out the window.

"What is next?" asks the Dane.

"Anand," says Gene. "No room on Western Railway, so we fly tomorrow at six thirty a.m."

"You will like Anand," the farmer nods. "Best accommodation in India!"

Trains

Wednesday, January 30. The men have a last drink at the Sun-n-Sands Hotel in Bombay, retain one room where they leave gear and fly to Ahmedabad, five hundred kilometres straight north: "big and pleasant, a sort of Calgary with ancient history." They eat at Kwality Café, a chain restaurant with excellent shortbread (!) and head to the Western Railway station. "[We are the] only whites on the vast long platform." I am thrilled that Dad is taking an Indian train. I have done it three or four times, always overnight. The open windows and ceiling fans do a surprising job of cooling a sweaty body even at high noon. Grahame joked about air conditioning, but the truth is it is much better to travel second class in India, non-AC. Now, if you have air-con the windows are sealed, usually dirty, and it's impossible to see.

Dad describes his sleep "like some Russian novel, only hot." The train pulls into Anand early. They rush to pull the luggage from under their seats, unlock chains around suitcases and open the door. To their surprise a boy leaps onto the train into their compartment. They look out at a "sea of turbaned heads and blackened faces into which we must plunge. Porters leaping at us for the gear! One wins."

They shake hands with Bhakan, the young representative from their next stop, Amul Dairy. He wears a crisp white shirt and brown-and-yellow-checked lungi. The porter insists on putting a heavy aluminum chest of equipment on his head and the men follow as he heaves and coughs his way through the crowds to a shiny black Plymouth. "Appalled sensation as thrust into Oli Baba." But then, "Whipped away through fantastic town, suddenly turn into garden with a sentry on gate. Surge of hope and relief." Relief? To be out of the "Oli Baba" crowd, by which I guess Dad means *Ali Baba and the Forty Thieves*, an Arabian folktale.

They enter the guest house to find Mr. Hanson, a New Zealander from Bombay, eating dinner. He points to his plate. "Pretty good, eh? I'll take this anytime." The three men toss a coin for the single room (only two available) and pull aside the curtain door, careful not to knock down the sparrow's nest tucked above. They have a short meal ("the food sandy and tastes like a steamed shirt") and, exhausted, tour the dairy. They talk (mostly Gene). They drink buffalo milk in an office and set off on a tour with the rep who met them at the station.

Dr. Someone, who talks loud but well, like a lecture, and keeps sounding his horn like trumpets, proclaiming his dramatic advance down an empty one-lane highway. We tour villages with names so strange we call them No. One, Two, Three.

A NECESSARY DISTANCE / *127*

Dad has a list of notes, the most interesting one from Town number two, where he observes a dentist dispersing little boxes to a crowd of people. "Paste?" wonders Dad. There is a temple on a walled lake with steps that allow people to descend to the water no matter what its level and cleanse themselves before entering the temple. The men watch two Indian movies with the director. Dad sleeps through part of it.

They return to the guest house for dinner. "Fried fish and God knows what. Afraid of water." Forty-six years later, I still don't drink the water, but now bottled water is for sale everywhere. Bad for the planet but safe for tourists.

They are tired.

Grahame looks reserved and distant. Gene is swearing. The attendant, an old fellow, upset because we don't eat all the fish.

They try to sleep. Gene has won the coin toss and has his own room.

The bed, dead. The bed is like the floor. Grahame changes film in the dark under his blanket. No soap or toilet paper or matches or hangers to be used washing my shirt.

"Hotels haven't changed," mutters Bill. When I first flew into Mumbai in 2006, my seatmate told me that he had grown up there and not been back in ten years.

"How do you feel?" I asked.

He peered out the window at the lights of the endless city and sighed. "Things don't change here. Nothing works. Nobody cares. It's all bribes. But I have family."

I glanced down at my faded grey bag, carrying the most recent letter from Vera describing the country she finds both frustrating and fascinating. Vera's husband, George, like Bill, grew up in India and agonizes about every inefficiency, every bit of nonsense, it's personal to him. To Vera, it is still a country she is discovering after twenty-seven years.

Dad's first assessment: "Seems a ghastly place to be trapped, but we have at last found India, after searching for three furious days. Sleep like a log (in a bomber yard)."

Experiment in Democracy

Dad and the team are about to visit the famous Ajarpura Milk Producers Cooperative Society. I stumble on a book of Amul advertising cartoons published in 2012. The images of the impish girl with blue hair tied up in a red polka-dot bow, red shoes and enormous black eyelashes have been famous since the mid-sixties. When I first visited India the child's cartoon face was stamped onto the ice cream George bought in the local grocery store.

Amul Dairy "emerged as an offshoot of the Indian freedom movement, to give poor farmers the best returns for their milk by eliminating middlemen. Since then it has grown into a national brand that is respected and trusted in every corner of the country. This book portrays how an endearing moppet and her tongue-in-cheek humour helped a milk producers' co-operative create a White Revolution. It traces how Amul evolved as a brand by commenting on the popular political and social culture of India over the past four decades."

Thursday, January 31. Anand, India. The team spend the day in Village number one, "arriving like men from Mars to Earth two thousand years ago. Stares, and like the Pied Piper gathered a huge crowd of children." They hire a man called Bhagat to be an actor. The shooting list for Anand includes:

A NECESSARY DISTANCE / *129*

Close on leaves and tilt up to Bhagat (nickname of one who worships) working in field wearing turban. Rises into frame, looks off at road as jeep passes. Hoes in irrigation ditch opening one ditch and closing off another. Feet in ditch, he digs. He walks out. Picks up shadows as he moves on.

They hire three men to keep the kids at bay as they shoot all afternoon in fields under hot sun:

Grahame climbed a tree and camera went up on rope. Got sunburned. Shirts off thirty minutes. Mouth dry as dust and passionately fond of lime juice and hot tea from thermoses supplied by Manners the butler. His packed lunch far superior to his dinners. In the evening, discussed the day's work and decided to throw it all out. Instead, we would hide Grahame, distract the natives with trickery and let Grahame shoot the real scene. Our guide, next morning, took to this idea at once, was brilliant in co-operating and deceiving as were the men in white who came in the second jeep to help.

End of Notebook Two.

The rest of the story of resorting to "trickery" to get "real life" on film comes several pages into Notebook Three. They decide to distract the children while Grahame shoots elsewhere on the sly. They have hidden him in an attic. Here's how Dad describes the antics:

Almost sixty children. Our guide senses they are becoming restless and calls for a real Polaroid shot to calm them. Elaborate pretense (real enough) to move them across square and line them up, small ones in front of house or along patio. Boys playing, dogs barking at us. Buffalo eating in front of houses under straw and stick enclosures. Bhagat is being shaved on his porch by his barber. The director and the writer (and interpreter) are among the kids with Polaroid camera, me making ostentatious notes.

Our guide Bhakan in his white sheets, sandals, brown vest and horn-rimmed glasses is talking to them and fussing without cause. Can see here how easily officials can manipulate these people. Gene orders the children to school and one is to take the picture to teacher but they themselves must decide who is to take it. Much raising of hands and crowding around and confusion. One boy is nominated by one other boy. Gene's experiment in democracy. The elections held – children vote for every candidate so start over and divide voters in groups. During counting some move over from right to left or try to stand between. Guide and Gene are both great showmen.

Interview with Actor

Bhagat is twenty-two. His father died at sixty and his mother at fifty-five of tuberculosis. He doesn't know about his grandparents or the history of his village. "Was your father ever unemployed?"

"Many times."

He was sad as a child. He was hungry and knew there was a crisis in the family. Seven years in school, from six to thirteen.

"What subjects did you study?"

"Mathematics, languages, science, history, geography, industrial [weaving]."

"Have you ever heard of Eskimos?" Dad isn't sure where this question has come from, but Gene is fuelled by questions.

Bhagat pauses. "I studied that five years ago. But I don't remember."

Gene thinks for a moment. "Cowboys?"

Bhagat looks puzzled. "Don't know."

A NECESSARY DISTANCE / *131*

Bhagat says his government is a democracy and the opposite of that is a republic. He knows about Japan, Germany, America, Africa. He heard about Canada as a student but doesn't know what it is like. He says China is thickly populated and has food shortages like India. "If nearby is my own field, I work for the sake of work. But if on someone else's field, it is for money. I enjoy most sowing the field. It was bad before the co-op and the canal, these are changes for the better."

"Is there anything you would like to improve this village?" asks Dad.

"Enough to eat and drink. More employment. Then there would be money for ordinary things. And celebrations, marriages. Purchase more land."

Dad has more than enough for the script, but Gene wants more. "What would you do if you had one million rupees?" he asks, looking at my father triumphantly. Bhagat doesn't hesitate. "I would spend it." He can't think how at first. But then he can. He would "organize an institution, the leaders would consult and with help, carve out a business, a charity."

A canal has been built here in Anand with help from the UN and UNICEF. The people in charge are in Delhi. Bhagat knows that New Zealand has sent money and machinery. He also knows the United States and Russia are "advanced."

Gene pushes for something more dramatic. "Do you know about any quarrel between those two countries?"

"I am not aware of a quarrel. It might be. Capitalism and communism are the same I think."

"What do you mean?" asks Gene.

"Communism means cultivation is done jointly and all are equal. No social status, high or low." Then Bhagat says he doesn't know what capitalism is. They ask if independence (1948) has had any bearing on village life.

132 / JULIE SALVERSON

"Yes."

"What changes?"

"We have come out of bondage."

Bhagat prays every morning after his bath.

"What do you pray?"

He says he prays silently. "Just become quiet and think about God."

Friday, February 1. Last day in Anand. They wait by the temple in a village for a breeze to stop rippling the water so they can get their shot. Across the road, a fourteen-year-old boy is trying to breed a buffalo bull to a cow. As the bull mounts, the boy grasps the phallus and struggles to insert it. The bull is not enchanted and slips back off. The boy tries this several times, then moves the bull away and examines the rear end of the cow.

Comes to some conclusion. Woman takes cow away. Second cow, waiting, is also examined. Boy walks away with his bull. Understand bull good for about six emissions a day. This one not sex-mad. All this at side of road by temple under large spreading trees. The cow's rear legs were haltered.

The three filmmakers and Bhakan go into the temple, leaving sandals on the stone steps. They pass under a dome with carved lions and shapes they don't recognize through a gate to an inner shrine. The temple is white and semicircular. There is a pole with a triangular weathered flag and one side descends to the lake. Around half of the lake are masonry walls, with arches and water channels. The opposite side opens to sloping hills where women wash clothes on the bank and the temple steps.

A NECESSARY DISTANCE / *133*

Bhakan waited for me as I put on shoes while others went back to jeep. Smiles at me and as we walked, talked in Hindi about my gaudy jungle shirt. I gathered he thought it too hot. I pointed to raw skin on my arm, at sun, and tried to indicate it was to protect me from burning. Not sure if either of us understood.

That evening the team have coffee at the house of Dr. Verghese Kurien, the Amul director. They arrived in a jeep after a hot ride in the setting sun. My father describes Kurien's "fascinating Americanized personality" and says the coffee is good. Kurien wants them to dine with the governor of the state the next day before they leave. "In our ragged state!" notes my father. It is a pleasantly cool evening and Gene and Grahame go out on the veranda to look at the moon in the bright Indian sky through their cameras.

Dad stays indoors talking with Mr. Kurien. "When the Queen of England came to visit, the government sent buses with fifty thousand people to give her a crowd. What got us was, two million came! When Eisenhower got off a plane in 1960, he was met by millions!" Crowds met Donald Trump when he came in 2020. Many Indians love a celebrity, look at Bollywood. Look at their weddings, where feeding a large crowd and attracting a famous figure is a status coup! A spectacle is a spectacle.

Word comes during dinner that they can't get their flight out and must scramble for new arrangements. This gets sorted: "Indian efficiency as such, we now seem to have reservations on the train and a telegram has come that someone has arranged space for 'the three Canadians' on a flight. But, as Kurien laughingly said, 'The time carefully left out.'" Dad finishes the Friday notes: "Will we dine with the Governor of the State and his fifteen servants tomorrow? Tune in for the next exciting installment."

I have looked at the India segment of the film. There is no trace of the willing children who practised democracy with Gene on a tropical afternoon. It is recorded only in my father's notebooks. An informal archive.

Farewell from Shiyapura
Saturday morning, the men return to the village and film an Amul employee milking cows.

"People here are not easy to convince of new things," she says. "They may socially agree I am right but don't like to admit something that discounts their own knowledge." There is a calf that won't feed, but it isn't sick and they can't figure out what is going on. They need to keep a calf with the mother nine months for the milk to "get let down." They won't kill it but will eventually sell it to someone who will. "That person may get calf to a slaughterhouse and take the sin on himself."

When we left, our guide said they wanted to give us a "party." Had horrible vision of some sort of feast. They brought three chairs but facing the wrong way. So when our guide said, "They want you to sit down," we sat together on the cement ramps of the Milk Collection Centre.

The village men gathered before us with their herd man in centre. He made a speech in Hindi, his face sober. Our guide, tall and serious, stood to interpret. "He says that countries like Canada have done much to help them for which they are grateful. They are pleased that you have visited their village and hope that you will come again."

Gene rose and said, "We came from Indonesia, and coming here to India, to a Commonwealth country, we felt we were coming home. It is our heartfelt wish that we may come again." The guide interpreted this while the herd man – standing in the dust of the street by the jeep, with the ox cart and the well just covered, and in the distance through the narrow street hooded figures of women, ghost-like, carried large jars on their heads – the herd man nodded throughout with little serious jerks of the head.

We could hear the guide enumerating the countries of the Commonwealth. I replied that from my interviews, they had no concept of the Commonwealth and he therefore had to explain it to translate Gene's reply.

Then we got into the jeep – suddenly at my front seat window a wizened old man (forty-five, I suppose) offered me blossoms in his cupped hands. I took them, and he gave more to Gene. We sat, waving and holding our flowers as the jeep maneuvered and drove away. All these villagers looked sad, and our hero Bhagat seemed positively stricken. We passed children coming from school in groups, and each gang shouted gaily to us and we drove on, waving, holding our flowers and deeply moved. We put the flowers in my sun helmet where they rode, all the way into the city. I looked at the strange sights and people along the way and suddenly none of it was strange any more, and the people seemed like brothers. The power of a simple gesture.

Thus ended our visit to Shiyapura. I felt as though, when we drove out, the centuries came surging back to swallow up the little village, as if time were a pool we had rippled for a moment.

The Governor's Cigarettes

The men return to Anand to discover they have third-class tickets overnight on the late train to Bombay. With a long day to wait, they sunbathe at the guest house, vultures floating in the hot sky, "must be a hundred, a cloud of soaring, weaving, motionless wings." Dad begins to read the novel *To Kill a Mockingbird*. A young man in white western clothes appears and takes them for a ride with his two little girls. The tiny one keeps saying, "Ay?," which their host explains means "This?" in Hindi. He runs production at Amul Dairy and drives them to see the Experimental Farm of the Agricultural College. "Saw grapefruit growing. And an odd bush called 'Watch me if you can' in which no two leaves or blossoms are the same." The man has lived five years in Massachusetts. He loved the snow.

Director Kurien appears with a young man in uniform, the general's aide-de-camp. The three visitors are indeed invited to dine with the governor. "No clothes. Assured it didn't matter." They return to find their guest house surrounded by soldiers. Waiting along with Kurien is the chief of police, the aide and another official. Dad offers Kurien the usual cigarettes, but he says, "No, we now operate on the Governor's cigarettes." Dad, Gene and Grahame each select a cigarette from a silver box, "the Governor thus appeased," my father writes later.

After the Indian Independence in 1947, most of Gujarat became a part of Bombay State until May 1, 1960, when the government split it into Maharashtra and Gujarat. This man they are dining with was Mehdi Nawaz Jung, the first governor of Gujarat from 1960 to 1965. A photo shows a man in his late thirties or early forties with alert eyes framed in black round glasses. He wears a black shirt buttoned up his neck and a black hat high on his head. He looks like someone I would like to have dinner with. The governor was born in Hyderabad, which makes sense as Dad says he married into the Nizam family, a nabob.

This governor established an auditorium hall for Ahmedabad. It is named after him, as is the first cancer hospital in India. He arrives at the guest house.

The familiar table has now become a formal affair. Dinner was excellent fish, cauliflower, some livery meatballs which would

A NECESSARY DISTANCE / *137*

have been delicious if not so highly spiced and rice. A custard pudding, coffee, cubes of pressed dates and a dish of spices to nibble, very aromatic. Grahame tried to pass them up, but the Gov insisted.

Gov to Kurien, who spoke of shooting panthers nearby, "That's not hunting, that's shooting. For hunting, you need horses and hounds."

Gene tries to make conversation about our not knowing the news. Gov spoke to a servant who instantly brought a portable radio. With great dignity the Gov pulled up the long antenna and tried to dial in some news, without success. Dinner over, he shook hands with each of us, more or less ordered us to listen to the news around the coffee table, and withdrew. Whereupon Kurien had the aide put away the radio.

We then talked about the war with China. Kurien said, "The Chinese have screwed us. While they were talking about the Great Leap Forward, we thought we were making it." Now all money for economic advancement is diverted to defence, doubling the army; purchasing arms abroad. This seems to be China's purpose, to slow down India's rapid advancement. But the country has been unified. Everywhere, people come forward with jewels, gold, rupees, for defence. Farmers in co-op asked to be not paid for one day a month, give it to defence. Sixty thousand farmers in this. A huge sum.

From the Governor's dinner, we were plugged into the Third Class of the Western Ry. 11:00 p.m. One small perch for each of us in crowded compartment. Sat up all night to 6:30 a.m. Hot and dusty bodies all over the place. Young father on floor wakened, stared incredulously at the white men.

We realized that these lower-middle-class people were not as dirty as the awful coach. We were dirty, not they. An unexpected generous concern for the white intruders. Man in upper asked me to take his bunk and get some sleep. I held up *Mockingbird* and declined. "Your friend," he said, pointing to Grahame, who also declined with thanks, though balanced in misery. It was startling to hear this English and generosity in what seemed an alien hostile atmosphere and was nothing of the sort. Later a man in lower offered us his bunk, to "get an hour's sleep before Bombay." We declined again. But these incidents made the ordeal of the night somehow easier.

They have a day off. Dad reads and sleeps in the sun, Grahame and Gene swim in the ocean. Swimming in Bombay! Was the water clean in 1963? They are a long city block from the beach, where vendors pass with brilliant windmill-type fans, each with two wheels revolving in opposite directions. Dad writes ten postcards and has two hot meals over the twenty-four hours: bacon and eggs, ham and eggs.

After strawberries and whipped cream and a banana split at Swiss Café downtown and a shop at Khadi's Emporium – dolls and an Indian vest – they walk by a movie theatre. "Chinta Sangam Presents" and a title in Hindi. It's a 1962 film called *Apna Banake Dekho*, directed by Jagdish Nirula and starring Asha Parekh and Manoj Kumar.

The next morning, Nago from Aarey picks them up in a Volkswagen bus and takes them to the airport. East African Airways. Extra luggage (film equipment) is paid for the flight to Nairobi. It is February 4. They left Canada January 16. It is a world away.

Lists

I skip to the end of the journals. I want to remind myself how he ended this whirlwind trip. Dad is home, not knowing what to do with his new thoughts. He is depressed. As I read this section I realize that today, as I type, is March 31. Sandra's birthday.

A NECESSARY DISTANCE / *139*

My mother's birthday has an unconscious claim on me. It was a ghastly day for the family, spent dreading her inevitable disappointment and drinking. She led with her emotions and the need to be loved and noticed. Sometimes we'd give her a birthday cake at breakfast, or in bed before breakfast, so she didn't panic that there wouldn't be one. I'm wryly amused at the last entry in Dad's journals, on March 29: "Sandra wants gardening gloves and a new hand spade for her birthday, Sunday. Tomorrow must shop with Julie and Scott. Also a new hose."

This entry is preceded by the one from the day before: "10:05 in bed. Worrying about clothes. Everything gone after the trip except a few summer items. Can I buy clothes on time? What clothes?"

This is followed by a line-by-line itemization of white shirts, underpants, suits, shoes, ties, cufflinks, socks and "Two years at app $40 per month – and if leaving country could liquidate debt from sale of house."

The entry about mom's birthday is the second to last entry. The last entry is this:

April 22. No notes since March 29.

End of Notebook Seven.

Sandra

My mother was born in 1923, so when World War II began she was sweet sixteen. Sweet sixteen, but she'd been kissed, by her first boyfriend, the high school quarterback at Runnymede Collegiate Institute in Toronto. By nineteen she was married to someone else. She barely knew her first husband, Ted. He went immediately to the air force base in Trenton and then overseas. I think she wrote him a Dear John letter, certainly when he came home they had nothing in common and they parted ways. Mom got a job in a bank and hated it. Her father told her she had to stay a year. "People are suffering and you are bored? You must learn discipline." She quit one year to the day.

"I always knew my own mind," she told me once. "Maybe my mother gave me that. She was an opera singer. There is a letter from a famous teacher in New York City inviting her to study, but she said no. Instead, she married my father and had two girls. She knew what she wanted but she only got some of it. I wasn't going to make that mistake."

My mom was the youngest, the glamour girl who cultivated her prettiness. In old photos, she looks a lot like Bette Davis, the Hollywood actress she adored. Her older sister, Lois, became a nurse and served in the war. My mom answered phones for the bank and then somehow talked herself into a job on the CBC switchboard. Anything to be close to show business. She was hopeless at it, she said later, but I've always wondered if she was deliberately bad at it because she didn't want to stay there. In fact, Andrew Allan spotted her and gave her an audition. From then on she had a career, independence, her own bank account. And she became, for a while, "Andrew's girl."

"Radio was really theatre," my mom would say. That was the place for the good parts. She had an instinctive talent – the recording of her playing Nora in Ibsen's *A Doll's House* is remarkable – but lack of acting training gave her a deep insecurity. She never knew how she found her way into a character, and so always doubted she could do it again. But she had many starring roles: Ophelia opposite Lorne Greene, Juliet opposite John Drainie. She played a woman who couldn't speak or hear but must communicate her experience of rape in 1900s' Nova Scotia in the play *Johnny Belinda*. She did this on radio.

A NECESSARY DISTANCE / *141*

When I was in university my mom got a role in the play *All Over* at the Manitoba Theatre Centre. Always nervous onstage, she flew west determined to do her best for Arif Hasnain, a director she admired. A few days into rehearsal she called me in a panic. "I have no idea what this play is about, do you know this writer Edward Albee? What on earth is he trying to do with this impossible play!"

I flew out to Winnipeg and sat nervously in the audience on opening night. I waited for Mom to be phony with her old tricks. She came onstage playing a nurse at the bedside of a dying man. She still had no idea what she was doing, but she trusted the director and had decided to be brave. It's the best thing I ever saw her in. She didn't know what to do. She just showed up. She was terrified and truthful.

Mom had a huge heart. At her memorial, John Drainie's widow, Claire, talked about how when John was dying of cancer my mom would show up every day with bottles of freshly squeezed carrot juice. Mom had read somewhere it could help. Bronwyn tells the story in her book but doesn't attribute it to my mom. "The carrot juice did nothing to halt the growth of my father's tumors, but it did restore his eyesight, which allowed him to read scripts up to the day he died."

I wonder if it was hard for Mom when Dad was away. Maybe she was reminded of her earlier independence. Despite two kids to look after, she spent a few months thinking for herself. When she joined him at the end in Mexico, I don't know who looked after my brother and me. When they were both safely home, perhaps her friends said, "Aren't you relieved?" I imagine her saying, as any spouse might, "Well yes. Mexico was disappointing. For one thing, I got sick. That happens in Mexico. But the thing I find harder to talk about – his habits came home with him."

Sacrifice for the Lord

It is 6:08 p.m. Friday, October 9, the beginning of Thanksgiving weekend in Canada. Downstairs, my husband is cooking rib-eye. I tell Bill about the meal with the governor, and his Hyderabadi roots. Bill's father was born in 1919 in Secunderabad, the sister city to Hyderabad, and I've heard the whole family tell tales of the Nizam and the wealthiest man in the world.

"When was he the richest?" I ask.

"Until they lost their statehood. Partition. Nineteen forty-seven. Although Hyderabad held out longer than anyone else."

"Have another go at the garlic, you've made it too thick." I am used to my husband's culinary requirements. His dad, Waldo, worked in a kitchen just after graduating from Central Tech high school in Toronto. He may have gone to a chef school, Bill isn't sure. Waldo loved cooking, but it only took a few days in a professional kitchen at Simpson's Court in Toronto for him to quit. "Too much foul language," he told his son decades later. Instead, he went to Hamilton and studied at McMaster for a Divinity degree. The cooking passed down to both his sons, but not the religion.

"It's odd a Nizam would be governor in Gujarat," says Bill, pressing down with the flat side of the blade, then swiftly slicing.

"Why?"

"Well, he's a Muslim in a Hindu state. And partition had happened just over ten years earlier, which set the two groups against each other. Years of violence." Then I remember that Gujarat is the state where Modi had been chief minister in 2002, when over 1,500 people had been killed in a targeted pogrom against Muslims. Now he's prime minister of the country, and wants to change the name "India" to the less commonly used "Bharath," a nod to the growing Hindu nationalism. In 2023, the word is engraved in

A NECESSARY DISTANCE / 143

dinner invitations and a formal nameplate at the G20 Summit in New Dehli, causing an uproar.

"What happened with Modi there? Can you tell me in a sentence or two?"

He looks at me in frustration. He knows I want a few lines for my book. "It's hard in a few sentences," he says.

I shrug, embarrassed. "Try?"

"There was a mosque in a place called Ayodhya, in Uttar Pradesh, that may have been built upon the ruins of a Hindu temple. This was done all over the place by conquering nations. Like in Cyprus and Istanbul where churches were converted into mosques. Standard practice. Ayodhya was supposed to be the birthplace of Ram, one of the gods, a sore spot with Hindu nationalists. Finally, a mob gathered and tore down the mosque. They are only just now building a Hindu temple, I'm not sure, maybe it has been completed."

"I can look that up later. Then what?"

"There was a trainload of Hindus going to Ayodhya. Whether it was deliberate or an accident hasn't been proven, but there was a fire on the train and a number of Hindu pilgrims were killed. It doesn't take much for these things to get out of hand. Rumour was, Muslim vendors from kiosks on the train platform firebombed the train. There was a backlash and mobs went on a rampage targeting Muslims and their homes and businesses. Somewhere between one and two thousand Muslims were killed in the process. Shops burned, all that kind of stuff. Modi was accused of not using his authority and power to stop it."

Last time we were in India, in 2019, Hindu nationalism was growing in disturbing ways. Friends from Delhi talked about how the Jawaharlal Nehru University (JNU), famous for its left-wing politics, was taken over by fundamentalist administrators. All over India, heads of institutions (including arts organizations, universities, cultural venues) have been replaced with right-wing Hindu people. People talk about this quietly and in private. In 2022, the Booker Prize–winning novelist and vehement political commentator Arundhati Roy publishes an opinion piece in *Al Jazeera English*. The country is transitioning from a fragile, flawed democracy "pretty brazenly into a criminal Hindu fascist enterprise." I hear similar accounts across multiple news services. The danger, says Roy, is how the bulldozing of Muslim homes gets the participation of municipalities, while magistrates and courts look away. What played the role of checks and balances in the old democracy "are now going to be used as weapon against you." The bulldozing is reported in the media as "being invested with a kind of divine avenging power . . . This spectacle is now beamed into every Indian home."

I stir-fry vegetables, cursing as the smoke alarm goes off. I pull it off the wall and Bill cooks rice as I read to him from Dad's account of the conversation at that last dinner in India. "After the governor leaves, the guy from Amul says the Chinese have screwed them, talks about a war."

"There are always skirmishes with India and the Chinese," says Bill. "They take turns saving face. There was one in the early sixties at the Himalayan border."

I check on my phone: Yes, it was October 20 to November 21, 1962. Just two months before Dad is there. I read out loud to Bill what Dad reports about everyone in the country contributing wages, jewels, rupees for defence. "It's feudal," says Bill. "We'll all sacrifice for the Lord."

I'm tempted to ask more questions, but I know that each moment of this trip, each page of the journal, can take me down more rabbit holes. Instead, I open a bottle of wine to celebrate. Dad is at the airport and out of India. And so am I.

India Section of Film

19:02 Music Changes. Sitar. Shot of water, men washing cows by shore, camera rising to see Indian temple structure in white.

Narrator:
And so we come over the rough waters into the placid pools of adult domestic responsibility. A period of life which stretches on before a man as interminably as the history of India.

Close-up of cow's face, rest of cow in water. Turns face toward camera, small horns. Man herds cows out of water. Cut to man coming out of mud hut in village.

One afternoon in Shiyapura, a family man named Bhagat, having finished his work, devoted himself to a period of energetic meditation.

Close-up of young man, moustache, large ears, smoking a long pipe.

Bhagat was a reflective fellow, sometimes quite mystical. Today Bhagat wished to contemplate per-fection. Particularly the perfection which had come to Shiyapura. It was getting to be like Ahmedabad, or even Bombay, they were so advanced and modern. He had seen no one in Shiyapura, not a single soul for over two years who had been forced to go without food. Not one single instance of starvation, and this was said to be true of this entire district of Gujarat.

Series of quick shots of people working. A young woman with pots on her head, a man carving a stick, a man cleaning something. Shot of baby being swung in cradle by a woman who holds a six-or-so-year-old in her arms.

Bhagat thought of himself as a small child crying with hunger, while his mother would sit transfixed by sadness.

Shot of cows.

A great change had come, the first change that ever occurred in Shiyapura, and it all came from milk.

Woman milking cow with her hands.

From milk, perfection. Bhagat saw his wife fill a jug with one link in the magic white chain. It made him glow with satisfaction at everything that met his eye.

He is still puffing on pipe while wife works.

He watched his happy village, thinking of the daily trek of the dairymen with the chemicals and the daily cash. He thought of the huge dairies like palaces at Anand and Bombay and of his own milk co-operative, 56,000 farmers like himself. It was amazing to realize how all this had spread out, making life so good there seemed to be no further room for improvement.

Two small girls playing.

How satisfying to be a father and to see your children playing happily. And all the children, not one crying with hunger.

Single guitar, shots of children, mothers, small child with eyes covered with flies.

21:35 We see a car pull up.

As Bhagat contemplated the benefits of change on the village, Shiyapura was visited by one of the agents of change.

Young people, a man with a pipe, women come to look.

Everyone became watchful, even old dodderers of forty. It was pleasant to have an advisor from the milk union visit, but you never knew what they were going to spring on you. They can be rather outrageous.

Shot again of Bhagat and his pipe. People gathered around the car.

Yet one must be generous and remember the good these people had done, as one remembered the foreigners who helped them do it.

Bhagat knew that where India had milk, children were getting milk —

Shot of hands carrying urns of milk.

— and that this protected them from appalling illnesses. He knew the dimly imagined strangers had conspired with his leaders to make milk possible, build the dairies, develop the collection and distribution systems. The whole complicated machine, from the care of the buffalo to the purification of the milk. There were experts from many lands.

Milk being distributed to a line of women. They carry pots away on their heads.

There was somebody named UNICEF, there were the New Zealand people who refused money for big dairy machines, saying, "Give the children milk." So, one must be grateful and listen with courtesy, even to the wrong ideas.

Young Indian woman talking to the group.

But listen to what she's telling them. The veterinarians can't treat your buffalos without touching

A NECESSARY DISTANCE / *149*

them. Now, everyone knows that hurts the milk, to touch them in certain places.

Shot of young calf.

And she says the male calves which are now left to starve could be used for food? What courtesy compels one to listen. And yet, she was right about the ear tags and the blood samples and the artificial insemination.

Shot of woman talking, then cut away to Bhagat with his pipe, watching.

They brought us satisfaction and they won't let us keep it.

23:25 Camera sits with woman. Then Bhagat stands and walks away from his pipe.

A shocking idea came to Bhagat, the front step philosopher. Shiyapura could not settle down to another thousand years of comfortable habit because change makes change and then goes on and on, like waves from a stone dropped into a pool.

Shot of cow swimming in water with temple from start of sequence in background. Sound of cow-bells like music, joined by flute.

CHAPTER SEVEN

Africa

Dad takes an East African Airways plane from Mumbai, departing at 11:30 p.m., Tuesday, February 4.

Glanced at Asian edition of *Time* mag. Same as US only cheaper paper. Rumoured that imports of *Time* will be restricted in future so subscribe now through your news agent. Also girlie magazine picked up by Grahame. 12:30 flying along Indian coast to Karachi. Desert country below mixed with villages. Quite a few rivers and a large desert in sight at moment. Vast area to the east pure white, as if under snow. Earth below dismal, tan-coloured, patches indicate some sort of farming. Must be worse than Dakota!

Drinking Tennent's Lager from a tin. African note in my pocket to pay for it (two shillings). Rather pleased to see Queen's picture on the note. First drink in exactly one week. My Paper Mate has been leaking in the heat like some twenty-five-cent pen. I get ink all over when I write. Had to keep letter to Sandra from becoming blotchy. Got Ronsonol lighter fluid, specially provided in the gift shop last night. Lighter now acting oddly. Dry one moment then later the entire lighter bursts into flame. The land now brown again with low ridges like lonely protruding bones or ribs, and patches of white in pockets, some of them black, indicating pools of water.

My beer is gone. I see an endless strip of canal below, like a long-bent pin. Where does it come from? Where does it go? The desert appears to be slipping behind. What will Arabia look like?

The Voice of Canada

Tom Power is interviewing Wynton Marsalis. The American trumpeter is talking a lot about his father, jazz pianist and educator Ellis Marsalis Jr. He speaks with warmth in his voice, such admiration and affection. Later that night I mention this to Bill. "Why don't I do that about my dad?"

"Well, you have affection. But you don't exactly praise him," he says.

This bothers me. I think of myself as a child sitting on the stairs late at night when Mom and my brother were in bed. Dad sat in the living room playing his harmonica soulfully. I listened to the sadness and hurt for how unhappy he was. But why did I think that?

A few weeks after hearing the interview I attend a symposium on the Cold War. Fifteen of us are in the Diefenbunker, the 1960s' shelter built near Ottawa to protect the government, military and other important personnel in the event of a nuclear attack. It's a bizarre experience. The archivist tells us that there had been just over five hundred names on "the list" and they would have been helicoptered in. "The staff had to find their own way."

The hour-long tour is surreal. We see the vault where all the gold would be stored, guarded day and night by two police officers. I mutter to another participant, "Where did they store the vegetables?" But then, around a corner we enter a CBC studio. Fully equipped and ready to broadcast to Canadians the daily details of life after nuclear attack. Five people were designated "the voice of Canada" and they would all be down there. I ask the archivist to please find me the names. Dad must have known them; everyone knew each other in that small world.

We are taken to the war room, where strategies would be debated around a rectangular table. On the wall are five clocks, five time zones. Four are different parts of Canada, the fifth is London, England. That's it. That was the world between 1959 and 1961 when the bunker was built. So, in 1963, this trip around the world that Dad, Gene and Grahame took was a very big deal. Very big. Nobody thought globally in those days. It takes seeing those five clocks for me to realize this.

Norfolk Hotel

Dad, Gene and Grahame are on their way to Kenya with a stopover in Aden, a port city that is now the capital of Yemen. It's humid in the small terminal building:

There are fourteen RAF fighters in one group. Big jagged mountains like dinosaurs behind the city. Used fan vigorously taking off. I said, "It's hot in Arabia." Gene commented on my powers of observation. An elderly Indian across the aisle laughed till his turban shook. Then, the flight to Nairobi, the lights beautiful after eleven hours of travel. Through customs with no trouble. Beautiful clean city. No one to meet us, but no trouble. Norfolk Hotel, very nice.

I can't resist looking up these places. Sometimes they are still there and sometimes they have history. The Norfolk was opened on Christmas day, 1904, only five years after the city was founded as a railway depot on the new line between the East African port

A NECESSARY DISTANCE / *153*

city of Mombasa and Kisumu on the shore of Lake Victoria – a service promptly dubbed "the Lunatic Express." It's a mock-Tudor building with a large interior courtyard garden that was advertised as the only stone hotel in East Africa. A 2010 article, "The Sad Decline of Nairobi's Norfolk Hotel," reports that most mornings "the lobby would be crammed with absurdly handsome safari guides, surrounded by admiring throngs of khaki-clad travellers weighed down with cameras, binoculars, and enough ancillary equipment to mount a major expedition to the Congo. And outside, a small herd of Land Rovers would be waiting, attended by a handful of dignified Masai [*sic*] warriors, leaning on their spears and robed in flaming scarlet."

Dad doesn't mention the warriors, but there would have been photographs of the historic guests who frequented the hotel: writer Karen Blixen, aviator Beryl Markham, Prime Minister Winston Churchill, naturalists Jane Goodall and Joy Adamson. Anthropologist Richard Leakey and Hollywood's top stars visited William Holden at his Mount Kenya Safari Club. The *Hideaway Report* editor, who writes anonymously of his travels in 2010, laments the banal furnishings and bad service of the hotel now owned by Fairmont. But that was over a decade ago. Maybe things have improved. I say to Bill, "If I had a million dollars, I'd take this trip!" But online I see a notice dated May 28, 2020. They have had a financial crisis (Covid-19?), paid off their creditors and given notice to all the staff. The hotel lasted for 116 years, "twice as long as Kenya has been an independent country."

The Norfolk Hotel has a history not known to my father. Playwright and cultural critic Ngũgĩ wa Thiong'o wrote of his experience trying to produce theatre in Nigeria. In 1977, Kenya was getting ready to host a UNESCO conference, the Second World Black and African Festival of Arts and Culture. Wa Thiong'o and colleague Micere Mugo, both teaching at the University of Nigeria,

English and Literary Studies Department, suggested the performance of their play *The Trial of Dedan Kimathi*, which performs Kenya's struggle for independence. It made sense to them that the play would be performed at the Kenya National Theatre, but the European directors said there was no room in the schedule. They were already committed – to the Jeune Ballet de France and *A Funny Thing Happened on the Way to the Forum*. Kenya's story was not as important as a French ballet and a Broadway musical. Here's how Wa Thiong'o brings the Norfolk Hotel into this story:

> The Norfolk Hotel overlooks the site where in 1922 African workers were massacred by the British police. The workers were marching to the central police station to demand the release of their leader, Harry Thuku, who had been arrested and later imprisoned for eight years because of his involvement in the nascent workers' movement. Their march was interrupted by gunfire from the police. The police were also joined in the massacre by the white lords on the terraces of the Norfolk Hotel. . . . The bodies of the dead and wounded lay sprawled on the ground on the site which years later was to house the National Theatre complex and the University of Nairobi. Harry Thuku became a nationalist hero, the subject of many songs and dances.

Nairobi, Wednesday, February 6
While admiring the beauty of the city and the gorgeous blossoms everywhere (Feb!) noticed a lovely golf course. No trouble to see who was playing and who was carrying the clubs.

Dad was in the lap of luxury. Not his usual accommodation. My Depression-raised father must have been stunned by all of it. No wonder he noticed who carried the golf clubs.

A NECESSARY DISTANCE / 155

Keenly aware that all this would be grass shacks and savagery if it weren't for the English, who have built everything. Certain in my mind that all will be a slum of incompetence in a couple of years, like Jakarta. The value problem is too great for me at this pace, so I am taking refuge in old-fashioned race prejudice. I am no longer certain that this is wrong . . .

The Africans would obviously (or would they?) be better off if the British remained in command. I am happy there were Englishmen here to help me. All the same, the beautiful city is not theirs – belongs to the Blacks. Should it be? Should such a city be built? Should there be a Montreal in Iroquois country? Or a Calgary in Blackfoot country? Yes, there should be. Practically. But there won't be – sentimentally.

In arguing with Gene, I come back to my own Scandinavian concepts (with American reinforcement – not too different, romantically) that I would offer no compromise if I were in the position of these people. But, of course, I am not. And, of course, they are not the same. And for their difference, I feel all men are not brothers, and that some are inferior to others. If I were a Black, and all my people Black, there would be no white people here. We would be living in grass huts and ignorance, but there would be no one making us, in our ignorance, their golf caddies.

This is narrow and Norwegian, but I think it's better than being the assistant manager of the hotel. And I wonder what will happen to Nairobi's beauty in a few years. In our evening walk we passed Negroes in white helmets with nightsticks. Do they expect violence? Such a comfort to be in such a beautiful, modern city, complete with Woolworth's, Kleenex, and enchanting English men and women. But everywhere, the servants are Black. If all this is given to the servants, can they use it? Should we give Ontario back to the Hurons? New York State back to the Iroquois?

My romantic ideals are all falling away. Bigotry is becoming a less obnoxious word.

So here is the paradox, interestingly recorded in this journal entry. On the one hand, he believes that the British have brought order, structure, "civilization" – and he admits that this is reassuring, comfortable, beneficial to the Africans even. On the other hand, he imagines himself as an African – as the serving staff and the golf caddies – and the emotions that he feels rise up in himself are rebellion, pride; better to be poor, "uneducated" and free (he thinks) than "civilized" and servile. Of course, he is not able to perceive anything but this choice, since he cannot imagine that the Africans, without the British, can be anything other than "ignorant" and, in a real sense, "uncivilized" and that they would not know how to carry forward the (of course desirable) British orderliness once the whites left and that things would inevitably deteriorate.

If the idea of "Orient" can include Africa, and if the narratives that westerners (including my father) were surrounded by in the 1960s were heavily influenced by "Orientalism," then Edward Said's writing might be relevant: "Every one of them [nineteenth-century writers] kept intact the separateness of the Orient, its eccentricity, its backwardness, its silent indifference, its feminine penetrability, its supine malleability; this is why every writer on the Orient, from Renan to Marx (ideologically speaking), or from the most rigorous scholars (Lane and Sacy) to the most powerful imaginations (Flaubert and Nerval), saw the Orient as a locale requiring Western attention, reconstruction, even redemption."

My father was speaking from a time where many from his world assumed that "order" and "civility" were desirable (there was nothing romantic about their opposite) and that these were the values of "civilized" cultures. This was deeply engrained in the status quo narrative.

But he was questioning it.

Thinking with His Eyes Closed

Bill comes with me to the barn. I'll ride my horse Henry with Diana and her mare and Bill will fix some horse blankets in the sewing machine room he has set up beside the viewing lounge. An hour or so later, after our ride, I am pulling the saddle off Henry's warm back and I call to Diana in the next stall, "I have a question before you go."

She comes over and stands with her Covid-19 mask slightly floppy on her face, her hair flat with helmet head. I ask her the question, "Who would want to know about a white guy in his forties . . ."

She thinks for a moment. "Maybe what he *says* is a red herring, maybe that's not what you want people to think about."

Diana asks me what the point of the book is, what message I want to get across. This soundbite question irritates me and I snap back, "You mean, what *Reader's Digest* paragraph explains it all to everyone?"

I get angry so fast these days, a flash storm, *bang*. I take a breath. This is Diana, I remind myself. And I *can* answer this question. Can't I?

I say, "People are complicated. People can do terrible things, dreadful vicious things. Also unbearably kind and generous things. And it's the same person."

Diana leans on the stall door. Henry noses her arm, looking for a treat.

"But what you are writing about isn't really what your dad *did*, is it? It's what he *wrote*. And it's his private notes, right? Not what *he* decided to publish. We all think so many things, and they aren't

– well, it doesn't mean they *are* what we think. They are how we *find* what we think."

Henry is now nuzzling my pocket and I give him the peppermints I'd forgotten were there. I pull off his sheepskin and saddle blanket. I put everything on the stall door. What would it mean if we couldn't think thoughts, *any* thoughts, and couldn't put them down in private notebooks as we tried to make sense of what we were feeling? What would it mean for this not to be possible or permitted? It would be like when I was a child, and then a teenager, so afraid my diaries would be seen and judged that I wrote in code. To protect myself. When I became an adult, I didn't know how to excavate my own convictions or even desires. I was too good at writing down what others wanted me to say.

Diana is still thinking. "You know, the other day I was riding around the driveway, just hacking. Morag knew I wanted to fix my riding position; I was leaning too far off-centre. She told me 'While you are riding, close your eyes. Lean forward, far. Lean backward, far. Do this a number of times. When you open your eyes, you will be in the middle.' Isn't that what your dad was doing? I wouldn't know I was off balance if I didn't try to lean too far forward, too far back."

I decide this is a good analogy. My father's notes are private, only for himself. He is leaning forward and back, thinking with his eyes closed.

Strange Bedfellows

Dad makes a few observations about the wildlife and their raft trip in Nairobi Royal National Park (the park remains, but "Royal" has been removed from the name) but it's his notes on the team's personalities that interest me. I read about fifteen pages and sit back in surprise. Here, by the pool at the Norfolk Hotel in Nairobi – what, three weeks into the trip? – Dad has an epiphany. He makes a decision and starts to write in a completely different manner.

A NECESSARY DISTANCE / 159

. Tomorrow we leave by chartered aircraft for Serengeti (Tanzania). Grahame delighted by the kind of aircraft. So is Gene. Have no bloody notion what they are talking about. Grahame called to have us in for drinks before dinner. Noticed Gene was well advanced in drinking. There is an intensity, a compulsive energy. A need to attack and argue. Reassuring because it is an extension of the sober personality; not quite reassuring, because the uncertain elements, the unpredictable, are also accentuated. Perhaps I should note more on this.

There are very interesting, though unimportant, facets to the relations of the three of us. If I record, for a while, not our trip, but our relations, I might learn something. I might, for example, not be as stupid as I seem.

And what is it that obsesses Gene? Can anyone so logical really care about the truth so much? Grahame is easier. You don't bewilder or fluster or rush the dear old British. (You don't the Scandinavians either, but I think, for all our stubborn singularity, we are in some way sneakier than the English. We stand back and say nothing, waiting for you to reveal yourself. If we seem not too alert during this examination, it doesn't matter. It's not us we're studying. This might be interesting. Rather than a travelogue of notes.)

Example of type of detail I could record. Without analysis. We three go to look at Norfolk Hotel swimming pool. Gene and Grahame stand at gate, looking, but I go in a few steps. I discover to my surprise that there is a bar just out of sight. In addition to the semi-nude western girls. I take another three steps to read the sign, regulations, how to sign in. I turn to convey this information, but at this moment G and G are turning away, deep in an urgency which is familiar to me (I know Grahame is hardly an urgent fellow), and they go walking away, as fast as they can go, imagining that some urgent accomplishment is about to be achieved. I look back at the swimmers at the bar, at the girls. I think I had better hurry out because there seems to be something terribly important going forward. I get to the gate. My two companions, who have not offered me a word, are vanishing around the corner, pacing forward feverishly, intent on some matter of overpowering importance. I wonder how this emergency could have arisen without my being aware of it. It's all so fast, so urgent, they can't wait to say goodbye to me or even to warn me.

I glance at the flowers along the long hall. Like prisoners going into cells, Grahame is at his door, Gene at his. Gene says, in an urgent driven sort of way, "Four thirty?" Grahame says, "Four thirty!" Both plunge into their rooms, like the Scarlet Pimpernel about to flout Robespierre. Left behind, and not advised, I decipher all this. My conclusion: at 4:30 we will go to the park and look at some animals. I stroll in and go to bed. Have a good and badly needed sleep. At 4:30, a knocking at the door. Gene. We go to the park and look at animals.

Basic thing here which seems to conflict with the personality. I would never rush away and forget that I had a companion. What does this mean?

I stop, typing this, struck by a memory. Not mine, my father's and I don't know when or why he told me. He is a small child, four or five. The family live in Winnipeg, his father working at the railroad, his mother writing. It's winter, something like twenty below. He has misbehaved, this small child, and his mother throws him outside as a punishment. He waits. An hour. Two. It's too cold to sit down, but he doesn't knock. The sun has long gone down. Eventually a neighbour sees him, knocks on the door, no answer. The neighbour takes him in for the night. I've never comprehended this story that my father laughed as he recounted. Where was his

A NECESSARY DISTANCE / *161*

father? Did both parents just go to bed? What kind of temper did my grandmother have? Or maybe she forgot, fingers on her typewriter, imagining the Icelandic sailor in her novel or the feminist fury in her essay. What kind of child waits for hours in those temperatures? My father, apparently. Now, over forty years later, he tries to understand his travelling companions. It's important to know who you travel with into the unknown.

He adds something, perhaps inspired by this new preoccupation. He mentions a collection he is writing, *Around the World in Eighty Limericks.*

During this long part of the trip, we present geological, scientific and spiritual limericks, to further enrich this experience:

> There once were two lovers in Hell
> Who emitted a sulphurous smell:
> They said, "We both think
> If we raise enough stink
> We'll get on in Hell very well."

It's a sort of never look back, the hell with the hindmost, and a fury of frustration when one is forced to remember there are other people. As when Grahame decides at the airport he won't be rushed and will take five minutes to buy some magazines. Gene is furious and races through customs, and then we all sit for an hour – reading Grahame's magazines! I think both are right. One must dive and attack. But to be so obsessed with dive and attack, one's values may become distorted. Everyone in wrong. Pakistan (seen from terminal) is a wrong horse. Noted Gene's bewildered impatience in Anand when Grahame was five minutes or so in the bathroom. Gene must have instant elimination. There is perhaps nothing like instant elimination to set up curtain of bewilderment, to destroy understanding of one's fellow man.

Gene is infused with a passionate urgency, but it so often expresses itself in trivia that I wonder what he is looking for. Never mind. An unusual man, unusual ways. He will either kill himself in some adventure, or have a stroke, or become one of the more famous names of our time. I have known many talented fellows, but few in this class.

But what class is it? A kind of mad fogey blown up at white heat, which leads to ruin because we move on so fast there is not time to answer it. Whole nations are disposed of with a phrase. Of course, this is easy, phrases are overpowering if voiced with a sound of authority. But surely there is no such world-encompassing and definitive authority here! What is the drive, the urge to condemn, to attack? As far as I can see, it is to attack cliché, or what is popular. Clichés are not always wrong. This is fascinating. What is Gene mad at? What does he want to do? Something he calls being "honest," but does he know how, or what, this is? Attack is not "honest." God knows what it is when you work within your own culture.

Must watch this interesting business of our relations on this trip for possible revelations of character. Much more interesting than more aircraft, more action, more villages, more natives, more lions, more beers.

It is 1:00 a.m. Now Thursday. So end this book and to bed. Up betimes at 9:00 ready to go on our next most urgent mission.

Note: In future, concentrate more on our relationships against the scenes we are in, rather than the scenes themselves. There is something here quite interesting – far beyond a travelogue or my personal reaction to new countries.

End of Notebook Three.

Wedding Dress

August 10, 2022. My parent's anniversary, they married in 1952. In our front room my mother's olive-green satin wedding dress hangs on the wall. She had the sleeves taken off to make it less formal. There is tubing down the front that flares out on each side to articulate a high waist. It is a beautiful dress. I kept it for years, then tried it on one day – fragile with age, the fabric of the skirt split right up the middle. Now it hangs there, torn, and I consider framing the still intact bodice behind a frame. But I want to be able to touch it.

Stories and Their Many Parts

The windows of the cabin overlook a blue lake. Bill and I are here for a week in October and for me it's a writing retreat. The house is a soft grey, several stories, red roof. I'm returning from a walk, starting up the last steep tree-lined bit of road to the cabin when my cellphone rings. I hear my brother Scott's recorded greeting: "Happy Birthday, sister. You haven't reached the top of the hill yet. Don't look down!"

I find Bill in the kitchen, in the one corner of the house where there is cell reception. He has been looking up the Gujarat riots.

"I have conflated two events," he says. "The razing of the temple was in nineteen ninety-two. The train fire was ten years later. But there was a fire. Muslims were blamed and it was pilgrims on the train. The body count was fifty-eight. Then there were riots, and the numbers say one thousand five hundred killed." "Pilgrims" in this context are mostly young men inflamed with a right-wing Hindu (anti-Muslim) agenda, who have the belligerent aim of "rebuilding" the temple on the land of the destroyed mosque. There were rampaging mobs with printouts of addresses of Muslim homes and businesses. A frenzy of rape and murder. People begging for their lives without success. A Muslim politician holed up with his extended family in a flat, him trying fruitlessly to call Modi to beg him to call off the mob, but Modi would not speak to him; the man going out to the balcony, offering himself if they would spare his family, going down and being killed, then they torched the whole flat and killed everyone. One boy survived who, years later grown up, told the story of that night.

All these events and stories overlap and connect to each other, layers of hurt and victory, resentment and relationship; the ground we walk on, the stories we tell. "Each of us is all the sums he has not counted," wrote Thomas Wolfe. "Subtract us into nakedness and night again, and you shall see begin in Crete four thousand years ago the love that ended yesterday in Texas." Time, the physicists tell us, isn't what we think – and not just the physicists but the dreamers too, and the grandparents, the story keepers. The twists and bends of coincidence and chance and inevitability shape the present moment. Too much attention to all this resonance leads to a trembling vertigo. Is it any wonder that after a few drinks and a night of remembering we wake up and hurry into the amnesia of our day. But we live thinly because of it. Our age of easy answers and oversimplification takes us nowhere fast.

My dad would philosophize and ponder. He was at home in the lost art of history. Colonial history maybe, western history, but he knew that stories mattered. Stories, unlike facts, are less likely to be reductive. They bleed into other stories. Opening, asking, inviting. The ripples on the water below the window never stop moving. But the lake remains. The stillness is an illusion.

Dad is in Africa. Browsing bookshelves, I find a slender 1979 paperback with the dated title *Tales from the Dark Continent*, "The bestselling sequel to *Plain Tales from the Raj*." The book is a reconstruction of Britain's imperial past in Africa assembled from recorded interviews done by the author, Charles Allen, "traveler,

A NECESSARY DISTANCE / *165*

writer and broadcaster, specializing in Third World affairs." Bill points out that the Indian *Plain Tales* is a play on Rudyard Kipling's *Plain Tales from the Hills*, which was itself a playful title.

"People either live on the plains or in the hills," says Bill. We laugh at the anachronistic phrase "dark continent" and he flips through the chapter headings: "White Man's Burden; White Man's Grave," "To Africa," "Keepers of the King's Peace." But when I start reading the book I am surprised. The book is interesting and the stories it tells are important.

Tales from the Dark Continent was published sixteen years after my father's trip, and its attitudes – taken for granted at the time – help me understand the 1963 world my father lived in. Allen states explicitly in his introduction: "I have made no attempt to confront the political issues of colonialism. I have confined myself simply to putting on record and in their own terms something of the manner and style of those who were there, placing them and their beliefs in the context of the times in which they lived and worked."

I look ahead in Dad's notes to see his Africa itinerary. From Nairobi they go to the Serengeti in Tanzania, then they fly to Rome for a few days. Then back to Ghana and Togo, and then across the ocean to Brazil. Okay, so a bit of east and west Africa. I pull a few fragments from Allen's brief history.

Britain's official imperial rule in Africa started in 1900 and ended in 1966. Hence my father while in Nairobi in 1963, "They get independence soon." But British involvement, says Allen, started well before the Crown. Business and money led the way: the Imperial British East Africa Company, the Royal Niger Company, the British South Africa Company in Rhodesia. This country is named for explorer Cecil Rhodes and I wonder about the original African names. Allen again: "But long before these chartered empire-building companies there had been other interests, for 'the first signs of the white man that the African ever saw were the slave-traders and the early traders in the oil rivers; the most villainous ghastly, dreadful people.'"

Material reminders of the slave trade remain: vast dungeons in Christiansborg Castle in Ghana, through which Gold Coast Society danced congas in the 1950s; iron rings on the walls of a bank building in Bathurst on the western coast of Sierra Leone. Bathurst was also the home of "recaptives" – Africans freed from slave ships by the West Africa Squadron of the Royal Navy, established after Britain's Act for the Abolition of the Slave Trade of 1807.

Traffic in slaves to the Middle East flourished in East Africa; suppression of that trade was of interest to the colonizers. I read this twice to make sure I've understood it correctly.

Stay in the Trouble

It was my mother who liked to fish and swim. Once Dad had hammered stakes into the ground and raised our dank canvas tent, he would retreat to a chair by the lake with a book. Late on one such summer afternoon when I was fourteen, Dad jumped up and walked to the rented rowboat pulled up on the sandy beach, grabbed the oars and pushed it out onto the water.

"Dinner won't be long, George," my mother warned.

"Neither will we," he said, nodding at me to join him. My brother looked up for a moment, then frowned back into the pools of minnows he had gathered into pails. Dad stepped into the boat and held out his hand. I flung off my shoes, waded out and climbed aboard. We glided out into the silence of the bay.

The dipping of the oars made a steady beat as we rowed by giant pines and cedars. He whistled, then got quiet. When we were about halfway around the bay he stopped rowing. We drifted. I scanned the shore for a deer, or a bear, or a moose. My reward was the scampering of two red squirrels, one after the other, in a race to somewhere.

A NECESSARY DISTANCE / *167*

Dad spoke from the back of the boat. "We don't belong here, you know." I looked over my shoulder, puzzled.

"It's not our lake," I said.

"It's not our country," said my father.

We sat for a while, the tiny rowboat slightly rocking, rolled by invisible currents. Then he took hold of the oars and rowed back to the campsite. I never asked about it, or if I did, I don't remember. It's only now, reading his journals, that I remember – what he said, but more, how he said it. Matter of fact. No drama, just a statement – that this place was more than I could see or know. Now, when people say, "this country some call Canada" – my father would have understood exactly what that meant.

Indigenous actors were cast and taken seriously in *The Beachcombers*, the comedy-drama produced by CBC between 1972 and 1990. Dad was one of a team of writers and the characters inhabited our house as vividly as they did the screen. Nick, Jesse Jim, Molly and, above all, Relic sat with us on the patio behind our house as Dad tried out story ideas. Sometimes we got to vote on the best one or make suggestions. The show ran 387 episodes and is the third-longest running series ever made for English-language Canadian TV. I expect he met Indigenous actors who after decades of "Tonto" parts were finally being cast in better roles. But I don't know. In the fall of 2022, plans are announced to turn *The Beachcombers* into an animated series. Dad would have been delighted. In 2023, reruns of the original *Beachcombers* appear on CBC Gem, CBC's streaming platform. I watch the season premiere and find it quirky, original, surprising. One of the episodes is Dad's.

As I read my father's journals, I am faced with both my father's complicity and his efforts to resist easy explanations. I experience all this too. I have been asking myself and my students the question "Who am I on this ground?" We talk about Tim Lilburn's book of essays *Going Home*, where he addresses the restlessness and

168 / JULIE SALVERSON

rootlessness felt by many of us with European heritage because of our detachment from the western wisdom traditions that could teach us how to live "undivided from one's earth." Lilburn says this happened to our ancestors long before they left Europe. My students think about their own lost heritages, their hidden resources. I invite them to consider whether a "settler" has more to offer than apology and shame. My students come from all over the world, although most are Canadian-born. I ask them these questions: From where and when did your ancestors arrive in Canada – whether eleven years ago or eleven thousand years ago? Did they work for someone or did someone work for them? What were they leaving, or fleeing, or seeking? I want us also to consider what traditions any of us might claim to help learn the exacting apprenticeship of knowing place. The white students are nervous; they think it sounds like white supremacy, or privilege. They don't think about class.

I tell my students about *The Book of Jessica*. It's the account of the development of a play created by a Métis playwright and an actor with Scottish heritage. Although the subject of the play was Maria Campbell's life, Campbell was impatient with how the actor – Linda Griffiths – was in awe of the tragedy of Indigenous history and kept saying, "I'm ashamed that I didn't know." Campbell tells Griffiths, "While you were being overwhelmed with my history and my oppression, you were making me feel like it was exclusively mine. I couldn't understand why you didn't know your own history . . . My great-grandfather was a Scot, hundreds and thousands of his people starved in Scotland, Wales, Ireland, not even six hundred years ago . . . You could say 'This is what happened to my grandfathers' and I could say 'This is what happened to my grandfathers.'"

In *After Fukushima*, scholar Jean-Luc Nancy writes, "We are being exposed to a catastrophe of meaning. Let's not hurry to hide this exposure." I have tried to learn the art of exposure through my study of a genre of clown with a red nose. The job of this clown – the job of being awake to alive reciprocal connection – is to stay in the shit: not to skip over, reify, sentimentalize or pathologize trouble, but to work through it. "Stay in the trouble," says scholar Donna Haraway. That's what I'm doing, I think, returning every day to these notebooks. And to the man who waited for me to read them.

Sounding Out These New Words

At the lake, I find *The Book of Woodcraft* by Ernest Thompson Seton, published in 1912. It includes eyewitness accounts of the betrayals of Indigenous Peoples by white men and governments, primarily American and British. Voice after voice testifies to the character, values, bravery and pride of different Indian (the word used then and still often used in the US) nations and individuals. It is both sobering and reassuring to listen to white voices categorically condemning the actions of their/our race at the time of settlement and occupation.

For example, Seton writes:

> We know now that the whites did use diabolical tortures in their dealings with the Indian, and deliberately and persistently misrepresented him in order to justify their own atrocities.
>
> The whites, however, had print to state their case, while the Indians had none to tell their story or defend them. Furthermore, it is notorious that all massacres of Indians by the whites were accomplished by treachery *in times of peace*, while all Indian massacres of whites were *in time of war*, to resist invasion. At present, I know of no exception to this rule.

And then a footnote: "Many supposed massacres by Indians are now known to have been the work of whites disguised as Indians."

The book is full of horrific accounts, brutality and butchery. Seton describes approaching a noisy, laughing group of children in a village: "My purpose was wholly sympathetic, but my presence acted as a wet-blanket. The children were hushed or went away. I saw shy faces, furtive glances, or looks of distrust. They hate us; they do not want us near. Our presence is an evil influence in their joy. Can we wonder?"

Grinnell became a renowned American conservationist. Many of his years in the late nineteenth century were spent building relationships with the Pawnee and the Cheyenne. But his closest relationships were with the Blackfeet. According to biographer John Taliaferro, he worked to document their past and to advocate for them as they "ran a brutal gauntlet of starvation, disease, corrupt agents, invasive stock raisers, and a steady onslaught of ineffective and downright bad policies drawn up by spoilsmen and would-be reformers in faraway Washington, D.C." The Blackfeet made Grinnell their broker with the Bureau of Indian Affairs, Congress and the White House. They adopted him into their tribe.

My dad would have read these kinds of histories. His bookshelves were full and his research for scripts was exhaustive. Grinnell and his wife, Elizabeth, arrived at the Glacier Park Lodge, Montana, in 1926, sixteen years after the creation of the national park he had first dreamed of in 1891. When I read about Grinnell checking into "a tourist temple on the grand scale," I think about Dad's dismissal of white imitation totem poles. According to Taliaferro, "Blackfeet Indians, fierce and far-ranging not so long ago, now loitered about the station and the hotel, selling trinkets and entertaining dudes with desultory song and dance." Grinnell accepted the need for tourists but never considered himself "a

A NECESSARY DISTANCE / *171*

full-blooded" one. In his diary at the hotel, he wrote: "Somewhat annoyed, but hope for better things tomorrow."

I don't have to think too hard to imagine what Grinnell, Seton or my father, for that matter, would make of what is happening in Canada today. The Truth and Reconciliation Commission, Kanesatake and the dispute between Mohawks and the town of Oka, land claims. *Resurgence* is a concept Michi Saagiig Nishnaabeg writer and artist Leanne Betasamosake Simpson learned from "a practice of life":

> This land has taught me that Nishnaabeg life is continual, reciprocal, and reflective. Sometimes, it is a critical engagement with my ancestors, those yet to be born, and the nations of beings with whom I share the land. It is a living constellation of co-resistance with all of the anti-colonial peoples and the worlds they build. This land has taught me that Nishnaabeg life is a persistent world-building process.

Simpson tells us that we can't learn about resurgence by googling or reading or researching. She isn't concerned with a response to colonialism, but with a "procedure for Indigenous life and Indigenous living is one that Indigenous Peoples used long before our existence ever depended upon our ability to resist and survive the violence of capitalism, heteropatriarchy, white supremacy, and expansive dispossession." I imagine my dad listening to a fiery speech by Leanne Betasamosake Simpson. I have no doubt he would have been captivated. He would have sounded out each of these new words and phrases. He would have tried to understand them.

This phrase "anti-colonialism" that Dad hears for the first time implicates the day-to-day encounters, people and lands of this trip that he is on. What Simpson calls "capitalism, heteropatriarchy, white suppression and expansive dispossession" are evident everywhere, embodied in every story. My father would have known about residential schools. He read and paid attention to history. He worked with Indigenous actors on *Beachcombers*. In these notebooks, he jots down fleeting thoughts as he experiences the vertigo of inequity, the embodiment of difference, the rattling of his comfort.

Dad is asking questions, but at the same time he is thinking and writing the same casual dismissals of peoples and cities for which he criticizes Gene. Even Grinnell complains about inefficient clerks and bad room service. The casual impatience, the assumed right to judge and the categorizing of people into who does and doesn't warrant courtesy that runs deep in our cultural conditioning clashes with what our intelligence knows to be unjust. Many of the soldiers involved in massacring Indigenous warriors and Chiefs, women and children, knew that what they did was wrong. But, like Hitler's henchmen and bureaucrats, we are all capable of constructing narratives that justify our actions or even make it necessary to act against conscience. It's easy to underestimate the complexity of our motivations for doing cruel things.

When I was at the Cold War symposium in Ottawa an Indigenous archivist, speaking about photographs taken fifty or one hundred years ago of Indigenous children on reserves, said of the photographer, "Of course he didn't care at all about the people." But how do we know this? Perhaps it is more insidious, more dangerous, if the photographer did care, and still took the photo. Cared, and still acted inside the apparatus of how things are done.

As I read through my father's notebooks, I ask the question so many others have asked – Germans in postwar Europe, landowners in the Caribbean or the American South, and now settlers in this country – what does it feel like to live inside largely unexamined narratives and feel them crack? Perhaps the 1960s marked the

A NECESSARY DISTANCE / *173*

beginning of more and more people like my father travelling "out there." Maybe it was the beginning of a new kind of looking.

Wouldn't It Be Nice?

I have a few of Dad's personal diaries with me at Blue Lake. Most of the comments about family are about drinking – "went on the wagon, went off the wagon" – and my mother's rages at me. Julie has emerged as a shadowy character who slips out of the house whenever possible.

Sad Mother's Day [My father's journal, 1970. I am fourteen.]

Julie gives Sandra a dirty novel (lesbianism) unwrapped. No card. No flower. Scott at Curtis's. S and I walked with dog in the rain. S cried. Said it's the way we live. Lois [Sandra's sister] goes to church with her daughters. They all love her. Julie went to mass with her friend Marilyn, not saying goodbye to S, which hurt her further. Julie returned and played guitar with Marilyn. I went to work, discouraged. No one to share S's show at 2:00 on radio so I will return from work to do so and tape it for her. Julie, recently enthusiastic about special occasions, no longer cares. She thinks she is sophisticated. Actually she is retreating from human involvements – she has only Marilyn and is escaping into love of horses. Animals offer no challenge in terms of relationships. It's the way I myself run out to walk with the dog. It's an escape seen in extreme form in the dreadful case of Miss Brown, the spinster vet, existing for creatures and terrified of people. Miss Brown gave up years ago. A sad, sad story. And of course, S mourns her own mother today. She feels, when the time comes, no one will mourn for her.

When my mother was in her late seventies she was hospitalized after a series of strokes. By this time, she was in a nursing home, tricked into going there by me. She had been drinking all the time and falling a lot. My father, in his eighties, could barely pick her up off the floor. I told Mom we were visiting the home to check it out. We locked the door behind her.

A few months later when she was visiting what was now Dad's apartment there was a knock at the door. It was a cab driver with a paper bag. She had managed to telephone the liquor store and make an order. I sent him away with apologies and a large tip. My mother fumed on the couch. She was a desperately frightened and lonely person. Dad told me once she started drinking when her mother died. She was in her thirties, engaged to my father, and over a meal with Mom's parents Sandra and her mother fought. Mom stormed out and her mother went to bed with a headache. She had a stroke and never woke up. Sandra blamed herself.

A year after the incident with the cab driver, shortly after Mom died, Dad drove me home from lunch. "Can you stay put a moment?" he asked. We sat in silence while he fidgeted. Then he apologized for ignoring her drinking when I was young. "She was terrible to you. I should have done something." I was amazed and grateful. After all those years, where had this come from?

Now, looking at the small notebook from 1970, I hear the misery in my father's words. I also see that it *is* the past. Everything is gone – the brutal and the whimsical, the joyful and the vicious. All gone. I decide that when I am done, I will burn the notebooks.

Or maybe sooner.

I wait until Bill is asleep and come back downstairs. The fire in the stove is still hot enough that new logs burst into flames immediately. A notebook will erupt like a matchstick. I gather the seven journals and arrange myself on the small wooden rocker. There are sharp crackles from the other side of the glass, glaring orange flames, almost white. I stroke the covers, black and wrinkled like old skin. A loud snap startles me, I pull the books back, as if the

A NECESSARY DISTANCE / *175*

fire could reach through the heavy glass and make the decision for me. I take a breath, then hold one out closer to the flame. Maybe Notebook One, Japan. Maybe Notebook Three, India. Or the one that contains his most terrible day of the trip, the one I'm just starting to record. It would be so easy. The pages would catch instantly. It would be over in moments. Would I regret it? Would it matter? My father's words curling, dissolving. Then nothing, only ash. No words, thoughts, no record. Nobody would know. It would be so easy. Even if it wasn't.

I have picked up James Baldwin's 1962 novel *Another Country*. In this Black Lives Matter movement, I read words published fifty-seven years earlier. The voice of narrator Rufus Scott: "How I hate them – all those white sons of bitches out there. They're trying to kill me, you think I don't know? They got the world on a string, man, . . . and they tying that string around my neck, they killing *me*."

What did my father write in Nairobi? "Noticed a lovely golf course. No trouble to see who was playing, and who was carrying the clubs."

Born Free

Notebook Four.

Thursday, February 7, 1963. Serengeti Plain.
    7:00 a.m. Heard Gene call in hall, knocking. Grahame, "It's me." Lots of noise and activity and Black men arguing loudly in their Lumumba voices.
    8:15 Breakfast. Alka-Seltzer, eggs. Poured coffee on my porridge. Badly hungover for some reason. Paid bill. Numerous cards. English women at gift shop are muddling humorously. Don't quite understand them but good rapport. Discussed

palm trees on main street. No one knows what they are, including Negro [*sic*] taxi driver. Waiting while boys buy fruit and fish to take to Serengeti lodge. Taximeter now reads four shilling, zero cents.

9:07 Joke about man who took Scotch, rye, rum, gin and soda, decided the common factor was the soda and this was what made him drink.

Flew to Serengeti in morning.

They fly in an Aero Commander 500A (two engines, six seats) and Gene complains that the English pilot is dull. He simply transports them, no conversation. "A man should delight in his work."

Below are herds of animals and the circular compounds that are Maasai villages. Mountains, lakes, dirt roads and a field of grass where they land. They sit waiting for their ride, Dad enchanted by odd green birds that gather on the wings and tail of the plane. Mr. Allan, a Norwegian, arrives so quietly in his Land Rover he startles the men. Tanned, in shorts, he has an accent and uses "jolly" a lot. His thin, handsome German wife is with him. She has had malaria but now is fine. "I wouldn't go to Nairobi no matter how sick I was," she says.

They check into the Seronera Wildlife Lodge, round cottages with high pointed green roofs. In the distance are mountains and umbrella trees. "Absolute silence. And the grassy plain."

They eat a blackened roast, boiled potatoes, carrots, rye crisps and noodle soup. Allan takes them out on the plain in the Land Rover.

Two ruts, sometimes dividing and getting thinner until they disappear altogether and we are sailing over a vast sea of grass. Sometimes you can't see the distant blue mountains, sailing this yellow sea. Islands of piled rocks appear. We sail around

A NECESSARY DISTANCE / *177*

the island seeking lions. Following circling buzzards. Ostriches stand about. Clusters of gazelles with black stripes and busy waving little black tails. A golden eagle perched on a rock. Then the birds, which had all moved because of unseasonal rain. The plain looks naked of anything but grass. Then you look through binoculars and it is alive. Thousands of zebras and wildebeests, strange cow or buffalo-like animals. Driving through the herds, seven thousand zebras, staring at us, trotting across the wind-shield with their neat, well packed, covered bodies. The hyenas in ant hole with black horns lying by them. The crazy "Great Bustard" strutting with his weird feathers, to entice his female.

They see a male and a female lion. On the drive back, the Norwegian states with confidence, "I have never seen anyone hungry here. The future of Tanganyika will be a tourist economy."

Gene asks, "But aren't the FAO talking about cropping the herds? How many are they thinking?"

Allan shakes his head and shouts to Gene and Dad in the back of the Land Rover, "Stupid. Ridiculous. Thirty thousand animals. Impossible. It would mean a slaughterhouse in this corridor. Would draw all the hyenas and the lions too. Lions prefer to eat what others kill. They're lazy!" He laughs. "But seriously, no, the lions would never return to the Serengeti, and they would turn on the domestic cattle. When you muck around with nature, you get trouble."

Allan tells them that once, during a year of famine, British Army trucks delivered American maize.

Heavy rain. Trucks bogged down. Hundreds of nations watched but not one moved to help a few soldiers get those trucks moving. Packed with corn. The British don't understand Africans – or anyone else! They say "please" and you can't say that to Africans. You must say, "This is what you must do or there will be trouble."

Back at the lodge they are joined over drinks by a pleasant young German in leather shorts and a young Brit in cotton. FAO men. They talk about fear. Dad's notes here echo a passage in a novel I am reading. Jan-Philipp Sendker's *The Art of Hearing Heartbeats* is set in Burma. He writes:

> Every one of us knows fear. . . . It encircles us like flies around ox dung. It puts animals to flight. They bolt and run or fly or swim until they believe themselves safe or until they keel over dead from exhaustion. Humans are no wiser. We see that there is no place on earth where we can hide from fear, yet still we attempt to find one. We strive for wealth and power. We abandon ourselves to the illusion that we are stronger than fear. We try to rule – over our children and our wives, over our neighbours and our friends. Ambition and fear have something in common: neither knows any limits.

The German at the Serengeti lodge throws back a whisky and tells them a story. "There are poachers, all kinds, looking for something to sell. The 'swishes' sell the most."

"Swishes?" asks Grahame, taking a crisp and making a face at its staleness. He is impatient for dinner, but a long drink is custom here, and these men are hungry for company.

"They kill the wildebeests for the tails." A bell rings, and the story is interrupted by the meal, but Dad brings it up again as they finish with coffee. It has given him an idea for the film.

A boy kills a wildebeest, the eternal hunt for food. But he leaves the food for the hyenas and goes off with the tails.

A NECESSARY DISTANCE / *179*

Later that evening, Dad settles on the front step to look at the full moon shining through the spreading canopy of an umbrella tree. He studies a bat hanging near a light bulb, radar ears twitching. The bat waits by the light for insects. Hangs by his feet, tan-coloured and uglier than the hyenas, which Dad describes as looking like different animals put together. Ears like bears, etc.

He thinks about the wildebeest and the boy. He had suggested, half-seriously, that this might be a scene in the film. Gene and Grahame got excited, "all hot on doing a western." He writes a letter to my mother. "Today we drove through seven thousand zebras, had tea at the Warden's, and a lion stalked in."

Dad isn't joking about the lion. There is a four-or-five-month-old cub they are caring for. The mother had three, took two away and forgot the third.

The humans are now looking after it. About the size of a young Newfoundland dog. Sleeps on their bed (Hey, Sandra!). But is doomed. Won't be accepted by the lions. And can never learn to hunt. Some say they must dump it on the plain, and it will starve to death. Lions must be taught to hunt by their parents. A family group, called a pride of lions, work together usually in hunting because the game is faster than they are. One lion herds the animals so they pass another lion, who singles out a victim and makes a kill. This doesn't come by instinct. The lions teach their young how to do this. So the local pet is doomed for lack of education.

I remember the 1966 film *Born Free*, about Joy Adamson, her family among the famous who stayed at the Norfolk Hotel. My parents took us to see the movie. This was after Dad's trip. Did he talk to us about lions, wondering what had become of the small, rescued cub?

The next morning, they worry their western idea might be vetoed, but the German FAO man has returned with everything set up.

The wildebeest will be killed for our camera with native with a poisoned arrow. The young English hunter will simultaneously shoot it in the belly so that it will be sure to duplicate the reaction to the arrow. When the camera has recorded the death agony, he will then dispatch the animal. Grahame said, "Somewhere out there tonight the wildebeest is peacefully grazing." We feel strange about this over-blooded plan. But oddly, I feel none of the compassion (?) or horror I would feel if I were home in Canada.

So let us see what happens.

The German has been to Indonesia and thought it the most beautiful of all countries. But as we drew him out, learned that he spent his time at Bogor in botanical gardens, had food in army and avoided Jakarta. Had never been to Hotel Indonesia. Mentioned the "coconut" project there was hopeless.

This is certainly the most beautiful and peaceful place we have been. People spend thousands for this safari-type experience. It's not at all like the gruesome jungle films. Here we are in a peaceful and beautiful resort, lit by the moon, about 68 degrees [Fahrenheit], with a thousand lions minding their own lordly business out there in the night. The weather couldn't be better. It is February 7 in the worst month of the year (at home). 11:40 p.m. to bed. Under my netting.

If This Was Africa

Friday, February 8, 1963. A few pages into Notebook Four, the men sit on the roof of the Land Rover driving to Banagi, a village

A NECESSARY DISTANCE / *181*

of round cottages with cone grass roofs. Gene leaps into his act as showman. They take Polaroid photos of two servants who delight in Gene's antics. They find the boy and father for the wildebeest hunt; the child is delicately beautiful, the old man ragged and full of character. "Can you shoot arrows?" Gene asks the boy.

He jokes, "I have already made my kill, will this job send me to jail?" The boy is afraid he will get in trouble for going over his quota.

One of the men that watches what's happening, a clerk, says he had to choose between going to school and learning to shoot. "Can write, not shoot," he says.

There is a discussion about the people of the Serengeti. "They have good memories but can't synthesize," writes Dad. "Can't follow a logical idea unless taught the whole pattern in detail. But working with machines, show a lot of ability." An Englishman says, "The Kikuyu at Nairobi are intelligent and well organized. The Maasai could beat them, but the Maasai don't care. They ignore politics and progress. Couldn't care less." My father writes in his notebook, "More power to them."

Everyone eats lunch: rice covered with stew, coconut, tomatoes, papaya and bananas all cut into small squares. It is "the best food since Canada." They go "hunting" in the afternoon, which means photographs. Their guides are two zoologists: Hans, the pleasant blond German, and Watson (as nicknamed by Hans), the Englishman – dark and curly haired like an Italian, with humorous gestures of face and shoulders like Peter Ustinov, the British actor who will narrate their documentary. Hans is cheerful, thin, with pale eyes. His home is near Frankfurt, and he has a convulsive laugh that reminds Dad of a German friend at home. Watson is "sly and mumbles in a Britishese I've heard only in films, using words like 'bloke.'" He makes a joke and then sinks into an expression of worry and doubt and seems like a child about to burst into tears. They find a leopard in a tree, innumerable birds and animals, and heavy rain.

At dinner, there is more talk of Kenya. Watson comments on the error of letting all the political prisoners go. "What will happen after Kenya's independence?" asks Grahame.

Hans swirls his white wine, "Everything will slowly, slowly become more . . ."

"More?" prompts my dad.

"Inefficient!"

"Ah," says Dad. He is feeling the heat, and something about this topic makes him tired.

"Yes. It will become more difficult to buy in the stores, to get services."

"And these are the important things? Stores and service?" presses my father. Dad is thinking, "Well, yes, food and water is now a service. Housing is now a service. But still . . . it didn't used to be."

It seems that Watson is a zoologist. "Men are different. This is what people mistakenly try to forget."

Dad decides to be devil's advocate. "This is not science talking when you put this idea forward, that people aren't equal, aren't the same. This is science as a religion substitute. The religion of who is better under God, or Gods, and who is heathen, or less. That's not science!" Hans is amused, but not Watson, who offers mildly that my father's remark is insulting.

Dad withdraws to his room. He pulls down netting against insects he sees no sign of and sleeps a dead sleep. No dreams. Heavy rain through the night.

In the morning Dad is surprised by a Black boy wrapped in green fabric bringing him tea. There are more visitors over breakfast; one of the women reminds Dad of my mother: "Thought of

A NECESSARY DISTANCE / *183*

Sandra often during this beautiful day and each time was in the most delicious agony."

Dad enjoys the Serengeti enormously. He is awed by the land itself, the seas of yellow grass that make him think of prairie horizons. "Every moment an adventure." It's as if the place has liberated him for the moment from human concerns; the pettiness of the politics, his own uneasy prejudices, his homesickness. They eat lunch with lions fifty feet from the car, wildebeests "circling like Roman legions. 15,000. Hyenas in sight. Incredible." Can he really mean 15,000 wildebeests? Or 15,000 hyenas? He is thrilled to get shots of the lions as he wants a dissolve from a schoolroom in Bolivia to a "lion on blackboard. Lions couldn't care less."

The plain seething with flea-hopping gazelles with busy tails. Rabbits and baby gazelles leaping out of sleep from under the nose of the Land Rover. Giraffes standing about grotesquely, looking down their noses at us.

They eat roasted meat and potatoes over a fire, followed by drinks. Mr. Watson, whose name is Murray, says that lions never bother people. "If they charge you, it's not seriously meant. It's only to see what will happen. If you run, it's a mistake. If you don't, the lion will veer off about halfway." Is this encouraging? "Lions have no notion what a car is, it holds no interest for them."

Gene asks about the notice they saw in the dining room at the lodge, about a lioness leaping on a car recently.

"Nonsense. Just to scare visitors into being properly cautious. A man was killed here two years ago."

"Oh?" Dad looks up from his plate.

"By a lion. The guy was sleeping in his tent."

"Jesus!"

184 / JULIE SALVERSON

"Fellow slept with his head outside the tent. Way too much temptation," continues Watson. "Died the next day."

The next morning Dad sits in his pajamas watching birds. Gene is on the porch too, reading *Serengeti Shall Not Die*, a 1959 chronicle by Dr. Bernhard Grzimek and his son Michael. Bernhard was a zoo director who said he had never done anything particularly "adventuresome" in his life until flying with his son in a Cessna from Germany to Tanzania. The two became smitten by what they saw and began the first comprehensive wildlife and migration study in Africa. Michael was killed when his plane hit a bird soaring a thermal above the Serengeti.

Now, as Gene reads and Dad watches birds, the sky is filled with white clouds, the sun occasionally breaking through. Two fortyish English women join them on the porch, wearing floppy khaki hats and baggy safari suits. They are here to photograph flowers, and Dad nicknames them "East African Flower Snappers."

Brandy at the bar in the evening. There is a discussion with Mr. Allan who came from Kenya recently. He makes no plans because of the political situation. "Could be thrown out tomorrow, they don't like us around here – not at all." When they take over the power, Allan says, that will be the end of it. Dad is appalled by the way the men talk about "Blacks." For example, about someone's son Thor at school: "Couldn't stand the thought of rooming with one," and "My God, you can't blame him."

"All this in a measured, practical voice," writes my father.

They discuss Kenya during the Mau Mau affair. I look it up. It's an uprising in 1952. There is a massacre of African collaborators (quislings?) and several Europeans. Thousands of Mau Mau were killed or executed in reprisal. The Mau Mau fighters came from Kenya's major ethnic group, the Kikuyu, a million strong and increasingly marginalized by white settler expansion and a British

A NECESSARY DISTANCE / *185*

divide and rule policy. Sounds familiar. I read online that the rebellion was marked by war crimes and massacres, particularly at the hands of British and Kenyan security forces. They suspended liberties and detained thousands of Kikuyu civilians. Brutal collective punishment and torture was exercised on the detainees, who had the support of South African archbishop Desmond Tutu. There are so many narratives of history. Including Mr. Allan's:

No. This is much worse. There they went around and took no nonsense (and told some women they would be safer to put away their guns). At any sign of trouble, you shot and didn't keep count. If they *had* shot a few more things would be better now in Kenya. But politics spoils everything. Now, we have to take all manner of insults from these people. Serengeti needs big investment, roads, lodges, but politics makes it difficult. The Blacks want to run it. Best thing to do is let them, so they will see what happens. Then we can come back and start over. There will be nothing left.

Then Mr. Allan tells them about a fishing research vessel given to Indonesia as war reparation: "The thing is now useless. Incompetence."

Dad: "I was struck by feeling all this – wilds, animals, and European versus Aborigine, was like America a century ago. We spoke of Indian wars in those days, 'Only good Indian a dead Indian.'"

Allan, speaking low: "We said the same in Kenya – 'the only good n [you can imagine this word, I won't write it for you] is a dead n.'"

I don't want to hear any more of this and I don't think Dad does either. He sits outside with binoculars looking at the moon in the clear night air.

Never saw it so vivid and three dimensional before. Sharp detail. Gene brought out a Canon tripod. Seized with an intense excitement, his voice tense, face strained, eyes starting out of his head – examining stars, listening to the cries of approaching lions, spying a hyena in the garbage. Hyena came around corner of a cabin and Gene kissed at it. Leapt in the air and fled. Gene had hysteria. Sitting in my pajamas under the moon 250 miles from the equator. But it got chilly. I began to shake. Got out my ski-jacket. But retired at 1:30.

In the morning, the boy in green appears again bringing my father tea in bed at 7:00 a.m. "Good morning, sir." He sets the tray on floor by the bed. According to Dad: "Rather a sweet soul in appearance. Find it hard to imagine shooting him to keep him in his place."

I think of a story told by Bill's brother George. He and Vera were with a friend from Ghana at a party in Hyderabad. They were leaning against the balustrade of the posh house looking down at the shacks below. Their friend said, "If this were Africa, those people would come up here and cut our throats."

Missing the Dark

Anthropologist Barbara Smuts was enjoying her usual stroll along a stream in Gombe National Park, Tanzania. Smuts has often made sojourns to study primate social behaviour, and she had already documented the social manners of her baboon friends in the African parks. On this occasion, however, something strange happened. The wild troupe of baboons did not proceed forward at their typical pace, but instead paused and sat motionless by the stream's still pools for moments of what she called "silent contemplation": "Without any signal perceptible to me, each baboon sat at the edge of a pool on one of the many smooth rocks that lined the

A NECESSARY DISTANCE / *187*

edges of the stream. They sat alone or in small clusters, completely quiet, gazing at the water. Even the perpetually noisy juveniles fell into silent contemplation. I joined them. Half an hour later, again with no perceptible signal, they resumed their journey in what felt like an almost sacramental procession."

Searching for some word to give to the astonishing posture of reverence among the monkeys, Smuts settles on a Buddhist term for a spiritual community: "I was stunned by this mysterious expression of what I have come to think of as baboon sangha."

I have an instinct that this story resonates with my father's time on the Serengeti. Then I think of the writing of a Vancouver friend, Patricia Fraser. She gives me another perspective on what makes it possible for us to "see" or "hear" something strange.

Patti is working with a group of seniors who are finding ways to tell their stories. She has done this for decades, with all manner of people. The seniors and everyone else are thrilled with how it is going – people love to tell their stories and others love the idea of people telling their stories. It fits into the contemporary narratives of truth-telling, authentic voice, popular rather than expert, all this – but something doesn't sit right with Patti even though the work is collaborative, group-led, democratic and validating, the process builds communication skills and affirms personal histories and, and, and . . . all the expected phrases.

Still. Patti senses that "the charming anecdotes intended to entertain the viewer," tales of domesticity and relationship, carried a "prominent and unexamined role of a *self* as the main character of all the stories." She asks herself, what is wrong with this? She reads psychologist James Hillman, who sees "autobiographical memory as being from a synthesis of knowledge of lifetime periods, general events, and specific episodes in one's life, a construction neither true or false, but rather, a synthesis of interpretation." Neither true or false, that's interesting.

Patti quotes poet and essayist Don McKay, who calls memory "the temporary domestication of time." She detects imposed orderliness all through the stories from the seniors in Silver Harbour, stories of selves "frozen in time" and set against images "of an increasingly domesticated world."

Patti looks up "domestic" in the dictionary: "to adapt life in intimate association with and to the advantage of humans, to bring to the level of the ordinary."

I look at my father's journals with a new question. How domesticated are his accounts? What couldn't he say? What could he maybe not even feel? Were there things he simply did not have language for?

Patti talks about missing the animated dark as we move steadily away from messy, swampy unmappable wildness into "flat, disconnected, uninviting, depersonalized, and literal appearances" of a world we have "de-animated." We miss the rich darkness when we "inflate the significance of the human person."

Not only stories and histories but places have become domesticated in the charming tales the seniors choose to remember and tell. Patti listens to their narratives in a brightly lit room with linoleum floors and no windows. She looks at archival photos: Horseshoe Bay, once a swimming hole and now a busy ferry terminal; in earlier times it had been a seasonal fishing camp named Ch'axáy by the First Nations after the swishing sounds of herring stirring the waters; Lynn Valley, turned from rainforest and river canyon to hamlet and then chaotic suburban shopping mall; the long-disappeared wildlife along the Burrard Inlet. Does my father encounter the not yet domestic?

One night in Quebec, Rose asked me why Dad went to the Serengeti for a film about hunger. "There was lots of food there." Rose told me she was taken to the area as a child to watch herd migrations.

A NECESSARY DISTANCE / *189*

"What they didn't tell me was that crocodiles wait for this. They lie in wait, and they rush and seize any animal they can catch." As a young girl, she was shocked. "My first reaction was to yell to my parents, 'We have to get fifty vets!'" Why did Gene, Grahame and my father go to an area lush with wildlife, with plenty of food?

Bloody Monday

Late into the evening on Sunday, February 10, the British zoologist Watson tells the three filmmakers bedtime stories. How hunting dogs kill an adult wildebeest. The lion who ate the man's arm off. Details. Dad lies awake with the candle lit, afraid to go to the bathroom. "Keen awareness of the dangers around." I am going to let Dad describe the next day:

Watson flew out at six to locate the herds and those outside park for our safari. We saw him land as we had breakfast. Two Land Rovers came. Put the three natives in Watson's [vehicle] and we went with equipment in Hans'. Drove off into the beautiful sunny morning through acacias, and out into the peaceful plain. Overtook a LR full of sightseers. Old type of Englishman driving. No harm. Hans flashing lights to pass, but they waved back in greeting. After some miles got the idea and pulled over so we could pass. Hans commentary on "smashing girl" in LR, he makes no bones about being woman-hungry.

No sooner past them than we found Watson out of sight. Stopped and studied horizon with glasses. Heat haze made glass useless. The sightseers passed us waving. We took off our shirts, basking in the sun as we waited. After a time, Watson appeared a square spot moving over the vast rolling plains by a picturesque mesa. When he came up, it seems his LR chose that moment to break down. He cleaned carburetor, but no luck. Tried towing it a couple of miles. During this passed two lions with manes, lying within sight of wildebeests migrating past Naabi Hill. A shout beyond the lions we gave up the towing idea. Watson set to work on carburetor, the three natives holding his tools. We decided to go ahead up the hill to film the herd.

Only a few yards on, saw a third LR and a fourth off the road, looking at a pack of hunting dogs. We joined them, taking pictures. The dogs lay about, looking at us with little interest. Hans told us these were the most feared and dangerous animals in Africa. Somewhat smaller than a police dog, large ears, ugly faces and a patch of blotchy coloration, jumbled blacks and browns and a disagreeable dirty red shade.

Since we were within yards of Watson, we drove back to him. The other two vehicles went on toward Naabi. I was looking at Watson and the three men at the front of his LR working across the radiator when Gene cried out, "Oh my god, look at this!"

Looked out my window and saw the hunting dogs running toward us. Coming at a fast lope, the whole twelve, an intent, evil silent flowing of dark bodies over the grass.

Glanced at Watson and the natives, in the open, in front of LR. They were all standing, heads turned, looking with startled faces at the dogs. I wondered why they didn't move.

Looked back at the dogs now saw a small brown (tan) calf running past back of our LR, the dogs a short way behind it. Took a fast shot catching calf and pursuers. (Later found camera in wrong setting!) We all seemed immobilized for moments as this column raced across the road. The fourth LR appeared, chasing. Someone out the roof, filming.

We followed, observing. The lead dogs were running fast, the others trailing behind. The calf ran into a nearby herd. The herd became a swirling mass of action, like a liquid violently stirred. The calf ran on, the dogs followed, intent on it with a

A NECESSARY DISTANCE / *191*

single purpose, ignoring the careening adults and the roaring pursuing LRs.

We came in close. A feeling of inevitable doom. A cry of helpless protest inside myself as the baby ran and the lead dog closed in. A grotesque floundering. The pack was on the calf. Dogs seizing and jerking horribly on legs, belly. In the first second a dog ran aside with a chunk of the living meat, chucking his head, swallowing down in typical dog fashion. In moments the belly was wide open and at least two dogs were eating their way inside it.

We watched all this with the most appalled sensations – A desire to shoot down all these evil creatures. Vultures flew down and stood near. A hyena ran in, standing within two feet of the dogs, waiting.

About a minute had passed when I began looking for the head of the calf. It must have been there, but seemed to have disappeared. The calf was now a torn mass of red meat, only the dainty legs jutting out positively identifiable.

Hans as moved by the scene as we were. He had never seen this. I said, "Cigarette?" He said, "After that, yes."

We drove back to Watson, got out, watched the scene through glasses. The vultures, dogs and hyenas all mixed in together, like ladies at a tea, having their dreadful picnic on the grass.

There was much looking at each other, attempts to laugh. Everyone strongly disturbed. The beauty of the peaceful golden savannah under the blue sky, glowing sun and magnificent clouds was now filled with a sense of savagery and murder and blood and death. The dogs were covered in blood.

While I type this story of the dogs, votes are being counted in Michigan, Georgia, Nevada and other states with red the leading colour. The front cover of *The Atlantic*: "The Election That Could Break America." Barton Gellman says there will be a constitutional crisis if there is no authoritative result. "Our Constitution does not secure the peaceful transition of power, but rather presupposes it," writes legal scholar Lawrence Douglas in a recent book titled, simply, *Will He Go?* Douglas, who teaches at Amherst, calls the days ahead a perfect storm of adverse conditions. "We cannot turn away from that storm."

The viciousness of the young man I saw on TV last night, his friends, all of them white, bunched up behind him holding guns like champagne toasts. "This is about protection and safety. For America. Without it we are lost," he declares. My father and the other men on the Serengeti in 1963 are stopped by the vicious primal violence of dogs, wild animals who are only feeding themselves. Dogs and hyenas, at least, tell themselves no stories. Where there is blood, there is dinner.

I pause to stretch and nervously check the latest vote counts. I don't want to. I don't want hope to disappear. My publisher posts, "We have to watch it doesn't happen here." I respond, "It was Baldwin who said, 'underneath rage is fear.'"

I get an email from Amnesty International. They are telling everyone in America to be careful. "As events unfold today and throughout the week, please take good care of yourselves. Take breaks, go for a walk, and be kind to yourselves. The fight for human rights, equity, and justice demands everything we've got – and I know our community will rise to meet the challenge."

The wildebeest, the old man and his son call me back to my desk. Blood on both sides of the story.

Bloody Monday cont. February 11, 1963
Watson having no luck with the broken Land Rover, we took the rainfall gauge (a plastic calibrated cylinder) and drove over

A NECESSARY DISTANCE / *193*

Naabi to plain on other side. Here were two areas fenced off with wire. In each, a metal container buried, with a filtered funnel to catch rain. Hans emptied each in turn into the gauge. The readings were 1.45 and 1.75. Then back over Naabi to Watson, Hans did quick work on the ailing carburetor, started it, got back into ours, saying, "Watson could have cleaned the carburetor all day."

We went up on the hill and filmed sixty thousand wildebeests below. The entire vista was filled with animals, some scattered, some milling, here and there organized columns moving. It seemed a vast military operation – and then at times like masses of ants.

It was now noon. Very hot. Hans said, "We have an hour to reach our location out of the park." We set sail over the plain. Over the grasses like two ships at sea, now close, now far apart. Mountains at times out of sight. Over fields of small yellow daisies, like buttercups. Long patches of small sagebrush, a clattery, jittery charge from ten to forty miles an hour. Sharp wild turns to avoid warthog holes. The oversized hyena watching us pass.

Suddenly a shout from the back. Grahame lost his safari shirt. Hans dubious about going back to look, almost no sight of our trail. We try a few yards. There is the shirt, with a hyena sitting near, watching us. Hans: "You're lucky the hyena didn't play with it." Chasing after Watson, now nearly out of sight – Along the park border, a shallow plowed ditch with occasional oil cans. Catch up in swampy area. Chains through water. Hans making jeering comments on Watson's chains.

Suddenly Watson stops. A lone calf running past, limping, holding up one misshapen foot. Watson kneels with gun, aims. Changes his mind. Runs after calf. The three natives join. Samson not so good, keeps taking wild awkward tumbles in the turf.

194 / JULIE SALVERSON

They take turns trying to run down the calf, without success. We wonder how the calf can have survived such fierce pain so long. They decide to follow in cars, presumably to shoot it. From nowhere the mother cow appears and leads it away. At this we break off and continue our safari.

NOTES
30 shillings for a wildebeest tail
Samson
Makuru
Waikoma Tribe
Bull weighs 600 lbs
300 lbs of good meat
Check with a butcher

Notes: Resume Bloody Monday
About 2:30 we left the natives in Watson's Rover and took off in Hans' looking for the quarry. Sighted a small herd, rejected because all cows. Moved on and found a herd with a suitable bull in the edge of an acacia wood. A lot of the thorn cactus, growing higher than seen previously.

It was now 2:45. We headed into the woods. Hans working around them, driving through the trees, to force them out on the plain. This worked well. Grahame set up tripod on back of pickup to be ready. Watson prepared his rifle. Hans searched herd with glass. A bull who tended to trail behind was selected. We moved in. The herd moved away. Some maneuvering to get in position, in range for both camera and rifle. It began to rain. Cameras dismantled. Waited about ten minutes till rain passed over. Set up again. Moved in, parallel to movement of herd.

Grahame rolled, on the bull. Watson hit the ground, kneeling and fired (smacking my ear with the blast). Hans followed

A NECESSARY DISTANCE / *195*

it with glass, convinced that it might be hit. Decided it wasn't, though unable to jump in that fashion unless hit.

Our bull ran on, seemingly unimpaired, but a little slower than the herd. "Cut him off," cried Gene from back. Hans speeded into gap between herd and bull, and he sliced off into isolation, running hard, with us alongside racing him. He stopped, faced us, stared at us. Hans yelled at us to stop. Before we could, he was gone again and the chase resumed.

The details became blurred in all the action. Moments are recalled. Chasing alongside the animal on our left and seeing the bloodstain on his shoulder. He crossed frantically in front of us, alarmingly close.

Close in on him, Hans angrily shouting, "Shoot him! Murray, why don't you shoot him?" But the moment was wrong for some reason. Murray had already fired several times. He would hand me the empty shells through the window so they wouldn't be found.

The bull fled into a wood before Hans could prevent him. We charged at an angle, a crazy careening path through the woods, the bull in the distance, running among the trees. It seemed we would lose him. But suddenly we went through a sort of gateway. Two trees tall and slender, spaced apart. We passed through this and found the bull in front of us and forced him again into the plain. The entry to the final act.

We got set, Murray on ground firing, as Grahame rolled. The gun fired. The animal staggered on and fell. We came up in the car. He lay to the left, his head turned back, watching his assassins. His breathing heavy, loud heaving sound coming in waves as the motor cut. Grahame filming, all of us in a state of horror at what we were doing. The bull stared over at me with an aspect of expectant anxiety. I felt the same despairing anguish I felt when the dogs were about to kill the calf. The day had progressed in a grotesquely agonized manner. We began with the horror of the dogs. Now we had taken their place.

Murray prepared to end the animal's ordeal. He walked to within a few feet of it and fired. Grahame rolling. Murray fired. The animal lay still. His head turned back, raised, looking at us, breath heavy. A kind of waiting, all of us waiting, the bull and the hunters in a long dreadful moment in which death was awaited. Then a kind of sad resignation. The waiting head, with a heart-breaking expression of the last surrender of all life, rolled over and fell sighfully to the ground.

It was now 4:00 p.m. The execution had taken an hour and a quarter.

We got out. Gene, in a horrified voice, to Murray. "That was exactly what we wanted." Horror in all of us. Looking at each other. I was afraid I would burst into tears. Gene wanted to vomit, he said.

But no time to linger on this. More to do with this dead actor of ours.

Hans and I went off for the natives and the other LR. On the way, Hans delighted us with a scaly anteater, very rare, which appeared in front of us. It rolled into a ball. Hans picked it up and put it in the truck. The astounding creature wound itself partly around the spare gas can. A nocturnal thing, nothing known about it. The natives believe it falls from the sky. Hans delighted to have one to study. This about ten minutes after the death of the bull, and I'm trying to live with this guilty thing, but out here too much happens, one strange thing on top of another.

We find the LR after some searching with glasses. I have to drive the other, following Hans. Surprised at how easy it is to drive. Enjoy this new experience over the prairie, slough-ing through swampy ground and deep grasses – feeling guilt

A NECESSARY DISTANCE / *197*

because the kaleidoscopic adventure leaves no time to feel the impact of our assassination.

Return to scene. Gene, Grahame, Murray have been at work. The arrow now appears to be embedded in the animal's flesh. We shoot, with much difficulty, the approach of the two hunters, the cutting off of the tail, and their walk into the distance with the tail, and the dead beast left to the vultures.

But turns out it was the allowed kill for the month of Murray and Hans. The natives cut the belly open. The huge stomach swelled out in a white balloon. The old Negro backed away, Samson helping, and dug deep into the shell of the body, ripping out the guts, his hands bloody, the air filled with a hot sweetish smell. We watched this indignity to our victim with some feeling.

At last the disembowelling was done. The body gaped open, the legs stood out dead and ridiculously graceful. We all had to help lift it into Murray's truck. We all got blood on our hands.

The interpreter brought a can of water for us to wash. I was astonished to hear Murray, as he washed, quoting Lady Macbeth.

Murray led off with Gene and Grahame and they disappeared. Hans pulled up to watch the vultures. Some two hundred had been in the canopy of trees where the bull had sought escape. This audience, on the withdrawal of the second LR, rose up and flowed across the sky. As the cloud of huge birds dropped down, we drove away. There was nothing to be seen of the bull but white guts and red blood, a gruesome spot on the beautiful savannah, sweeping away past the lonely acacia trees into the open range and to blue mountains beyond. This was a life now ended, and a scene now vanished, for one creature who had been singled out for our film.

Now the beautiful plain was felt to be filled with savagery and death.

Night overtook us. The road was mud and water. Owls flew up in the headlamps. As the Rover battled the mud with screaming gears, two lions, white in the dark, crossed our paths. I put my head out, and saw that the huge male let us pass, then came padding after us for several yards. I now regard myself as the only member of the party who has been pursued by a lion. After ten seconds of looking out, and wondering if the savage plain was about to exact payment, I drew in my head, informed Hans and closed the window. Hans said, jokingly, "Help!" and fought the car forward at increased speed. But within three minutes of five miles per hour, he stopped, got out and in the dark cleaned the windshield. I held my breath. Later I realized he didn't believe me about the lion. He still doesn't.

Water flew in sheets over the car, looking like flames in the lights. Twice we stopped, waiting in the dark as wiring got wet. Each time Hans decided to get out and clean it. In the back, the three negroes laughed and joked in their language, safe under the tarpaulin cover while Hans washed over the motor by the light of my gas lighter. I wondered what procedure would be required of me if a leopard came down on Hans from the surrounding trees, vaguely visible in the wet night.

Suddenly Seronera. Dinner, drinks in the bar. Lights out. Struggled our way into bed with the stump of one candle to share between our two rooms. The night now beautiful out there, the grasses receding under the acacias. A postcard scene. I could feel the murderous stalking through every mile of it. Decided not to walk the few feet to the bathroom. Locked my door, thinking of Watson's tale of lions smashing down doors with their fists. Tucked my net around me, thinking of Hans' theory that lions don't know what net is and won't touch anyone inside. (They also do not chase Land Rovers, but ours was chased tonight. I saw it.) Turned off the light. Expected to lie awake all night. But suddenly it was morning and the little youth in the green dress was bringing me tea.

The Real Drama of the Serengeti

Denys Finch-Hatton was a private man who was famously the lover of writer Karen Blixen, played by Robert Redford in the movie *Out of Africa*. A British aristocrat and a big game hunter with classy clients, his outrage at the "orgy of slaughter" by tourists motivated him to agitate the British parliament, whose oversee of Tanganyika Territory had begun after World War I. In large part thanks to Finch-Hatton, the almost twenty-six thousand square kilometres of the Serengeti was included in a closed reserve in 1930, declared a game sanctuary in 1937 and established in 1951 as Serengeti National Park. In 1981 it was declared a World Heritage Site by the United Nations.

Scientist Sean B. Carroll, in his 2016 book *The Serengeti Rules*, describes the Serengeti as "one of the last remaining great concentrations of large mammals . . . that have largely disappeared from or been exterminated on other continents. It is the site of one of the last remaining mass animal migrations on land." As he describes the web of relations and balances between each life form, he keeps returning to the wildebeest. Decades of study of the Serengeti stopped in the late sixties because Tanzania adopted an extreme form of socialism, collectivizing agriculture, banning private ownership and closing borders. By 1977, the wildebeest had not been surveyed for four years.

Biologists Tony Sinclair and Mike Norton-Griffiths took off from Kenya on May 22 of that year and flew back and forth across the border into Tanzania taking photographs. According to Carroll, they noticed lines of trucks moving north toward the Kenyan border and when they landed were arrested for spying by Tanzanian guards and placed under house arrest. Their cameras were seized, but they managed to hide the film. After three days they escaped and weeks later the images revealed that the wildebeest population had reached 1.4 million animals, five times what it was in 1961.

"It was now the largest wild ungulate herd in the world."

Lions and hyenas had also increased, which made sense as there was more prey. But more puzzling was an increase in giraffes.

Their studies revealed that fires in dry season had drastically reduced since 1963. Fewer fires meant more young seedling trees and more food for giraffes. But why were fires decreasing? More wildebeests meant more grass was eaten, so less dry brush to burn. "For decades, researchers and conservationists had been fretting over the disappearance of mature trees on the Serengeti and blamed elephants for their loss. The possibility that more young trees were regenerating had largely been overlooked." More astounding was the discovery that grazed grass regenerated more than grass that was left to grow. "The shorter grass allows more light and nutrients for other plants, such that many more species of herbs grow. These herbs in turn support larger numbers and a more diverse community of butterflies."

And on it goes. As Carroll puts it, "contrary to essentially every depiction on television, the real drama of the Serengeti is not a cheetah or lion chasing down a gazelle – it is a wildebeest munching on grass."

Driving home from the barn in 2023 I listen to an interview on CBC with Bob Rae, Canada's representative to the United Nations. He is asked what Canada needs to do at the upcoming summit in the face of the huge crises facing the world. "Collaborate," says Rae. Nobody works alone.

This is Carroll's message too. It is one of the "rules to live by," together with: coalitions are powerful; objectives may be global, but implementation is always local; the measure of civilization is

A NECESSARY DISTANCE / 201

how people treat one another; global efforts are possible, so be optimistic; and solutions rest on good science, but implementation depends on good management.

Carroll tells the story of the eradication of smallpox, much of it credited to Donald A. Henderson, an American tasked with leading the global vaccination campaign in 1966. At a 1978 meeting in Kenya, Henderson was asked by the then director general of the World Health Organization (WHO) what was next. "[He] reached for the microphone and said that the next disease to be eradicated is bad management."

Not to Be Trusted

That's about it for the Serengeti. The next day they have tea at the warden's with his wife and two young children. The family have a Siamese cat who is locked in at night. She got out once and was blinded by a spitting cobra but recovered. Back at the lodge they buy a bottle of brandy and polish it off while dining on the wildebeest. They buy Maasai swords and wildebeest tails. I think I remember the tail among Dad's souvenirs.

Gene is trying to find someone to bring him a giraffe-tail bracelet; he is willing to pay thirty shillings. Nothing turns up so the hotel bookkeeper gives Gene his own and refuses any payment. Gene gives the man a Gurkha knife in return. The man is moved to tears and insists on taking Gene's address so he can send him something more. "Most un-Indonesian," comments my father.

The three Canadians are asked to move rooms and spend their last night in one large dorm with bunks. This is to make room for a new group of German tourists. Dad dislikes them instantly. One member of "the pack" is called Ribbentrop, who

has a giant cold face. Across from him sits a man with red splotches on his weak-looking features. His eyes are sick-looking, as if bearing some grudge, as if his money has just been stolen. I can see him making lampshades. Another big fellow who wears a knife all the time is Prussian-cropped (hair) and looks reportedly cheerful and somehow crude. I suppose they are all lovely people when you know them, but they look cold and indifferent to me. One of them blows his nose like a trumpet. Anyway, I didn't care to sit and listen and look at this crowd with evil connections to the past. About as pleasant as the hunting dogs.

He writes this less than twenty years after the end of World War II. He lost friends in that war and as a documentary writer and journalist saw photos of concentration camps early on. I'd forgotten how Dad had felt about Germans, but now reading his words, I remember. I also remember Carin, the young German immigrant who often looked after Scott and me as children. Once, sensing something was wrong, she rushed to my brother's crib and pulled him out moments before the ceiling collapsed. She became my parents' great friend, a kind of aunt to Scott and me. But her scowling autocrat of a husband confirmed what Dad had already decided during those war years; powerful, entitled German men were not to be trusted.

On one last outing in the Land Rovers, Dad watches Hans shoot zebra with an immobilizer gun. The weapon fires a narcotic, allowing them to attach ear tags and a yellow plastic identifier collar. The researchers cut the hair off the tail at the first vertebra; this distinguishes it from the others when they follow the movement of the herd and observe social behaviour. Once the zebras have taken the anaesthetic, Hans drives the vehicle alongside and a crew member catches it by the tail, holding on (the man is tied in) while the car slows. The zebra stays immobile, an instinctive move as the

A NECESSARY DISTANCE / *203*

only chance of escape if seized by a lion is to freeze and hope for a moment of escape.

At 2:50 p.m. the same pilot in shorts arrives to fly them to Nairobi. They take on board a sick child and her mother; the blond girl has gastroenteritis from drinking bad water in Aden. The father wants to come but the plane is too heavy, loaded with wildebeest meat that Ribbentrop wants transported to the city. When they arrive in Nairobi, Dad picks up the film he had dropped off. The two test rolls of Tokyo and Indonesia in good shape. The cost of development: $14.50. Dad estimates it will cost $150 to develop all his film when he gets back to Toronto – one of each shot. The men drink excellent Beaujolais in the hotel bar, admire beautiful girls and retire to their rooms. Dad writes my mother about the Serengeti, mostly Bloody Monday, and settles under the mosquito net. It traps the air so he pushes it aside, is bitten and pulls it back despite having been told there is no malaria in Nairobi. He has strange dreams all night, driving through fields of mud.

Shopping, Nairobi, February 15
Flashlight
Shirt and socks
Kleenex
High boots (?)

There is a crude sketch in ink on the back cover of this notebook. A circle with two wings coming out the bottom. It looks like a child's drawing. Written beside it:

Tsetse versus house fly. (Closed wings.)

End of Notebook Four.

204 / JULIE SALVERSON

Serengeti Section of Film

11:12 Shot of young youth and old man.

Narrator:
Today the youth Samson would become the man Samson. He would make his first real contribution to the livelihood of the family. He would make his first kill.

Shot of lion, then father pointing, son looking. Herd of wildebeests.

The spirit of the lion was abroad the morning Makuru took his son Samson into the Serengeti plain of Tanganyika. This is in protein-hungry Africa where the masses half live on cassava root. Within range of his eye, sixty thousand wildebeests, an astonishing, irresistible treasure house of game. Samson, of course, knew there could be danger. The government men with their guns tried to keep them from their rights. The notion of officials that the herds could disappear was obvious nonsense.

Shot of boy and father climbing over rocks, after the herd.

It's only politics. And where there is a need, and a youth is to become a man, he can't bother his head with nonsense.

A NECESSARY DISTANCE / *205*

There were other kinds of officials too, sometimes, to be seen here, intruders they were, called scientists, who went about writing in notebooks, counting animals, measuring rain and following herd migrations.

As we hear this, we see the man talking to the boy, explaining, gesturing as they walk.

These strangers thought the animals should only be killed in certain ways and at certain times so the herds wouldn't vanish, and the best use could be made of the meat by their peoples. All this.

We see the two prepare, pulling the bow from the sheath.

All this was perfectly ridiculous.

12:30 Where there was a need, and thousands of animals at hand, an enterprising new man like Samson would not wait idly for notebooks to be filled, he would use his poisoned arrows.

Arrows prepared, drumming in background. Shot of the herd. Arrows shot by both men. Herd starts to run, the men run. Drums increase. More shots from the bow. The men run. The animals run. Final shot, boy smiles.

The arrow hits home. And the rest was time. A handsome animal must die. His power and grace and freedom condemned by a little black tar on an arrow tip.

Shot of one animal running, slowing. Then boy and father running across wide plain, animal far ahead, moving slowly. Big sky. Single guitar, slow, replaces drums, one bird in sky circling, vulture. We see bull close up, limping. It turns, looks. We see the boy and father hurrying close. Bull staggers, falls. Shot of vulture.

But this is truth in the Serengeti and around the world. Some die so that others may live.

The men approach the fallen bull.

There is no waste.

Boy gets on knees, starts to cut the animal's tail.

To the victor, the spoils. To youth become a man, the honours. But there is no waste. To the man, a fly swisher, worth thirty shillings on the souvenir market. And to the vulture, six hundred pounds of meat.

We see the two men walk away, swishing the tail. They leave the rest.

A NECESSARY DISTANCE / *207*

To a million other Africans, only cassava and millet. And there is no waste.

We watch the two men walking away. Silence.

The Railroader

I keep thinking about the hunter in the Serengeti and his son. And I think about that *other* son, my brother, and the birthday that isn't mentioned. And yet there is Dad's gift, the Mexican sombrero. Then I wonder about Dad's father, George Senior. Pa. He was never talked about in our house. Too many bad memories, too much disturbance. But now, with my father dead almost twenty years and the old man gone closer to fifty – now I want to know more. It seems to start with a horror story, one told gleefully by my father at bedtime.

"Once upon a time there was an old couple with one child they loved very much." Or, no, it doesn't start this way. It starts like this: "Without, the night was cold and wet, but in the small parlour of Laburnam Villa the blinds were drawn and the fire burned brightly. Father and son were at chess, the former, who possessed ideas about the game involving radical changes, putting his king into such sharp and unnecessary perils that it even provoked comment from the white-haired old lady knitting placidly by the fire."

"The Monkey's Paw" is a story of superstition and the grotesque. It was written in 1902 by W.W. Jacobs and is a classic "be careful what you ask for" tale of three wishes and an old man's stubbornness. It scared the hell out of me. I have no recollection of Mom reading to us, although doubtless she did. It's my dad's ghost stories and songs from the Old West that I remember. He got so carried away with the suspense, the rise of the narrative, the creepiness of it, he was completely oblivious to the nightmares it gave his children.

"Hark at the wind," said Mr. White, who, having seen a fatal mistake after it was too late, was amiably desirous of preventing his son from seeing it.

"I'm listening," said the latter, grimly surveying the board as he stretched out his hand. "Check."

I'd forgotten the father and son playing chess. Dad taught the game to both Scott and me. I played until I was around nine and finally won. I felt sorry for Dad and started to lose deliberately, at which point he abruptly withdrew. "You play a game or you don't," he scolded. He was disappointed in me. What had I done? It was a lesson I didn't learn for a long time – don't patronize people by withholding your skills and knowledge. My brother was clever at chess and did well in school tournaments. When he was thirteen he went to a provincial championship. Something turned the game sour for him, some *Lord of the Flies*–type experience I think, though he wouldn't talk about it. He never played again.

"I should hardly think that he'd come tonight," said his father, with his hand poised over the board.

"Mate," replied the son.

"That's the worst of living so far out," bawled Mr. White, with sudden and unlooked-for violence; "of all the beastly, slushy, out-of-the-way places to live in, this is the worst. Pathway's a bog, and the road's a torrent. I don't know what people are thinking about. I suppose because only two houses on the road are let, they think it doesn't matter."

"Never mind, dear," said his wife, soothingly; "perhaps you'll win the next one."

Mr. White looked up sharply, just in time to intercept a knowing glance between mother and son. The words died away on his lips, and he hid a guilty grin in his thin grey beard.

A NECESSARY DISTANCE / *209*

"There he is," said Herbert White, as the gate banged too loudly and heavy footsteps came toward the door.

As the story ends, White is so terrified of what he might encounter, he wishes all possibility away, slamming the door on the unknown. What comes to the door in the story is fate, or greed, or opportunity. Three wishes, in the form all stories love. Are you satisfied with your life? Will you roll the dice and risk your soul? Will you accept your children as they are? What happens when the world creeps up to your door and knocks?

In March of 1977 my father drove from our village of Whitevale to Toronto to interview his father. Pa was eighty-seven years old and lived alone in a house on Putman Avenue in Toronto. Dad used the transcripts – which I still have – to write a radio play called *The Railroader* starring Mavor Moore. Three years later it was produced for CBC Radio. The only other character besides the railroader himself is called Interviewer – the railroader's son.

George Salverson Senior, or Pa, was born in 1892 on a pioneer homestead near St. Croix, Wisconsin, and lived there until he was five. The closest doctor was twelve miles away and he never saw one in his boyhood. From the interview with my father: "Settlers in the wilderness, for God's sake – innocents abroad."

Pa's oldest brother was Tom and there were two sisters and a younger brother. Pa's family came from Kristiansand, a seaport town in South Norway. A family of sailors, they came to Indiana in 1875, tried farming and failed. Pa's father went to Duluth, Minnesota, on the tip of Lake Superior, to get work, seventy-five cents a day for a twelve-hour day. My great-grandfather hated the sea.

Pa left school sometime during grade three and went to work in a shirt factory for a Mr. Sharagrunski on Central Avenue, cutting out buttonholes for fifty cents a week. Then he got a job as an errand boy on the railroad – and never left. One day in Duluth, he heard a young woman give a firebrand speech about women's rights and justice. He thought she was interesting, she didn't just talk about clothes and boys. When he realized that she was from Winnipeg he asked the railroad for a transfer. He got it.

Interviewer: What do these memories mean to you?
Railroader: Don't mean a damn thing, I guess. What do memories mean? They're just there, that's all.

Pa read everything. All his wife's books and everything that she read, including his favourite, *Caesar and Christ*, published 1944. "I read it three times!" He edited a national union magazine. And then, avidly researching my grandmother, I find out quite by accident that he was an alderman! In Port Arthur! Not only that, he tried to start a union. But not just any union.

My grandfather is mentioned in historian Ian Radforth's book *Bush Workers and Bosses: Logging in Northern Ontario 1900–1980*. In a chapter about the complex relationships within the Lumber Workers Industrial Union of Canada (whose members were largely Finnish but also French, English, Swedish, Slav and other new Canadians), Radford describes tensions between radical strike workers, the general worker population, the companies, the Communist Party and Soviet influence and infiltration. Into this scrappy story, Radford inserts this paragraph:

Another development that grew out of the 1933–4 strikes was a new woodsworkers' union, the Canadian Bushmen's Union (CBU). This affiliate of the All-Canadian Congress of Labour was led by a Port Arthur alderman, George Salverson, formerly a member of the Brotherhood of Railway Telegraphers. Salverson hoped to recruit unorganized bushmen who, he said, "have determined that these Bolsheviki

A NECESSARY DISTANCE / *211*

side shows shall cease." According to the CBU leader, his organization stood for "peace in industry, intelligent discussion, goodwill regarding workers' problems and a fair deal." Salverson reported that the union had been organized by "Canadian-minded workers of several nationalities." He appears to have tried to unite White ("Canadian-minded") Finns with "Anglo Saxons," although much of his appeal was blatantly nativist. An Ontario Department of Labour correspondent at the Lakehead reported that "at the time the CBU was organized, the officers were nearly all . . . foremen, superintendants or timekeepers' in the employ of the Pigeon Timber Company." In other words, it was a company union.

A company union? My grandfather? In the transcript of my dad's interview, Pa rages about the bosses, about who has the power and about the endless crushing of the workingman. He lived his life alongside my socialist grandmother who wrote endlessly about injustice and saw the miseries of poverty first-hand not only in her childhood but all through her life with her husband.

Curious about the thirties and the anger my grandfather expressed against Bolsheviks, I decide to read the diaries of Russian revolutionary anarchist Emma Goldman. Goldman immigrated to America as a young woman and was so emotionally affected by Chicago's Haymarket Square riot (the bombing of a labour demonstration in May 1886) that she began a life-long campaign for higher wages, abolition of the draft and, among other things, birth control. My guess is that both my grandparents knew of and admired her. "Red Emma" is forced to return to Russia in 1921. She stays for two years, growing in shock and disillusionment at the rampant political opportunism, industrial militarization and increased use of deportation as a political weapon by the Soviets.

212 / JULIE SALVERSON

In Russia, Goldman visits with old friend and fellow revolutionary Peter Kropotkin, who tells her this:

"You see a small political party which by its false theories, blunders, and inefficiency has demonstrated how revolutions must *not* be made." It was unfortunate – Kropotkin continued – that so many of the Anarchists in Russia and the masses outside of Russia had been carried away by the ultra-revolutionary pretences of the Bolsheviki. In the great upheaval it was forgotten that the Communists are a political party firmly adhering to the idea of a centralized State, and that as such they were bound to misdirect the course of the Revolution. The Bolsheviki were the Jesuits of the Socialist Church: they believed in the Jesuitic motto that the end justifies the means. Their end being political power, they hesitate at nothing. The means, however, have paralysed the energies of the masses and have terrorized the people. Yet without the people, without the direct participation of the masses in the reconstruction of the country, nothing essential could be accomplished. The Bolsheviki . . . have been trying to eliminate and suppress the cultural forces of the country not entirely in agreement with their ideas and methods. They destroyed the co-operatives which were of utmost importance to the life of Russia, the great link between the country and the city. They created a bureaucracy and officialdom which surpasses even that of the old regime.

In a chapter of his edited volume *Canadian Working-Class History*, Radforth calls my grandfather "a propagandist par excellence" in his attempt to "offer an alternative to the radical unions." These efforts were undertaken in 1933 and 1934, when Pa was

A NECESSARY DISTANCE / *213*

"a former Port Arthur alderman and member of a conservative railwaymen's union." That is the extent of what is written about George Salverson Senior. What was he agitating against, and for? What was "conservative" about the railwaymen? I wish I could sit down with my grandfather. I wonder what I have inherited from him. I am a moderate. Like my father. Like, it seems, my grandfather. But perhaps "moderate" is the wrong word. Goldman's *My Disillusionment in Russia* was published in 1923. It's impossible that my grandparents wouldn't have read it. Pa knew first-hand the gruesome conditions of labour, but he was not a romantic dreaming about the revolution and he seems to have had a fine eye for bullshit. No armchair socialist, he may have had justifiable suspicions of radical organizers and the infiltration from Soviet communists. I can't know.

As a young teenager, my grandfather worked running telegrams down to the docks for five cents a telegram. His mother wrapped his feet in rags to keep his toes from freezing. He met people from the railroad, got involved in a railroad strike, climbed poles and cut telegraph wires. The strike was for Chicago and North Western railways. Clarence Darrow was the corporation lawyer for the railroad. Darrow went down to the tracks to see the people striking. He changed sides. He said the people he had been representing would never miss a meal no matter what happened, while the strikers would starve. From then on, he defended the underdog. To his last day.

My grandfather read every word Darrow published.

Morning Glories

Laya visits. She is American, a former dancer who I haven't seen in fourteen years. Two months ago, she emailed to say she was coming to the Toronto area and wanted to visit. I was thrilled but the night before her arrival I don't sleep much. What do you say after fourteen years? I needn't have worried, her infectious deep laugh outside the door as Bill brings her in from the train reminds me, I *know* this woman. I open the door to a broad smile, a more fleshy but still sensuous frame in a vibrant green swinging top and black pants. In her early seventies, she looks great. Hair streaked brown and grey is gathered into a loose knot behind her head. Her hug is as robust as her laugh.

After fifteen minutes in the kitchen I can see how tired she is. I'd thought her silence over the past six years had been due to our cancellation of a plan to house-sit for her and her husband on their sheep farm in New Zealand – something which now seems a sad lack of courage on our part, but this is what we do in life, dodge the unknown. It turned out, however, that she was taking care of her partner through serious illness and of her parents in their last years. She so obviously needs rest that I immediately relax and rest too. For three days we talk, walk, sleep, play with the cats. I tell her about Dad's trip. Laya had lived in the Ivory Coast for a few years in the late sixties. She studied at a university there and then spent time with the Yacouba learning about their family and social structures. She was invited to rituals celebrating the transition of boys into men. But Laya wants to talk about America: "Trump is rewiring the constitution, provoking war and burying everything we believe in, including the people who support him," she says, to which I respond, "If he wins this time, he'll change it enough that he can't be voted out." She looks at me, assessing my innocence. "He already has."

A few days ago, explosions on two oil tankers in the Strait of Hormuz triggered a war of words between the US and Iran. A headline screamed, "West Asia on the Edge." This is more than rhetoric and it makes me remember the urgency I felt as a teen-ager, seeking out information on bunkers and wondering how to stay safe in a nuclear winter. For a long time now, I've refused to

A NECESSARY DISTANCE / 215

live in that heightened state of terror, but as I read the headline I feel it returning. "A lot of people are buying up property in New Zealand because it's so far away from all this," Laya tells Bill and me as we escape the hot sun in a shady neighbourhood café. "You should too," she adds. I start to laugh and then stop. She's serious.

These conversations with Laya about politics remind me that my father's trip happened in the heart of the Cold War. Dad, Gene and Grahame circled the globe when western journalists understood the world as east and west, America and the Soviet Union. The term "Third World" was coined by a French journalist in 1952 and referred to countries not aligned with NATO or the Warsaw Pact. The distinctions were political, not economic. Our understanding of "north and south," of "first, second, third and fourth" worlds, of "developing nations," was in the future. And it wasn't the environment the three filmmakers were thinking about, not really, it was the production of food from a planet everyone assumed would keep providing forever – if we organized ourselves right. That's what really characterized the urgency with which President Kennedy spoke in the spring of 1963 when he launched the "Year to End Hunger." This was the initiative Gene's film was part of.

Laya and I drink tea in the fall garden. A breeze flutters the large Norway maple in my neighbour's yard, its grand branches waving like a benediction, its dying trunk a reminder. My Zen teacher says that gardens teach us everything. "Nature doesn't do arguments." I look at the strands of fading morning glories climbing the side of the old barn at the back of the yard. In the spring, I had tied up lengths of twine to help them find their way, then spent hours untangling insistent spurts of green that shot in all directions. The slender vines wound themselves into furious knots, twisting back and down toward the ground or nudging their way under the barnboards that cover the wall. I pull the long pale strands back into the sunlight from the dark crevices where they curled, pale and dying but stubborn in their impulse to grow. "Like us," says Laya.

She tells me that morning glories are considered an invasive weed in New Zealand. They are routed out, poisoned. But the world is filled with desperate life struggling for the sun. Do we eradicate, or do we garden?

Laya leaves. I get back to work.

Roman Holiday

Valentine's Day, February 14, 1963. The documentary team are in Nairobi for a stopover. Gene knocks on Dad's hotel room door with a pot of tea, which Dad drinks in bed as he catches up on writing postcards and letters. He dresses and meets the others at breakfast. They discreetly study an airline hostess at the next table – "decided she was the right age for Grahame, it was up to him." There is lots of this gentle teasing of Grahame in the notebooks and I wonder why. Soon I will understand. But not quite yet.

It's a glorious sunny day. Gene arranges passage to Rome and Dad goes shopping. "Bought large flashlight and white 'mukluks' in army surplus store." I remember these boots – they occupied different spots in our successive homes and survived various moves. We all tried them on in the snow. The word "mukluk," I discover with new post-colonial eyes, comes from the Yupik word "muclak," meaning bearded seal. They were usually reindeer or sealskin boots made and worn by Indigenous Peoples in south-western Alaska and northern Siberia. What were the boots doing in this store in Nairobi?

It's midnight. The three adventurers drive along Princess Elizabeth Way to the airport past blossoms under orange streetlights. They take off in the early morning on a South African Airways

A NECESSARY DISTANCE / *217*

plane; below them zebras are running. Six and a half hours later in Rome they check into the Grand Hotel Plaza.

Marvellous hotel, grandeur, marble staircase with huge lion at base, on ceiling of dining room an illustration of a seventeenth-century minuet, a Roman orgy with drinking men in togas pouring over bare bosomed beauties. Went for a furious walk. A sidewalk café on Via Veneto where we drank coffee with milk, all foamy like hot chocolate and whipped cream. Ate delicious pastry, but not outside because of cold and rain. We're a source of interest in parkas, ski jacket and the eternal balaclava, hastily donned at airport. It's forty degrees [Fahrenheit] in Rome.

I think it was my dad's first latte. They walk, take pictures of the Spanish Steps and the poet Shelley's house. There is rain in the camera; the weather is chilling after the tropics.

The guys have plans. An afternoon tour, then an evening deluxe affair that includes Rome by moonlight, dinner and four nightclubs. Dad opts for the soft bed and spacious bathroom.

Have noted with curiosity that the better the food, the more critical of it both Gene and Grahame become. No explanation comes easily to mind.

He soaks in a hot bath and then rests with a book about the Serengeti: "Except for some lion information, the old man is a bore and an atrocious writer. Switched to C.P. Snow for relief. Cambridge politics – rather dully absorbing, a sort of bored and polite accumulation of concern, perfectly fitting my present mood."

218 / JULIE SALVERSON

He naps until just after 6:00 p.m. and looks at the clock. The thought of going out horrifies him. This might be the last good rest for a month.

Beginning to feel relaxed and a little better. A knock at the door.

Gene and Grahame parka clad and at the full charge, highly organized. "We're going down now for a cup of coffee and then we'll meet you at eight o'clock for the tour." My reaction, "Silent." Good God, what is this constant need to go tearing out for coffee? Confronted by the urgency, the agonized state and the need to slow down the sinus with the rest and with some need, I suddenly decide that a tour of nightclubs held no interest for me and it might be better saved for some more suitable moment in the future, even if it never comes. I said was having too good a time relaxing and would prefer not to go.

Gene, in his intense way, looking at my pajamas: "Have you been here all day?"

I felt I had done something incredibly unambitious – wasting a whole five hours in Rome when it was expected we master the whole earth in two months. I had a picture of the two of them crashing about on mysterious errands all afternoon. Suddenly realized my growing problem – I needed a rest from external organization. I'm used to running my own life, and while it's pleasant to let someone take over, there has got to be a break, and today's the day! At such a moment, I would have a fight with Sandra.

Gene then said, "We'll have to try and get a refund on your ticket, we've already bought it." I felt a further strong reaction to being trapped by all this external organization where something of no consequence was involved. I said, "See if you can because I'm having more fun here." "All right." The two of them bashed on down the hall. No further pressure, though no doubt

A NECESSARY DISTANCE / *219*

expressions of incredulity. However, I need a day off to be my own boss and do what I feel like, rather than what I ought to feel like. Anyway, they need a rest from me blowing my nose into Kleenex – and it's fierce today – a sure sign I need to be by myself and rest. This way I'll feel better in the morning, less in a mood to hit the two of them over the head. How can they stand so much fellowship? Especially Gene? He's the impatient fellow who tears up letters that remind him of CBC politics, who suddenly closes doors with what seems a need to be alone. It's possible he doesn't recognize or tolerate this in others? He seems to swing through moods, in which he makes a snap judgment about Pakistan or Roman breakfast rolls, then evaluates it and comes to a more moderate judgment.

Tonight nothing could make me feel remiss about not going on a pub crawl. Tonight, Rome means a rest and a little psychological and physical adjustment in a civilized place. An escape from the strange into the familiar, long enough to arm myself for the second half of the tour.

How like my father I am when it comes to the limits of other people and a horror of being organized. But Gene is a good friend. Four years later in the summer of 1967 our family will drive across Canada to spend time with the Lawrence family in Vancouver. Gene will introduce his friend to Simon and Garfunkel, whose records Dad will play endlessly for months. We will camp in each province and then stay in the Sylvia Hotel in Vancouver, where our collie dog is terrified of the elevator, so my father carries him up three flights of stairs.

Dad is fed up with Gene, but it's the kind of impatience you feel for someone you have affection for, the tired rubbing-up-against that is inevitable in intimacy. Travelling can bring out the worst in us.

He tells a few more stories, including an argument as to whether the woman with the sick baby on their plane from the Serengeti might have chartered a flight and not waited for them. "She should have realized how serious the baby's illness was," says Gene indignantly. "They were told about the ailment at Arusha Hospital."

"No," says Dad. "It was diagnosed falsely as dysentery." Dad is frustrated by Gene's impatient sarcasm, and writes in his notebook: "Besides, children are always getting sick, and you don't rush off and charter an aircraft at great cost every time they have a stomachache, especially if you have no loot."

In a torrent of feeling from this man of few words connected to his own emotions, Dad adds:

Of course, snap decisions of a derogatory nature are always anathema to me. Even though I make them myself. It's disturbing to be attacked because not coming to the same conclusion, you are accused of not having witnessed the same event. And suppose you hadn't? Suppose your thoughts were elsewhere, or your observation? Why should it matter? I can see that I'm in bad shape tonight – I think more of Sandra. What a marvellous fight we could have, each understanding the other! Wish I had similar notes made by Gene and Grahame about me and each other. Bet they would sizzle!

Weddings and Mothers

They leave Rome and fly to Ghana on British Overseas Airways Corporation. They land in Accra, and make plans to travel by car. At their hotel – the Ambassador – they discuss visas for Togo and Dahomey. I peer at a map of North Africa and can't figure out their route. Ah, a bit of research, in 1975 the name Dahomey was changed to Benin. The King of Dahomey remains in a ceremonial position that was handed down through French colonial rule to

A NECESSARY DISTANCE / *221*

independence in 1960. Dahomey had become wealthy by agreeing to sell Africans to European slavers. In 2022 *The Woman King* hits the screen. It is a story about Dahomey women soldiers that is both fascinating and controversial.

A short YouTube video tells of "The Dahomey Mothers," who "struck fear into the hearts of European colonialists." By 1800, they were an army of four thousand women who "fought for the expansion of the kingdom." Selected for their teenage beauty by successive kings and then trained as soldiers, they sang of being better than men. In 1890, King Béhanzin ordered the Dahomey women soldiers to attack the French. Any women who refused were killed. After four hours of fighting they withdrew. After two years and several more battles, the French took over the country. It was the end of the women warriors, but their dances live on in what is now Benin. I read a press release from Hollywood: *The Woman King* is directed by Gina Prince-Bythewood and will star Viola Davis; it is "inspired by true events in the Kingdom of Dahomey."

The film is released in 2022. It does well at the box office but provokes an uncomfortable conversation. It is accused of whitewashing slavers who, in this case, were Black. The kingdom captured men and boys and sold them for tobacco, alcohol and weapons. Some were kept on plantations that supplied food for the army or the court. Davis, speaking to the press, says "We entered the story where the kingdom was in flux, at a crossroads. They were looking to find some way to keep their civilization and kingdom alive. It wasn't until the late 1800s that they were decimated. Most of the story is fictionalized. It has to be." Her husband, co-star and co-producer Julius Tennon calls the film "edu-tainment" and says it is meant to entertain people, otherwise it would be a documentary.

I wonder what my father would say to this, fiction displacing fact to please audiences. I suspect he would not agree with the concept or the execution. But our minds and attitudes are shaped by the times we live in, so perhaps this is one more instance where comparing 1963 to 2022 is a limited project.

Ghana gained its independence in 1957. In 1961 Queen Elizabeth visited, although her trip was almost cancelled at the last minute. President Kwame Nkrumah was on his way to becoming a dictator and on October 19 of that year Winston Churchill wrote to the British prime minister, Harold Macmillan, saying he was uneasy "both over the physical safety of the Queen and, perhaps more, because her visit would seem to endorse a regime which has imprisoned hundreds of opposition members without trial and which is thoroughly authoritarian in tendency."

Five days before the Queen's trip, bombs went off in Accra and a statue of the president was hit. Elizabeth was worried that Ghana would leave the Commonwealth and that the regime was getting close to the Soviet Union. Nkrumah had visited Moscow. Elizabeth told Macmillan, "How silly I should look if I was scared to visit Ghana and then [Soviet leader] Khrushchev went and had a good reception . . . I am not a film star, I am the head of the Commonwealth – and I am paid to face any risks that may be involved. Nor do I say this lightly. Do not forget that I have three children."

The Queen travelled with her year-old son Andrew. The visit was a success, she was seen dancing with the president and a neo-Marxist Ghanaian paper hailed Elizabeth as "the world's greatest Socialist Monarch in history." The trip also helped Ghana get American money for the Volta Dam, a hydroelectric project central to Nkrumah's plans. Macmillan wrote to John F. Kennedy, "I have risked my Queen. You must risk your money."

My father sits in the hotel restaurant reading an editorial in the *Ghanian Times* attacking neo-colonialism in Nigeria. He notes that there are very few ads in the paper. The porter at the hotel desk covers Dad's letter home with large colourful stamps: "Should make a sensation in Willowdale."

A NECESSARY DISTANCE / *223*

While their travel arrangements are being sorted, Dad and Gene visit the Nigerian FAO director for Africa. He greets them wearing a brightly coloured robe and a handsome pillbox hat. When Dad admires his full beard the director suggests my father grow one too. "I've tried. The result was horrible."

The man laughs loudly and tells him they should do more filming in Africa. "Nigerians won't go to your show unless they are mentioned."

The director has been to Canada. "I have visited Toronto. When I was in politics. No longer. I resigned and got out in time to avoid an explosion and land in jail." He laughs. "But this is part of the fun."

Dad asks how stable Africa is.

"Not advanced politically like your country. The only stable spot in Africa is Tanganyika, but this is only because they have had independence only two months. In two years more it will be the same."

"He is a Nigerian and speaks freely," writes my father.

Our guardian here is a young worldly and good-looking Dahomian named Tevoedjre. He's the one who met us last night. Took us on today's protocol visit. Chatted about politics freely. Thinks there will be lots of trouble in this part of Africa. Says Nkrumah has done a lot for Ghana, that he's a clever man, knows how to get what he wants bit by bit, says he doesn't know what will happen and vigorously pronounces, "Hitler was a clever man too."

They are driven to the customs office to get their equipment, looking out at a well-paved Independence Avenue and huge estates. Only their tripod has arrived from Nairobi, so they wait a few hours for another plane with their cameras and other bags.

One of the officials is interested in Grahame's airline tags. Grahame explains the trips each tag represents.

"Must be nice to go around the world," says the man. He signs and stamps Grahame's form.

Dad, Gene and Grahame drive east across the border to Togo and south to the port capital of Lomé. They spend a night in a hotel and drink too much whisky arguing with Tevoedjre, then drive the next morning in "appalling heat" through miles of coconuts and straw beach houses. Togo is "one family, one million people, one plantation – not a nation but a coconut farm." They cross the border west into what is now Benin.

They are here to shoot a wedding in the village of Ganvie, founded by the Tofinu people. Afah, the groom, has been in the French army. Houwe (Ooie), the bride, has had five years of schooling. "There is difficulty for such people to return to the traditional life and this is one of the problems of the country. People with these opportunities want to gather in cities where there is nothing for them to do. Afah was a 'sous-officier' – a sergeant."

For the filmmakers, the wedding provides a setting against which to profile fishing techniques. The scene is the beach at Sèmè. There is a flurry of excitement as FAO visitors and cameraman join the party and locals gather around. There are clowns in a boat, with gay French masks and yellow and red costumes made to look like feathers. They dance on stilts and Grahame dances with them, shooting film to the astonishment of dancing couples, "all mad rhythm and motion."

The Village! Ganvie. Acadja (Akadya): The technique of fishing. Bushes are brought in by dugout and placed in the lagoon. Fish are fed off the bushes and the net is thrown around. Then the dead sticks are thrown out and the net drawn in. The technique of Acadja is unique to Ganvie. Arrive at Chief's house – waves,

A NECESSARY DISTANCE / 225

shouts, the drum beating. Whistles, and an old man scolding over which canoe to use comes ashore from launch. Fish. Tilapia, around three pounds (3,000 Francs). Sell 50 percent, eat 50 percent. Twelve thousand people. Man gives dowry to woman, cash and gifts. This began 150 years ago as a refuge from the slave trade. Many here are religious, but the wedding ceremony is not religious.

Then the couple walks to the exotic shore, the startling surf and the explosion of activity as the Senegalese come with their boats, six to a vessel, tough men of the sea. Our hero sees what can be done with courage and skill. Our hero throws net over camera, pretending it is a fish.

We shot late afternoon on the beach at Sèmè. Sand, surf, sun, sweat, and in need of Entero-Vioform. Quite ill. Too humid, too hot, too much water drunk at hotel, first time on trip and paying for it. Despite this, stunned at sudden drama as the longboats of the Senegalese come soaring ashore on sand, and the crowd rushes down and they all battle surf, getting the boats up and getting out the big fish. One is a shark.

Back at Hotel La Plage, exhausted (me quite ill) to find we made date with a Canadian oilman who has overheard us speaking English. He mumbles and has had malaria three times. Last time in December, just recovered. Three days in a coma in Paris hospital. He told us if we were too tired to accept his invitation, he would buy us a drink in the outdoor restaurant under palms with the sea breeze cooling us, and let us go. I asked for lemonade.

Over dinner there is pleasant joking about the proprietor's daughter who is an exquisite young innocent protected-type French girl. We have engineered Grahame into a bet between he and Gene to buy her a drink. Obviously, the money will be lost, but this sort of nonsense seems essential. The girl a natural object of a kind of lewd idolatry. In fact, I should think she becomes a symbol of our own way of life and values, of what we think we are and of what matters to us. I am increasingly surprised to find how I come to evaluate and symbolize degrees of civilization and worthiness in terms of women.

To bed full of pills. My French tonight didn't work so well placing a call for "Sept heures et demi." This because a friendly Frenchman intervened to pronounce it correctly. He reappeared at breakfast when I was trying to say, "Jus d'orange" to waiter. Why must these helpful people always interfere?

Wedding Section of Film

14:59 Group of people dressed up, sound of drums. A wedding?

Narrator:
Having grown up successfully, Houwe and Afah got married in Dahouie, their old hometown. It was a quiet affair with old customs like flinging money around. But that's marriage, and only a few hundred guests. Just enough to drown out any doubt on the part of the bride and groom.

Children, drums, dancing, singing. Bride is young, beautiful, adorned with scarf, headdress.

Marriage is a time of decisions, even in the oldest and most unchanging of villages with the most inflexible of customs. Having babies was one inflexible custom and it was astonishing to realize that there were now twelve thousand people living in the stilt village of Ganvie.

A NECESSARY DISTANCE / *227*

Shots of boats. Man throwing a net. Small houses on stilts.

Afah, new husband, may have wondered how many little lagoon fish would feed twelve thousand people. Afah was not an untutored villager, he had been to school, he had been "sous-officier" in the army, he had returned to village life because he was too smart to follow others into cities which could not employ him.

Shots of the men gathering in the nets as they stand on long narrow boats.

But he had no wish to be the head of a primitive household. He was a bridegroom in need of an opportunity. He cast his net upon the water. And the opportunity came.

We see three men in white coats approaching in a small narrow boat. Two Black men, one white.

It came in the boat with the tribal chief, and a man from the government, and a stranger from another land. The conversation wasn't really so cheerful. The lagoon was silting in, the fishing would deteriorate, there were too many mouths to feed. If you want to live better you must increase production.

Close-up of these men, white man looking at net.

But how? Go to the ocean. But a man doesn't shrug off his heredity that easily. His fathers had always fished the shallow lagoon. You could wade across it. The ocean was alarming, unknown, dangerous. His skills and equipment would be useless. And, imagine what Houwe would say, the timid bride. Oh, it was utterly out of the question.

Shot of groups of men on boats around the chief and visitors.

So, naturally, it must be investigated.

17:40 Couple and FAO man walking along beach at ocean.

When the FAO expert had driven Houwe and Afah to Sèmè on the coast, to demonstrate the outboard motor school, the bride may have felt she was already losing a part of her so recent husband.

FAO man in white shorts and shirt and sunglasses, Afah and Houwe in wedding robes. Close-up of Afah talking.

A deep-sea school for inland fishermen, the sea was the school. Tough professionals from Senegal were the teachers.

Group of Senegalese around small boat.

A NECESSARY DISTANCE / *229*

The outboard motor was the chief instrument. When a man had learned he could buy his own motor with his enormously increasing catch. The sea was inexhaustible. What a strange furious school of pounding waves, organized by a Belgian, with Senegalese at the helm —

We see them pulling fish from the boat.

— and Dahomey men taking to this battling life. Appalling to the gentle bride. But to the groom, a revelation. An escape from his dilemma, a way out of the village.

Close-up of bride's face.

Unheard of. Not the way of her easygoing people. An alarming marriage.

Shot of waves breaking. Settling on the water. Sound of waves.

There is a mad rush back across the border to Togo and Gene argues with their host (they call him Laughing Boy) because of a mix-up between Canadian and African time. Dad goes to bed sober. Laughing Boy escorts them seamlessly through heavily guarded customs back into Ghana where they wait for visas at the Senegalese Embassy in Accra. They will transit through Senegal on their way to South America. In Mr. Tevoedjre's air-conditioned office the FAO director sorts his mail.

Brought up a letter for "Mr. Lawrence," then another for "Mr. Woods." My heart sinks. I said, "Can I read yours?" He smiled. I've been thinking steadily about Sandra the whole way from Lomé. Looking at an Alitalia calendar, realize that we hit Mexico City three weeks from today. Two months has become three weeks. A joyful sensation, despite all the fun of this expedition. I don't want it to go on forever. I begin to sense there will be an overpowering excitement to meeting Sandra in Mexico and then a softened secondary excitement about getting home.

If Lost

It is December 9, my grandmother Laura's birthday. She was born in 1890, the year of the Dahomey women soldiers' attack on the French. I read in an article by Terrence L. Craig that she became "a fervent traditionalist," arguing for qualities that she valued in the face of the rampant materialism she saw around her. She felt that Icelanders, "with their remarkable history of exploration, parliamentary government, and inspiring sagas, could only be the poorer if they assimilated into the vulgar and materialist society she saw in the Canadian West."

I pull out her first novel, *The Viking Heart*. I am captivated by its easy charm but more than that, by the details of what drives the family from the life they love – farming and fishing in the shadow of a large mountain – to immigrate to Canada. As far as I can discover, this is the first novel written in Canada in English about western immigrants. The date of publication is 1923 (McClelland and Stewart). Laura is thirty-three years old and has a seven-year-old child, my father.

A few years ago, I read Wallace Stegner's 1971 novel, *Angle of Repose*. It was Christmas and I didn't leave my armchair for a week, gripped by his language and by the precision and artistry

A NECESSARY DISTANCE / *231*

with which he evokes the narrator's frontier-era grandparents. It was the first time, amidst all the conversations about colonialism, that I realized "settler" wasn't a homogenous category. In Stegner's novel a few very rich people back east (New York, Chicago) run, well, everything. The protagonists go west to escape poverty, looking for a life that challenges them. They barely survive what they find.

In my grandmother's novel, it is only the restless teenage son Carl Halsson who dreams of leaving Iceland. Barely fifteen pages into the book, the mountain they have dreamed under for decades erupts, spills over, "[turning] loose upon them the smouldering fires of its pent-up rage." As the family rushes to escape, Carl runs back to help his dog rescue the sheep and is killed in the avalanche. This is one of a number of volcanic lava flows in the 1860s and 1870s that wiped out families and farms.

The fictional Halsson family join 1,400 other settlers, many of whom have lost everything: "The period prior to 1876 was one of unusual suffering and distress even in that land of great privations. In addition to the losses and suffering brought about by this last eruption, the fishing in Iceland waters – the one industry upon which the people then depended – had greatly fallen off. So unproductive were the fisheries that large numbers of people were rendered destitute and were on the verge of starvation."

Laura wrote pointedly of the misleading and exaggerated promises "of the Land of Plenty" and the misery of exile. "Hunger is a sharp sword and severs every tie." All her writing addressed inequity and human greed. Although she, like my father, insisted on not joining organized causes, she wrote and spoke for the rights of the poor, of working people. As Daisy Neijmann writes: "Her personal experiences in the cities, as well as her second-hand knowledge of the Gimli community's terribly tragic beginnings gained during research for *The Viking Heart,* had taught her that most non-English immigrants had little to look forward to except hard manual labour."

I finish my grandmother's novel in tears. It is a moving story, but more than that it is the realization that she is a good writer and a principled person and that I share her politics. There are powerful depictions of poverty and of the hardship of women's lives; and, although the references are few, she is damning of how "Indians" have been treated. What a force. No wonder Dad lived in her shadow. And maybe I wasn't ready until now to know what a force of a writer and person she was. How would the young me have measured up?

I also realize that my father was the first in his generation post Iceland and Norway to not live in poverty. He read widely and was a learned man. He struggled, but we lived well. He must have been astonished to get those cheques – for stories. I hope his mother was proud.

I go through more boxes. I find a gold case five centimetres square. On the cover are etchings of two children's faces, a boy and a girl, and the words "Just happen to have . . ."

I open it. Facing me from a scratchy black-and-white photograph is a girl of about five, dark hair to her shoulders, big smile and eyes squinting from the sun. She wears a bathing suit and perches on the side of a sandbox. In her hand is a plastic shovel and behind her on the grass is a small black spaniel. The dog is Smokey and the child is me. Next to the photo handwritten in bold old-fashioned letters are the words "These precious photos are my valued treasures. If lost please return to Laura G. Salverson, 56 Putman Avenue." A Toronto address I recognize.

There are eight small photos in the case, including one of my dad in his forties in a bathing suit. He is sitting in a lawn chair, a book in his lap and a towel wrapped around his head. It is one of the few photos I have and the only one where he has much flesh on his bones. Another picture is much older, probably Dad is in his twenties, a tall winsomely thin fellow flipping through a magazine. Come to think of it, I don't know that I have any photographs of Dad where he isn't holding a book – except the commissioned sketch of him in pastels in a sailor suit at the age of five.

What does this have to do with anything? Here on my desk, Dad's journals are open on one side of me, *A Viking Heart* open on the other. I've also found documents – a letter from Canadian writer and director Mavor Moore to Dad about an early draft of *The Railroader* and my father's eulogy to actor John (Jack) Scott. I posted something on Facebook yesterday about my grandmother and her birthday. A flurry of friends responded, most of them surprised. I guess I don't talk about my grandmother.

One response came from John Scott's daughter Laura – who, I realize only as I type this, must have been named after my grandmother: "My father adored her," she writes. Laura Scott is one of the few people who knew Dad who I can still talk to. The other person who responded to my post was Dad's goddaughter and Hugh Horler's daughter Georgia. I send her a text and we arrange a phone call. "I would love to talk about Uncle George."

"What do you remember first?" I ask when we talk.

"Hmm." There is a pause. "His face."

"His face?"

"Yes, he had a most extraordinary face. And his kindness. And his attention. He really wanted to know what you thought, even if you were a muddled seventeen-year-old. He really listened. And music. He was always playing the piano."

I tell her, "That is how he met my mother."

One winter night, after recording a drama at the CBC studios at the Jarvis Street building the CBC had taken over from girls' private school Havergal College after the war, there was a party. Everyone adjourned to Algonquin Island, a ferry ride away from the downtown Toronto shoreline. Dad had an earache, but he went anyway, and when he got there, he did what he always did when he was shy at a party, sat down at a piano and started playing tunes by ear.

Shortly afterwards, an actress arrived in a silver blouse. She crossed the room and sat beside him on the bench. It was my mother. He already knew her professionally, but that's all. Afterwards they took the streetcar up Yonge Street to Fran's Restaurant on St. Clair and talked for hours. She confided that she "seldom saw a microphone without feeling a pang of fear." A few days later Dad lost his hearing in his right ear from the infection he got on the ferry. He said it was worth it.

A few months later my mom was playing on stage in Kingston in Noël Coward's *Blithe Spirit*. Andrew Allan was also in the cast. My dad showed up pretending he had work there, and promptly got the measles. Mom figured out he had come to see her and figured she'd better visit the sick fellow. Years later, she told me that she sat in the doorway of his room wondering what kind of father he might make. He was certainly capable of loyalty and devotion! When my mom died in 2000, her full-page *Globe and Mail* obituary included this: "When she accepted his proposal, 'I was very surprised,' Mr. Salverson said. 'She was a glamour girl. I couldn't understand why she was interested in me.'"

The story of my mother meeting Laura Goodman Salverson and Pa is very different from the brutal episode where Laura humiliated her son's young Catholic fiancée with words, devastating my father and leaving his friend John Scott overcome with emotion and throwing up in the bathroom. Dad brought his new love to the door of his parent's Putman Avenue house and knocked nervously. When Laura opened the door, my mother greeted the old couple enthusiastically, marched into their living room, flopped onto the couch and dazzled them. My mother was emotionally honest and perhaps my grandmother recognized it.

A NECESSARY DISTANCE / 235

I find more papers and a file with a letter Dad wrote to his father in the 1970s. He is telling Pa why he wants nothing to do with him anymore. I put the letter aside. For the moment, it's too much.

In Rome, Dad collapses in his room, then soaks in a hot bath. Wait! I've typed this part before. It's all starting to run together.

I need to get Dad home as quickly as possible. And release myself from the past.

Black Whites

The outdoor bar of the hotel in Accra, Ghana. Dad finds Gene and Grahame deep in conversation with a New Yorker married to a Ghanaian who studied law in the US and at Dalhousie University in Canada. Dad marvels that the American looks barely thirty but has a thirty-three-year-old daughter and grandchildren.

Her Canadian-American accent and outlook (used expressions like "those cats") seemed to give a special credibility to what she said. She and her husband are called Black Whites. Other lawyers here are annoyed because he wins cases citing case histories in British Law, which applies here. The lower courts are corrupt, but the Supreme Court is made up of excellent men who are incorruptible. Ghana, however, is a police state and political cases do not come to court. This couple fear for their grandchildren, and if they want to talk freely at home they go to the bathroom and run water. Nkrumah [president] is a delightful man and her husband can argue with him in private, but not in public. Their mechanic has warned them about cars of friends which are bugged. There are no secrets in Ghana.

It is known that a man arrested for having a bomb from Lomé at a Nkrumah rally was really a police agent posing. Another man who was shot escaping jail could not have escaped because of a system of slats barring the windows. Press photo showed the slats intact. Later one slat at the window in question has been removed. She said she would not talk freely like this again, for perhaps two months. She only does so because she knows Canada. We observe a remarkable difference between an American Negro and an African. She is the only American Negro we have encountered here. She was introduced to Gene by Tevoedjre, who came to the hotel "looking for celebrations" (Gene). She promptly insulted Tevoedjre, who left, and she remained for over four hours to talk to Canadians.

As they leave Accra on Sunday, February 24, their taxi is searched for bombs. The customs officer at the airport asks, "Why were you four years in Ghana?" They are charged thirty-four Canadian dollars for overweight luggage. Grahame stays behind, I don't know why, and Dad reaches back across a customs barrier to shake hands and wish him luck. Dad buys Liberian knives and drinks a "Sterilized Girl Chocolate Milk" from a can.

On the flight from Accra they drink pineapple juice and "real coffee." My dad writes a paragraph about the dazzling perfection of blondes. Pan Am blondes, blondes in Africa, dimpled blondes. They disembark in Dakar, Senegal, and their plane, the Queen of the Pacific, carries on to New York City. The last hours on African soil are spent on a Riviera-like beach loaded with French girls in bikinis. Both Dad and Gene are too shy to take photos, they miss Grahame and the fun they would have had, joking and teasing him about women. "Why do we pick on Grahame? We miss him."

Alive and Well

I am at a friend's off-grid cabin for a few days of writing. It is spring and the woods are full of red trilliums. I send Bill a text asking him if he could try to find out about Gene Lawrence, Grahame Woods

A NECESSARY DISTANCE / 237

and the editor, whose name will be on the credits. Before I'd left, Bill had showed me how to download the film onto my computer so I can watch it here offline. It's crazy, I've written an entire draft of the book without watching it. Now, I'm ready.

I make supper and decide to write about preparing to watch. A message pops up from Bill. "Grahame Woods is alive and living in Cobourg."

Cobourg is ninety minutes from my house. It never occurred to me to check. How old is he? Dad would be 105 this year. Whaaat?

A minute later another text: Grahame's phone number. I stare at it, perched on the creaky single bed on the second floor of the wooden cabin. It's almost suppertime. I could call him. Now? In the morning? I stare at my phone, dumbfounded. Why did I assume they were all dead? Because Gene and Dad are. Because it was so long ago. But then, another text. "He'd be 85 or 86, born in 1934." Oh! That's not so old. I quickly calculate. He would have been twenty-nine in 1963. My God! No wonder they thought he was the fun one with the girls. And already a senior cinematographer. On an international shoot!

Bill texts me Grahame's email. Branches scrape the window and the rain rattles the roof. Without thinking I type a note. I am George's daughter. I am writing about the trip you took together. In 1963. I would love to talk to you.

I send it. I have never hoped for something so much in my life, that this man is healthy, is well and would like to talk to me. As soon as I send it I wonder, will he mind? Did he know Dad kept a diary? Did *he* keep one???

I can't get over that I have planned to watch the film tomorrow. For the first time. Grahame's footage.

I'm trying not to keep looking at my phone to see if Grahame has replied.

"Sleep on it," texts Bill. "Whatever happens was meant to be."

Bill keeps sending information. Grahame Woods was a cinematographer and then a television scriptwriter. He won all sorts of awards, then quit the business to become a mental health counsellor. But there is more.

Bill finds something Grahame wrote for a local Cobourg newspaper, in answer to the question, "Why did you raise money for kids/HIV/AIDS in Africa?" He'd gone back? In fact, he'd spent years in Africa. His trip with Dad and Gene must have been his first of many. It made an impression. It really surfaces now, my blind spot as I translate these notebooks: I have not written about the very substantial *good* these men were trying to do. But talking about Canada's good deeds can be complicated.

Canadian film and television producer David Hatch is arranging for me to be interviewed in *Atomic Reaction*, his documentary film about Canada's part in the atomic bomb. "Canada likes to think it's a squeaky-clean country," he says over the phone. "But no." As an example, he cites what he has learned in his own research about uranium mining and what has been revealed about the brutalities of residential schools. "When I was growing up in the seventies, I was told we were the NATO good guys, the peacekeepers. Canada tells itself it is innocent of history." I don't disagree with him. But what do we leave out when we focus only on the damage? "The west is imperialist, racist, uses its science and technology to conquer," says Vladimir Putin. How do we respond?

Speaking with Hatch reminds me how different it is to make a documentary now than when Dad was writing *The Secret Hunger*. "The funding formulas have become extremely complicated," says Hatch. "For producers, it better be a passion project. Not a great way to make a living."

It's after ten, one more trip to the outhouse. Sitting on the toilet, staring out at the leaves lit by my flashlight and shivering with rain, I have a ridiculous revelation. I haven't seen the movie because I

A NECESSARY DISTANCE / 239

am afraid. I'm afraid it will feel cliché, and shallow, and silly. And I don't want it to be. And now Grahame is alive and the film is real. Grahame is real.

I think about how amazing this thing was that they did. Flying around the world in 1963 to get to those places, trying to get people on film talking about their lives, trying to get footage. And now I am ashamed of myself. For not giving them more credit all along. Grahame's emergence into my life, ninety minutes away, breaks the glass bubble.

I ask myself, why does the film have to be amazing? Excellent question. Why indeed. Because it's my amazing dad! I'm smiling as I think this. All the standards of my family, the adulation my father carried for the people he worked with. They were stars – Mom, John Drainie, Gene. Dad saw himself as the servant to all that talent and passion. But he had to serve brilliantly. I mean really, the most important night of the year in our house was the Academy Awards. That was the metric. Maybe it's time to let go of these impossible standards.

I say to myself, why not just carry on finding out what it *was*? Try not to make it be what you need it/him/them to be.

I go out to get firewood and as I step onto the grass from the cabin I hear a loud rustling in the woods, something crashing, then silence. I stand for a moment, listening. A slight flutter in my belly, but I'm not nervous, just startled. It's twilight. I peer into the crowded brush, new leaves competing with dead branches and imagine shadowy figures. It couldn't be a bear, could it? It's a porcupine, or an ambitious chipmunk. My chiropractor the other day looked at me as she escorted me out of her office. "I don't think I could be alone like that, in the woods." She looked tentative, this woman so solid in her skin. I suppose to some people it's a kind of bravery.

No credit cards mentioned in Dad's journals, just Thomas Cook traveller's cheques. Barely phone service in emergencies.

Talk about dependent. Not something the old Icelander would like one bit. But with no cellphones, how much more could happen, what else could a person experience? More unprotected but more available.

Late at night by firelight in the cabin I watch the movie. I sigh with relief as I close my computer. Peter Ustinov reads my father's words! They sound like him. The whole thing is a compact and skillful plea for compassion, education and nutrition. I'm proud of it. There is hardly a white face in the entire thing.

CHAPTER EIGHT

South America

At 2:30 a.m., February 26, the two men take off on a de Havilland Comet aircraft operated by Aerolíneas Argentinas. It is just under five hours to Recife, Brazil. They land at 4:30 a.m. and the first sign they see on the side of a mountain says "Cinzano." They are driven downtown in a 1960 Ford V8 with a running board. Steamy heat and carnival.

Young people dressed as clowns, Ku Klux Klan, Indians, Roman slave costumes, etc.

Ku Klux Klan? They sit in a café drinking a beer called Brahma Chopp and ignore beggars and women who pull at their arms, some with babies. They have learned to do this from locals everywhere and they finally practise it. The ignoring. The carnival overlaps with the Feast of Ramadan.

Gene and Dad wait for a cable from Grahame. They try to find a Mr. Fernandez but have no luck. A Mr. Richardson from the FAO, English and desiccated, tells them everything will be closed for two days. There is mail for them, but Richardson makes no effort to open the office. Oh, and by the way, "The drought area you are going to film is now green and rainy."

/ 241

242 / JULIE SALVERSON

These two old friends from Canada, tired of each other's company, lie in the sun on a crowded beach. Dad escapes into the novel *The Leopard* by Giuseppe Tomasi di Lampedusa. It's the best thing he's read in years. The surf is grey and wind ruffles the coconut palms. "Like elegant windmills. We're suspended in tropical futility."

They decide to bypass Brazil and so there is nothing more to be done but play in the hot surf. Beautiful young women in bikinis are too much for Dad, he escapes to his hotel. He is bored in the restaurant by "loud Americans who we have been missing so much."

Back in his hotel room, he writes at length in his journal. He is appalled and self-judging. Although, if I look twice, there is an element of self-mockery. I have been taking my father very seriously. Perhaps I am forgetting his love of the dramatic. After all, he married my mother.

He's doing what Diana said that day at the barn. Feeling his way. *Leaning forward, leaning back. Eyes closed.*

I have decided no one is any good except Canadians and only the Canadians who live in Willowdale. Another astonishing day, idyllic on the beach, frustrating in terms of work. I find I am getting used to being astonished and have come to expect it as a right. What does this portend?

We had a conversation in which we decided that you can generalize about people, and it is a Canadian weakness not to. The exceptions are exceptions only because the generalization is the truth. If clichés weren't true, they could never become clichés.

Back in our rooms, immobilized, unable to communicate with anyone, wondering what happened. Mr. Richardson not very helpful. Suspect these FAO missions are a kind of racket.

A NECESSARY DISTANCE / *243*

Word arrives from Grahame at 6:45 p.m. He didn't get their cable cancelling Brazil so they must wait until four the next morning for his arrival. Dad reads a bad book about Oscar Wilde. They finally find the FAO's Mr. Fernandez, at his tenth-floor apartment. He is "an Esquire type bachelor, an Indian from Goa, who prefers to be Portuguese. Says Goa is not happy at being liberated after five hundred years."

In the early hours of Wednesday, February 27, they reunite with Grahame at the airport and Fernandez coaches the trio in the gentle art of bribing their way onto a flight to São Paulo en route to Peru. They are in their fifth day of getting from Accra to their next location. The three men scramble onto the plane, Fernandez calling, "Run, Run!" The aircraft is half empty, they have their choice of seats. The hostess notices Dad making notes on his briefcase and inserts a detachable table in front of him. He feels he should go on writing to please her.

There are several pages of notes about getting to Lima via Rio and Buenos Aires. Dad makes point-form notes about Rio and the onward flights:

Grahame had a date – Gene to beach. I to buy a swimsuit on Avenida Copacabana; Adrift with no language, drinks on sidewalk café, loners on the beach; Christ in the Sky, Rio – Sugarloaf Mountain, white rum called Viva Montilla; Buenos Aires – European boulevards and a highway like 401 and lots of political signs. Victoria with revolutionaries. Streets with no cars, a good idea. Santiago, Chile – Smart Europeans in a handsome terminal.

Pan Am jet takes off in horrifying display of lifting, sinking, thrusting. After takeoff, lights of Rio horribly low. Seat belts sign remains on very long time. Scared stiff by maneuvering. Man in back seat sounds like professional musician, sings

244 / JULIE SALVERSON

and plays guitar all the way. Latin American music. Probably returning from Carnival at Rio.

They land in Lima and Dad mails home a Sancho doll he buys for my brother at customs. Sancho Panza, says a contemporary website, is "fantastic for an original gift." Sancho was the "loyal manservant of the Indigenous hidalgo Don Quixote of La Mancha," and the dolls are sold to "help you know the literary heroes of Miguel de Cervantes." When I told my brother that I was writing this book (last week, too nervous to tell him before) he said, "I have all the knives from Africa."

"He brought back knives?"

"Several. They are all here."

When I mention the Sancho doll, Scott remembers that too.

"Where is it?" he asked, excited.

"I have no idea."

"Too bad." He sounds disappointed.

Finding Grahame

Bill and I sign in at reception at the seniors' residence. We present the proof of our Covid-19 tests. We are free to take the elevator and remove our masks. It's an older building and feels comfortable, lived-in, not medicinal. We stop beside a door marked Grahame and Glorya Woods. I collect myself, and knock.

Immediately the door is opened by a sharp-eyed woman of medium height, tidily dressed. She gestures us in with no fuss. Grahame sits on a sturdy armchair. He is thin, his spine bent and his sweater carefully buttoned. When I had called the week before I heard his voice on the message service, confident and musical with a soft British accent. I left a message. An hour later the phone rang and it was his wife. She told me he had advanced dementia and

A NECESSARY DISTANCE / 245

couldn't really see or hear. Yes, I could come. But she was warning me, "He has good days and bad days."

Glorya takes a seat across the room by the window and Bill is somewhere behind me. I sit in an upright chair right next to Grahame. I offer my hand. He takes it. His handshake is firm and he looks at me intently for the entire visit. About twenty minutes. For twenty minutes I am sitting beside Grahame! It's the closest thing to being with my dad and I am almost overcome with emotion. But I manage not to be that selfish. Instead, I talk directly with the man listening with such attention in front of me.

I mention the World Health Organization, Dad's name and Gene's, that the film was about food sustainability.

"So many trips, it's hard to remember which is which. If it's Tuesday, it must be Mali."

"You went to the Serengeti and there was a wildebeest hunt."

He nods firmly. Then with a laugh, "I was just a young lad!"

"What was it like? Being in these countries, trying to make a documentary?"

His fingers twist the thick gold ring on his hand. His replies are instant. "You feel a guilt. You've been in an impoverished village and then the hotel door closes behind you and you choose what's on the menu."

Immediately I can feel the intelligence of the man, and his politics. He was a child in the bombings of England in World War II. No chitchat with Grahame.

"It was like a double life," he says.

"Dad writes at the beginning of his notes that Gene had to fight to get you. And that you were paid less per diem than the others?"

Glorya straightens in her chair by the window. "He made up the extra two dollars with equipment," she says.

"Did you work for the CBC too?"

246 / JULIE SALVERSON

"I was a production unit manager."

"Did you know my father?" I ask, surprised. I hadn't known this.

"I saw him coming in and out of meetings," she said. She doesn't elaborate. I wonder why they didn't know each other more, hadn't kept in touch socially like so many – Gene, for instance – but I don't ask. But there is a curious lack of response about my father.

It occurs to me that Glorya might have gotten letters from Grahame on that trip. I ask. "Different wife."

I turn back to Grahame. "What do you think about those trips?"

He doesn't hesitate. "The hotels were another world. Nothing to do with how people lived. You walked inside and you were in a fantasy. Most people think that's real life. People here – they have no idea how other people live. No idea."

I ask about his time in Africa. Grahame got involved in an HIV/AIDS orphans' care program in Mzuzu, Malawi, and raised money for it. He wrote provocative editorials for the local paper and became a counsellor based in Belleville.

He says now, "All over the world you listen to all these interviews. It can provide a different perspective. Counselling seemed like a natural thing to do."

"Did that help you understand people's troubles here, and their mental health?"

He gives me a hard look. "People here have nothing like those problems."

This shuts me up. I feel the innocent that I am, and not for the first time wonder what it was like for these men, not so much to encounter what they did in places worlds away from Toronto, but to try to communicate what they had seen and learned when they got home. In the documentary certainly, but that was the job and they were skilled at it. What about among friends and family?

"This is bringing back so many memories," says Grahame.

A NECESSARY DISTANCE / 247

I am tentative. "Anything in particular?" I think he hears me, but he sits quietly. I try to memorize his thin light hair and the spots on his scalp and hands. He has hearing aids in both ears.

"What is your project?" he asks. I think for a moment.

"Your film was about sustainability, world hunger, how to provide food for the world. I'm asking, what does the world need now? What is sustainability now? What are we hungry for now?"

Glorya speaks sharply, "We're facing extinction."

"Yes." I turn to her. Then back to Grahame. She has given me a new thought.

"The world had so much optimism in 1963. Kennedy called it the 'Year to End Hunger.' There was the sense, 'We can do it!'"

Glorya harrumphs. "We blew it."

I tell Grahame that I have the film.

"How's the cinematography?" he asks with a twinkle.

I pause only a second. "Not bad," I say.

He smiles. I feel Bill behind me, reminding me these are elderly people, and I stand to leave. Just before we go, I say something to Grahame, a comment about this trip he made, the many trips he made, that so few people could understand then and maybe can understand even less now. I say some phrase, and whatever it was, he shoots back, "Good title." I laugh. It was a moment where I was really my father's daughter, understanding something of the professional life, of show business. But I can't remember what I said.

When I get home I find a novel by Grahame in the Queen's Library. *Bloody Harvest* was written in 1977 and reissued in 1982 by my grandmother's publisher, McClelland and Stewart. It's about a working-class labourer from Sudbury who spends his summers picking tomatoes alongside immigrant workers. It's about class in Ontario and I have hardly read a novel that addresses this at all, never mind one written so well. It looks like I am the first person to read it. What a shame.

I tell Glorya I will send the sections of my dad's notebooks that include Grahame. I do this, excluding a few of Dad's personal comments about Grahame and girls. Probably silly but you never know. I notice something, and I put it in my note to Glorya. Grahame turned twenty-nine in India. With Gene and my father. I hope they raised a glass to the young pup.

In the spring of 2023, a friend lets me stay in her house in Brittany, France, as I finish this book. I take a break, feed the three cats their supper and go out to hike up a nearby hill. By a stone fence beside some white daisies, I pull the phone from my pocket and google Grahame. Maybe I can visit again when I get home. But no. There is an obituary from the *Globe and Mail*. He died six months ago. I feel a grief that is out of proportion to the short amount of time I spent with this remarkable man. But of course, he was one of the last links to my father. I walk a very long time that evening. He died in November, the article says. "Grahame lived a very full – and at times, extremely dramatic life; he was a romantic; a Renaissance man; a proud Canadian. He loved his wife, Glorya, profoundly. He was a good person and he will be missed."

I read Grahame Woods' article on how he got involved in the Mzuzu AIDS/HIV Orphan Care Program (MAOCP), Malawi:

When asked to write a short essay for MAOCP, a question was posed; "Who am I and what prompted me to want to raise money for AIDS/HIV orphans in Mzuzu?" The immediate, easy answer to who I am is that I'm a retired mental-health counsellor and former television playwright who lives in Cobourg with his wife Glorya, writes a bi-weekly column for Northumberland Today, belongs to the Cobourg Poetry Workshop, volunteers at the hospital with Glorya and attends St. Peter's Church, but not on a regular basis.

A NECESSARY DISTANCE / *249*

Giving the question deeper thought, I came to realize I'm someone who came to Canada and, over the years, discovered himself; only I wasn't conscious of it until I retired and had time to think about it. What truly focused me was a heart attack and subsequent bypass surgery eight years ago. In another life, I was also a cinematographer for the CBC, shooting documentaries that took me around the world, with a great deal of time spent in various African countries. I mention this because, a few years ago, I heard Colin Turnpenny give an illustrated presentation about one of his trips to Mzuzu, telling of AIDS/HIV orphans, their meagre lives of sparse opportunity, of sickness and in many cases, premature death, his images recalling my own experiences. His words stayed with me, parked in a compartment of my mind.

All it took was a letter to Canon Peter Walker suggesting a Classical Star competition as a Mzuzu fund-raiser. Peter put me in touch with Heather Godfrey. We hunkered down to try to make it work. Seven months later, on a cool November evening, the finalists played to a packed church and $2000 was realized.

It was during one of my rides in early spring of 2008 that it occurred to me that I should put my cycling to even better use. I had an idea. Why not have people sponsor me to raise money for Northumberland Hills Hospital? For me it was a way of saying thank you to the hospital where, at its original home on Chapel Street, my life was saved following a heart attack. I called it Thanks for Life Ride. It raised a lot of money. Fast forward that to 2010. I had an idea. Why not do it again, this time to help the Mzuzu feeding and clothing program?

Which is how my 1000 Miles For Mzuzu came to pass. There was one small but important change around the 500 mile mark. I learned from Colin that students going into high school in Mzuzu have to pay tuition fees. No money? Then no school. It was information that excited me, gave me a focus. I pledged to raise $2000 to send five students to school for one year. It was something tangible, providing an additional incentive. Five young people will have an opportunity to reach for a future – as I did when I stepped onto Canadian soil for the very first time on that journey of discovery. It's a great feeling.

Interlude

Saturday and Sunday, March 2–3. Lima's Hotel Crillón is excellent and has an all-night bar. Luxurious bath and excellent breakfast. Gene, of course, has been up and out, walking through Lima. A short walk during which we managed to buy Coricidin tablets for our colds, acquired in Argentina – we are now soft tropical types and can't endure normal weather.

Now on Toronto time, Dad reads Colin McDougall's 1958 novel *Execution*, picked up in the Rio airport. The story came from the author's Second World War experience and is based on the real-life story of Private Harold Pringle, a Canadian soldier who was executed by his own army in Italy. It sounds like the kind of tale Dad would tell. It is interrupted by terrible news.

Gene calls at my door, upset, having just heard that a three-man team, like ourselves, has been killed in a small plane crash near Calgary – Norman Caton, Len Macdonald and Charles Riegler. The last two were with us on A Winter's Day. Should he tell Grahame – they were close friends? Yes, otherwise he'll hear by mail or read in paper somewhere – besides no point in concealing it.

A NECESSARY DISTANCE / *251*

Concerned for Sandra reading such news – while we continue to careen around the earth on a multitude of flights. Alarms me to think of her seeing heading in paper – "Three-men CBC team die in crash." Well, I hope not. A very sad affair. I see Len and Charles as we all stood on Mount Norquay and filmed the magnificent dawn.

The next day, in a "subdued mood," they drive in an ancient Packard limousine to the bullfight arena,

with a mountain looming above it topped by a cross. Under this symbol of execution six animals were dispatched to quavering band music, by men in shabby costumes.

The picadors seemed bravest, taking on the fresh bulls without arms. The man in the white suit the most efficient, stepping in to dispatch the bull with an ardent knife. The greatest showmanship displayed by the attendants . . . they hooked up the carcass and did a running exit in Vaudeville or Ire Follies style, to music. Women next to me smiled, chuckled and gossiped when a bull was given the mortal thrust – as mother might comment on a school play or performance of their children. One bull was a fighter and leaped right over the fence after being wounded. Threw the matador, who had to go to fence and drink Coca-Cola to recover. Bull with the most sense kept backing away. They chased him all over the ring, while people shouted and whistled. The audience makes the most noise when the bull is smart enough to refuse battle.

It's all an orderly execution in ballet choreography. We saw nothing to touch the brutal, tragic drama of our wildebeest hunt. I doubt if any such exploit, hunters or bullfighters, will impress me now. We saw the moment of truth in Serengeti.

252 / JULIE SALVERSON

We left in a state of depression. Grahame very disturbed in his quiet way. My cold has affected my ear. The city seemed dream-like, almost silent. Couldn't hear the girl's high heels on pavement.

Norman, Len and Charles, I realize, were killed a week ago today. We were bathing on a beach at Dakar.

Air of Death

From a biography written by Pip Wedge the month after Dad's death in 2005:

> In addition to his fictional dramas, George was also capable of top quality work in the field of documentaries, of which he wrote many for the CBC. Most famous of these was his 1967 documentary, Air of Death, which dealt with the problem of air pollution and was produced and directed by Larry Gosnell. The CBC won the ensuing lawsuit that had been brought by companies claiming they had been libeled, and the documentary was the precursor of many similar hard-hitting documentaries to be broadcast in Canada.

Air of Death was a documentary about air pollution and concentrated on allegations of fluorosis poisoning from a phosphate plant near the Ontario town of Dunnville. The show helped start the environmental movement in Canada, was broadcast on Sunday, October 22, 1967, and pre-empted *The Ed Sullivan Show*. I am excited when I happen upon a scholarly book from 2014 – *The First Green Wave: Pollution Probe and the Origins of Environmental Activism in Ontario* – that gives the program and the subsequent court case the attention it deserves. Ryan O'Connor reports that the show was seen by 16 percent of English-speaking Canadians over the age of twelve (1.5 million people) – 12 percent of whom

A NECESSARY DISTANCE / 253

were teenagers – and had great critical success. One example from the *Toronto Star*: "This is a well-researched, highly documented program that must have shocked thousands of easy-breathing viewers from coast to coast. For taking a firm journalistic position that Canadians have been living in a fool's paradise of pollution, the program did the nation a service."

But as I read through the chapter about *Air of Death*, I am increasingly bewildered – where is my father, the writer? The focus is maverick producer Larry Gosnell. Dad worked with him countless times. The other name mentioned frequently is broadcaster Stanley Burke, the face of the show and a media star. In O'Connor's book, all the words from the documentary seem to be attributed to Burke. But Dad wrote all the words not spoken as interview questions or personal remarks.

Dad joked about how when the CBC set up the "war room" on Jarvis Street to fight the lawsuit he was paid full-time. "Two months! The only real job of my life! A steady paycheque! It was industry attacking the CBC. Doc makers from all over North America, even Mexico, came to help us fight the case. The question was huge – could a documentary say what it wanted to say, and name the villains, or did you need to give equal weight, say, to Adolf Hitler?"

CBC won the case. I find G.S. in a few footnotes as someone who attended meetings. It takes me a while, but I track O'Connor down and talk to him one winter morning just before I submit my final draft of this book. We talk about *Air of Death* and his experience writing the book and he puts me in touch with Gosnell's family, who still have all of their father's papers. Then I say, "Can I ask you an awkward question? Why didn't you name Dad as writer?"

There is a pause. O'Connor is stunned. As we talk, he pages through the chapter, looking for my father's name. He is surprised not to find it. I am relieved, and grateful for his concern at the omission. We talk a bit about how strange a process researching in archives is because files are labelled in ways that mean you only find what you are already looking for. In O'Connor's case, he found a lot about Stanley Burke. I say that actor Peter Ustinov had narrated the 1963 documentary. "I can see why someone might be more interested in Ustinov than in my father." I thank him for his time, adding, "Who knows what I will discover I have missed in this book, six months or six years after it comes out."

Among my pile of Dad's things – pitifully small, he threw so much away – is a meticulously filed binder with every media clipping about *Air of Death*. This show was perhaps the proudest accomplishment of his life, but he's accidently invisible in the only significant discussion of the show that has been written. This is so often the case for writers, and perhaps even more true with non-fiction stories, of which there were many. As early as the 1950s, supervising producer Sydney Newman (who had come to Toronto from the National Film Board in Montreal) says in an interview with Mary Jane Miller, "The best way to capture the imagination of your public is to speak to them about the questions that are on their minds at the time. That is the way to build audiences and give your stuff relevance." Miller wrote two books on early television drama, and she says that in the early days the amount of dramas produced was three or four times that done in the 1970s. Miller asked Newman about responding to headlines in the 1950s and how it was possible to do a script and get it on the air in a couple of months.

Yes, providing I could get the writer to do it. When Russia invaded Hungary, I said, "We must do a play for *GM Theatre* about a family caught up in this." . . . I wanted a story on the Hungarian invasion by Russia, right away. I had on

A NECESSARY DISTANCE / 255

my staff George Salverson, a very good writer . . . I called George in and I said, "George, drop everything. Burn the midnight oil." He wrote a one-hour play in about four days. I sent telegrams off to get the newsreel footage from France and Britain of the Russians. We went on the air about four weeks later . . .

Newman also told Miller that they wanted young talent. "When television began in Toronto, they would not allow anyone over the age of thirty-five to join the production services. I was the oldest person hired . . . I was thirty-five."

A bronze medallion sits on my desk. It is an award called the Christopher, and illustrates the saint carrying a child on his back. Above the image are the words: Honoring George Salverson, May 6, 1957. Written on the back: better to light a candle than to curse the darkness. I also have the broken-off bottom of a 1956 CCAA Award for my father and Max Rosenfeld for one of several productions Dad wrote called *The Discoverers* – it's about Canadian scientists Banting and Best, the discoverers of insulin. Dad won awards but rarely talked about them. His lack of acknowledgement for *Air of Death* makes me think about arguments in our family kitchen about Dad not standing up for himself. He might script it this way:

Mum: "You are not asking for what you deserve, not being paid enough."

Dad: "I'll see what I can do."

Mum: "They will get away with whatever they can."

Dad: "You don't understand the situation . . ."

Mum: "We need the money!"

Dad: "I don't want to be pushy."

Mum: "Jesus Christ, George, what is your agent for? Call Matie! I'll call Matie!"

256 / JULIE SALVERSON

Dad: "You will *not*, why do you always *always* go on like this?"

Exit father figure to hide in office. Sandra pours Scotch and swears.

Mum: "Hell, damn, spit!"

Matie Molinaro, Dad's agent for over fifty years, was born in Long Island, New York. She founded the Canadian Speakers' and Writers' Service and represented early authors like Earle Birney and Marshall McLuhan. Matie told me stories about her work with the Red Cross in World War II and with the Office of Information in Algiers, Naples, Rome and Trieste. She was also a war correspondent in the Psychological Warfare Branch. I wish I had recorded our conversations. I remember her as incisive, warm and terrifying.

Dad loved collaborating, and he brought that affinity and skill to his jobs. In the daily notebooks, he is constantly scribbling story ideas for shows. But I suspect it was hard for him, that pitching part of the game. It wasn't his nature. He rumbled along quietly fabricating stories, an easy and comforting way to interpret the world. His scripts were tender, mischievous, romantic, but he didn't slice open bone. He didn't spill blood. Today, you might say he didn't integrate his dark side. Oh, he had one all right. It spilled out in rages, fists pounded through walls. He knew a lot about deprivation from the poverty of his childhood, his mother's forbidding intellect and his father's alcoholism. My brother tells me there are stories he'll tell me someday. "Not for your book."

People liked my dad. They admired his calm, his graciousness, his lack of ego. All these qualities infuriated my mother. Perhaps she was my first teacher when it comes to seeking not who to admire, but who to blame. But Mom's feelings for Dad were more than that. And so are mine.

I am developing a pride in my father and what he was doing on this trip. The three men were professionals contracted to see and

A NECESSARY DISTANCE / 257

document what was felt to be a rapidly changing world – a world many saw as changing for the better, becoming modern. They brought their cultural perspectives and assumptions with them; a certain First World arrogance blinded them (although not, I think, Grahame) to the impossibility of their task and made them overlook the fact that it takes a long time to *see*. It was a flawed project that was seriously undertaken and carried out in good faith. It was part of the important heritage of Canadian documentary filmmaking.

I am finally speaking up for my father. Perhaps the worst I can say about him is that he was an ordinary man of his time who produced – with his team – an extraordinary small film with its scratchy soundtrack and images from half a century ago. A document, a record, a reckoning. An act of witness.

Bolivia

They fly over desolate sand and clay mountains to La Paz, landing on a gravel runway in a cloud of dust. It feels like the surface of the moon. They drive between adobe houses to the rim of a valley, below which the city spreads

in a giant hole – like buildings spilled from a bowl, falling in crazy unordered angles.

Rarified air – lungs sucking fast and deep – a vague sensation in the head. Deep uneasy sleep in afternoon – walk to FAO. Cognac in bar hits me hard, but kills pain in head.

They meet a woman called Joan Astel, who tells them of incredible adventures she has had travelling here over the past few years: tales of revolutions and shots in the street. When I google her, I keep getting Joan of Arc. Dad is overpowered by the altitude (La Paz is 3,640 metres above sea level) and by his cold. He can hardly hear. He gets a long, necessary sleep but has a persistent chill, as if recovering from a long illness.

La Paz is unbelievable, a moon crater colony full of pueblo type Indians in shawls and bowler hats. But my senses so fuelled I feel no power to comment, letting optical effects slip over me almost unheeded, but perhaps remembered at leisure. South American Indians stem from old civilization and it shows. Pictures in mail welcome – but can't recognize Julie. Have we been gone so long?

Dad is suffering from the altitude and what will later turn out to be hepatitis. But it's more than that. Tim Lilburn writes about the collapse of competence that precedes knowing. It's a kind of nakedness. When we drop our frameworks, our guarded certainties and our coping mechanisms, an emptiness follows which is a space for receiving. But my father is not well. Don't we have to be strong for the collapse of competence to provide a space for learning? If one is ill, doesn't just keeping up become the priority and the focus of all one's energy?

The exhaustion Dad is experiencing is an opportunity. But he's also there in a role. He's a professional. There are expectations. Where in all this is the possibility for something truly new? I think this applies to most of us. What conditions make it possible to recognize what Lilburn discovered in the woods, trying to look with unencumbered eyes – that he does not know how to see a deer?

Dad, Gene and Grahame want to *see* the people they are meeting. I, swimming in this postmodern critical time, am preoccupied with their inevitable failure. But what of the attempt?

The three men drive to Pillapi at Lake Titicaca but are told everything is closed so return to shoot at La Paz. There is no hotel

A NECESSARY DISTANCE / *259*

available so they stay in an old Spanish house with high ceilings
built around a courtyard garden.

Lots of notes from Dad, including about the script:

Agrarian reform. Experts in agriculture. Bring in seed, sell to
Indians and teach them to use it. School Programs. Eighty
thousand Indians in Dept. of La Paz. On Altiplano to Argentine
border, one and a half million. All same people, not divided into
tribes. Descended from Incas. Eat mostly dehydrated potatoes
and lima beans. Maize is a delicacy. Barley for animals or sale.
Meat on Sundays and only a few strips. Labour chief is of the
opinion that a poor family is sometimes without enough food.
However, people are not "hungry" generally, but everyone
speaks of malnutrition and a high infant mortality.

"Production of potatoes is down 75 percent since the reform,"
writes my father. A little research tells me a few things about the
1952 Bolivian Revolution.

The MNR, the Revolutionary Nationalist Movement, is
described as a middle-class coalition choosing nationalism over
Marxism. I read that they were "a centre-right, conservative political party" and the leading force behind the 1952–1964 revolution.
When they took power, they established a universal vote that
included women and Indigenous Peoples; they also nationalized
the tin mines and undertook major land reform. Before 1952,
90 percent of agricultural land was in semi-feudal cultivation
and owned by 6 percent of the population. Just over 9 percent of
that land was in the hands of absentee landlords and less than 3
percent in Indigenous hands. The new government encouraged
Indian farmers to develop modern cultivation, but this did not
happen, although strong peasant unions (syndicatos) developed.

260 / JULIE SALVERSON

A significant element of the revolution was the incorporation into national life of the Aymara and Quechua peasants who made up 65 percent of the population. This was a significant turning point in Bolivian Indigenous-State relations. The general Dad mentions below (Ballivián) headed a military junta that negotiated the change to the revolutionary government, but he was not particularly revolutionary himself.

The walls are three feet thick, and warm air has not penetrated since the days of the General. Production of potatoes is down 75 percent since his time, since the reform. This must mean the people have just what they had before, assuming the General took the profits which now don't exist. How has this benefited the people or the country?

In the notes about the script I see the story of the funeral procession that starts the film. A midwife tries to help but is resisted. The sick child is referred to witch doctors. There are three pages of examples of children dying from neglect – stories from the midwife.

Dad, Gene and Grahame are beyond exhausted. "The air is too rare to smoke or walk without losing my breath. I am told cars react oddly, so driving style is in accord with the sluggishness from little oxygen." For two days, Dad has only eaten tinned Danish cocktail sausages, which come with their own opener.

The hotel, they say, is like a field hospital, a recovery zone. They consider Bolivia "an endless wretched experience, for all its quota of fascination."

Sick with intestinal ailment, two appalling nights in the hacienda at Pillapi. Total lack of any convenience. An old man brought out two bottles for us alone, a special treat, and I forced myself to drink this musky potion, in that dank and chill-

A NECESSARY DISTANCE / *261*

ing tomb of a dining hall, while dead Spaniards wept. Night in the black, lighting cigarettes to have something to see, wavering my luminous dial to keep from going mad. Walked at dawn, hating the place. The double mud fence along road a dissolving grandeur with old trees, all speaking of decay and neglect. Bitter wind, distant shepherds and flocks, an escape into fresh air and this rugged nature such a relief after the dank big hold of the General's one-time grand reception hall. With Gene, some bitter conversation about the inadequacy of the people allowing such conditions. Two English girls we meet living in filth, going to La Paz for a weekly bath.

They drive to the gloomy airport building, the highest commercial airport in the world at 13,580 feet, and escape to Lima. Dad finds himself surprised to have such confidence in Peru. Exhausted and drained, he writes: "So once more civilization surrounds me. Once more South America's beautiful women are in sight. Once again, I come to the conclusion I have been drawing all through this trip. The cause of underdeveloped countries is underdeveloped people."

I have stopped trying to edit my father. He is writing privately from inside experiences I can't imagine in a time I only saw from the perspective of a seven-year-old child. From the perspective of a young girl and her adored father. Her hero.

Something Difficult

This afternoon I went to a documentary at the Kingston Canadian Film Festival with my friend Deborah Windsor. When the lights came up, we were told that the festival is closing because of Covid-19. We stumbled in bewilderment down the stairs and out into the winter sunshine. In what turns out to be my last drink before lockdown, we pull up chairs at the Chez Piggy bar and order wine.

"Can I talk about something difficult?" she asks. She is comfortably in her late sixties, always smiling. She isn't smiling now.

She wants to talk about Canadian Catholic theologian and philosopher Jean Vanier, the founder of L'Arche – communities around the world where people with and without intellectual disabilities live together. He died in 2019 at the age of ninety-one. Last month it was revealed by women close to him that he was a sexual predator. My friend is reeling. Deborah spent part of her youth in France at L'Arche. Vanier, her godfather, was one of her heroes. Was? Is?

I too have a connection to Vanier. I knew a family that ran a L'Arche home in Toronto. Vanier's work represented everything good, human relationships disarmed and loving. At the time, the embodiment of hope gave me something to strive for, to believe in, and it directly influenced the theatre company I started, working with people with mental challenges. But now it seems Vanier isn't what we all thought. Or rather he is more, or less, than we thought.

The story has exploded in the news. A man many considered a saint, who created a movement of dignity and equality between disabled people and the internally disabled rest of us, abused his power. No doubt about it. He did not acknowledge what he had done before his death. Now he is a violator, a liar. The rage, anguish and confusion is palpable. A friend writes that her husband, a man of seventy, "was heartbroken when the news broke about Vanier. Paul had really thought of him as a hero."

Why are people shocked to discover a deep flaw in a hero? In a novel, what we value and expect is not what we demand of real life. Characters are dismissed if they are one-sided, called superficial if they are too full of goodness – or, for that matter, evil. The writer is lazy or unskilled. In a contemporary novel, high praise would be lavished on an author who created a character as complicatedly flawed as Vanier was revealed to be. This understandably horrifying news about Vanier – and I don't pretend it isn't horrifying – reveals another view of the real Vanier. (How we love the word "real," what fragile reassurance it gives us.) If a film makes a character only heroic, it is called a "reductive Hollywood depiction." But a life full of inconsistency – great acts of kindness and intelligence, desperate blindness and sometimes brutality – that's unbelievable. The truth is, we are all partially blind to ourselves. That may be what causes our shock, our outrage, our grief – the frightening realization that it is ourselves who are being outed.

I call my friend Cameron. He is in his seventies and lives alone in an apartment near the Danforth in Toronto. We have decided to have weekly chats to relieve the Covid-19 loneliness. Immediately he brings up the explosion over Vanier. What, we ask each other, drove him to behave that way, a man with such deeply held values and beliefs?

"Can you imagine how lonely he was?" asks Cameron.

I say, "Most people treated him like a saint. Idolized him. Who does a man like that talk to?" The question doesn't release his enormous culpability, the way he preyed on the loneliness of others, but it is a question. Are we partly culpable when we turn people into heroes?

When I hang up, something else occurs to me. The element of grief that comes with hearing this news. Grief – how to understand this as distinct from judgment? Grief that Vanier could behave that way. Grief that all of us, even our heroes, are capable of at least some diminishment of others. Over and over.

The Last Shot

They fly to Panama en route to Mexico. Dad has a window seat:

I enjoy moonlit undulations of snow-capped Andes, and also sleep against cozy angle of chair and window. Plane stops in

264 / JULIE SALVERSON

Guatemala – a city on tablelands divided by interesting ravines full of foliage and surrounded by mountains – no snow here. Very hot. Pleasant terminal an old-country look to it, stained glass windows. Bought a Coke. Flew on just above massed white convolutions of cloud above which rose alarming peaks like islands in a foaming sea. A volcano rose above the port wing.

They land in Mexico City. The last filming will be in Tlaltizapán, 125 kilometres south. They seem to drive back and forth in one day, there is no mention of transportation. The main notes are about the script and what they have to shoot. It's a boy, a doctor and a clinic. I remember it from the film, where the story of the child's funeral in Bolivia dissolves into a boy in Mexico:

Narrator:
A child is born, new life is begun. There's a boy growing here.

Shot of more ornate coffin, high up on a pedestal. Young man walking around in graveyard. We are now in Mexico.

Where a boy grows in energy and health and imag-ination, there will be a very good thing. There will be a hero. The boy Juanero was the possessor of a genuine grade A hero. He longed to emulate his hero, to dream of glory, of fighting for the common people of Mexico.

Close-up shot of face of statue with moustache and penetrating dark eyes.

A NECESSARY DISTANCE / *265*

As his hero Zapata fought, land reformer, on this very spot by the bullet spattered church.

Shot of church against sky, boy looking up.

Oh, to be a hero.

Camera pulls back as boy — we see he has a guitar in his hands — runs up the steps to the church, and the guitar has become a gun, which he points and seems to fire. We hear gunshots in the distance.

The boy runs toward the gate of the church, turns, right toward the camera, seems to leap over it, then alone against a blank building. Then camera looks between wide-spread legs in white pants, and the boy approaches, then gunfire, then boy falls.

The mighty reformer bit the dust at the hand of an old friend. It was Doctor Ortiz from the clinic, who used to tap Juanero's chest with chilly instruments, and tell people the children who were sick could be cured by such things as sprinkling fish flour in the tortilla dough.

Boy and man walk away down the street, friends.

The experiment was a success. The money for it has run out. Gone now also were the workers at the protein-rich fish plant.

Solo guitar, boy and man wave at each other as they part. We realize this is the doctor.

Dr. Ortiz remembered it in less simple terms, and with sadder contrasts. There were those who accepted change, and those who did not.

Shot of boy running off, with his toy gun.

The experiment had been an attack on the single principal of diet which produces pot-bellied children with matchstick legs and adults too tired to care.

Shot of young woman making tortillas.

Like millions of others, Juanero's mother served up cornmeal tortillas and excellent beans, and served them exclusively all day long.

10:37 The same occurs in Asia. And Africa. No one ever guesses why he's unwell, or why the measles carries him off so easily. Physicians and nutritionists are the revolutionary fighters today, spread thinly around the world, wearing those new labels: FAO, WHO, UNESCO, UNICEF. Fighting the invisible plague of hunger.

All while mother makes tortillas.

A NECESSARY DISTANCE / *267*

```
And ignorance. And like Dr. Ortiz, enjoying exper-
imental success in the growth of a boy with dreams.
```

```
Shot of boy eating tortillas.
```

They spend days trying to get their equipment from the Mexico City airport. The FAO tries to help but they are busy with Freedom from Hunger Week activities. The FFH campaign launched by the FAO in 1960 was a five-year affair. The film is part of this.

Dad is confused by a familiar face at the Hotel Geneve, "a round-faced young German with the formal look of a waiter." He is indeed a waiter – from the Celebrity Club in Toronto, a bar in an old mansion across the street from the CBC studios on Jarvis. It was a showbiz hangout for decades – where everyone headed after work. As a child, I was as much at home there as anywhere. Sometimes more.

Heinz. His name pries open a memory of exuberant conversation. Everybody's children were welcome at the Celebrity Club, more so if they wanted to join in the roaring debates that were already in full swing when you sat down. I loved the recognition I got and loved being welcomed into an argument. Both my parents were happy there, it was their reward for a day's efforts in the studio. Sitting among colleagues who respected each other, they felt valued and fulfilled. The drinking was shared with colleagues who enjoyed challenging each other.

Heinz is on his way to Acapulco, where Dad is headed to meet my mother.

I won't tell Sandra and she'll have a surprise.

268 / JULIE SALVERSON

There are fewer notes now. The men are ready to be home. Gene is a wreck, hands shaking. He has "called Benson" and heard that the director Paul Almond is having trouble on his film in Jordan with overexposed film. It was Benson who told them of the plane crash outside Calgary, he seems to be their contact back home. Even after they leave, money keeps arriving to their last shooting location. The doctor in the film, Bartolomé Pérez Ortiz, jokes with Dad in the hotel bar:

Dr. Ortiz: You speak very good English.
   Geo: You speak very good Spanish.
   Laughter.
An unseen group sat outside in the narrow dark street with guitar and Mexican harmony. Still at it as we went to sleep about 10:30. Aroused several times. The singers having gone, the dogs came. In a choir of hysterical voices they seemed to be surging through town. Made me think of the hunting dogs of Serengeti – except those were silent.

Saturday, March 16. Tlaltizapán. 1:15 p.m. Took last shot of whole film – a donkey's close-up – and went to square for Cerveza.
   Tore into Mexico City at a hundred kilometres per hour. Dropped Dr. at hospital. Returned to Hotel Geneve to find Gene gone leaving letters and Courvoisier. Sad apologies in letter to Grahame. We agreed Gene worries too much.
   Grahame and I felt the boy was at times quietly amused and serving dutifully as good son [in the scene]. He seemed to regard his performance as rather a silly bore. He at all times refused offers to join us in soft drinks, candy, or to share something at breakfast when he arrived early. Dr. Ortiz had warned

A NECESSARY DISTANCE / *269*

us they were proud people. Certainly no one was grabbing for our money.

I read with fascinated horror how a *Time* correspondent spent weeks going over the desert into Yemen to report the war with the Egyptians. He went by donkey, jeep, truck, on foot, with six Yemen guards, two of whom were killed, and one wounded. I must say, this stern adventuring must be beyond me. The other thing I must do is cable Sandra about our next move. If this is really the eleventh she comes to Mexico in five days. Two months had become five days. Well, that's something. My real life now seems so far away, like a dream.

Finally, his first words about being in Mexico with Mom: "The energy I spent preparing for Sandra's arrival. She now seemed an imagined creature from another world. The Britannia Canadian Pacific Air Lines (CPA) was late. My nervousness mounted. At last she appeared, unfamiliar in a hat, with a tunic, white face, smiling bravely."

And so it ends. All that is left is Mexico with Mom and the return home. For Dad, and for me reading, the finish line is in sight.

CHAPTER NINE

Re-entry

Note attached to the top of Dad's computer:

A word of advice:
Look to the blowing rose about us: Lo,
Laughing, she says, into the world I blow;
At once the silken tassel of my purse
Tear, and its treasure on the garden throw.

From Omar Khayyam

Pink Tequila Cocktails

Dad meets my mother at the airport and kisses her awkwardly. They have a drink at the hotel and then wander in search of a restaurant. Turned away from exotic places that are full, they wind up at an all-night cafeteria eating vegetable soup and excellent oysters. I think of their first real date after the party on Algonquin Island in the 1940s, talking through the night at Fran's Restaurant on St. Clair Avenue. I have inherited my parents' preference for local diners.

Retired in our twin beds, both exhausted and rather polite, despite grateful momentary embraces. Sandra alarmingly tired.

/ 270

A NECESSARY DISTANCE / *271*

Mom has looked after two young children for more than two months. She later confesses to her husband that she has been nervous about the reunion and shy around Grahame, who she doesn't know. These men have been around the world. My mother is still the girl who grew up in small-town Peterborough, Ontario. Dad persuades her to wear the silk he has bought her in India. She looks marvellous and starts to relax.

The next morning, they have breakfast in bed, shop for a "Mexican Cowboy Suit" for Scott and decide to wait until they return from Acapulco to add a sombrero to the gifts. Too hard to pack. They have lunch with Grahame – Carta Blanca beer and club sandwiches.

He took my air ticket to be signed over to CPA by Air France and Pan American. Will leave at desk. Very grateful, as this is a fussy business. Suddenly, with little formality or ceremony, Grahame and I were saying goodbye and the Great Adventure simply dissolved, fading into air. It was over.

My parents fly to Acapulco and settle into a delightful room with a balcony and a pebbled beach below. That night my mother starts throwing up. Eventually they call in a doctor. She tries to get Dad to go swimming. "I refused to leave her to her misery in a hotel room in a foreign country."

She recovers and they spend an afternoon at a beach. They meet "an American lady whose pink husband showed interest only when he learned I had been around the world. Then cruise on the Fiesta – American tourists, felt out of place. Rather superior – having been travelling so far in dead earnest, sometimes with hardships."

They return to Mexico City and visit the opera house – Ballet Folklórico de México. The next day my parents depart for Canada on Aeronaves de México, both drinking pink tequila cocktails with maraschino cherries and an orange slice. It's a four-hour flight. At 5:00 a.m. they land at Malton Airport in Toronto and, despite nervousness over an amethyst and some Peruvian silver, have no trouble with customs. Mom's cousin Bill Scott picks them up and drives them home. Everyone opens gifts and goes to bed. My dad is too tired to sleep. I imagine him sitting in the living room playing his harmonica. Preparing for re-entry.

Fencelessly Flowing Yards

In his 2015 book *Reaching Mithymna* Steven Heighton describes the Canada his mother found when she left Greece in the 1960s:

> The fencelessly flowing yards of a new subdivision, the bland chatter of cocktail-calm neighbours in the soft twilight, the shouts of children off somewhere playing cops and robbers or war in perfect safety, the white noise of sprinklers on weedless lawns. A place where vices, rages and bad smells are suppressed or decently contained. Grief or exaltation likewise. Death above all. Most folks white, in fact WASP, straight, courteous, middle-class. A near-theological belief in the existence of Normal. The complacent, depraved fantasy of being the nicest, or the greatest, nation on earth, far from the weaponized frontiers where crazy shit goes down.

Heighton had made a last-minute decision to fly to Greece and volunteer on the frontlines of the Syrian refugee crisis. He spent a month on the island of Lesbos, wading through NGOs, refugees and other volunteers and haunted by memories of his deceased Greek mother and the residue of his childhood. Like my father he was out in the world – though a different one and for different

A NECESSARY DISTANCE / 273

reasons – for only a few weeks. He too was trying to help. He too felt the bewilderment of returning to the "First World."

In 1963, my parents lived in a new subdivision in North York. God knows what brought them there, maybe their good friends Joan and Perce Curtis, Stacey's parents, who lived over the back fence. After a few years, Mom and Dad retreated downtown. Normal was not the religion in our house, but the exuberant eccentrics that made up my parents' circle may not have ventured so far north. I don't know. In the puritan Protestant Toronto of that time, "vices, rages and bad smells" were certainly suppressed and contained. But there are always other stories, darker versions, and maybe my late friend Heighton is too harsh.

My father returns on Monday, March 25, 1963. He has seen so much more than most of his friends. Than his wife. He will read the news differently. Stories of governments falling and accounts of independence struggles will now be reports from places he's been. They will involve people he's met, sat down to dinner with. He'd been there. Perhaps for the rest of his life he will think differently about the poverty and hunger that he'd come to believe could be fixed. After all, he had seen the solutions with his own eyes. Will he think, as Grahame's wife Glorya did, that "we blew it?"

My father returns to an insular world and to a family with financial struggles that are blunted by the release of alcohol. He loses touch with Grahame, who goes back to Africa and makes documentaries all over the world. He resumes his Canadian life and tells stories from there, many with an international connection.

Home

That drive from the airport back to North York would have been so different for each of my parents. For Sandra, perhaps regret to be back in the dull browns and greys, the snow, it was still March. For

274 / JULIE SALVERSON

Dad, like landing on the moon. He had been gone only nine weeks, but he had literally been around the world and *his* world had been upended, inside and out. Perhaps he sat in silence, wondering how to put words to it all. Aware of the journals that he'd stuck in a drawer while unpacking – had he kept them close at hand on the plane, safely visible to him and not trusted to checked luggage? Aware he was implicated by these journals? Did he show them to anyone? Could it be I am the first to read them? Seems unlikely at first, then almost definite.

Notebook Seven is three pages long. Dad notes a "marvellous sense of luxury" being back. Gifts are opened. He drives the babysitter home and goes to renew his driver's licence. The car feels "luxurious and powerful."

On Tuesday Mom accompanies him downtown for the first look at the rushes. The film footage of Indonesia disappoints Grahame but he says there are enough good shots for a thirty-minute film. I had always thought my dad was writing the script during the trip in some other notebook. But in his notes for Tuesday I see this:

To screening of Indonesia in a.m. Grahame brought me six malaria pills for six weeks – bought in Ghana for six dollars. Grahame disappointed at some scenes, but Gene insisted we have lots of good shots for half hour. Home for short rest, then to office. Had terrible time trying to write outline for use in editing film, but began to see opportunities, and felt encouraged. But slow – will have to finish in morning and deliver it at noon I hope.

I check the dates again to make sure I am reading this correctly. They arrive home on Monday, look at the footage on Tuesday and Wednesday, and Dad delivers the finished script on Thursday. My

A NECESSARY DISTANCE / 275

students complain that they have only three weeks to revise an assignment.

Dad is unhappy with the wildebeest section, "the most tragic moments missed. Including the actual death of the animal." It was his idea, the hunt. The day of the animal's death is the worst day of the trip for my father. It haunts him for years, and he mentions it again in the last pages of Notebook Seven, after he has returned to Toronto. This won't make sense to people who have lived close to the land and know there is nothing sentimental about animal behaviour and those who hunt for food, not sport. But the experience shakes him.

Dad gives us the Maasai sword and wildebeest tail. How could he bear having such a thing, after how he had felt? But in many of life's decisions, one thing does not at all lead to another.

He keeps feeling an urge to embrace my mother, "an instinctive natural feeling which I had to restrain." These words make me unspeakably sad. Should I delete them? But there is no escaping the collision of my parents in Mexico, excitement quickly turning to irritation, then retreat. Had Mom received the letters? Had he said anything to her except travelogue notes? Did she ever read these notebooks?

Dad describes the dinner on Tuesday night with old friend actor Alfie Scopp and his wife, Doris:

Showed pictures and the obscene silver from Peru. Later Alfie and I quarrelled vigorously over my new bigotry. He told a tale about ordering a dress suit from Hong Kong for thirty-five dollars and getting a Nazi customs officer who made it as difficult as possible for this Jew. Another officer told Alfie the German was fighting the war all over again as a Canadian customs man. At end Alfie asked where he was from. "Hamburg." "Oh yes, I know it. I was in the Air Force and we dropped a lot of bombs there!" Alfie and I parted friends at 2:00 a.m. and I, rather drunk on soothing brandy, decided to soften my bigoted line. Coughed a lot.

The coughing is a prelude to the oncoming hepatitis.

There are pages of entries about my mother's birthday, Sunday, March 31, just after they got back – and not a word about my brother Scott's, March 22, when they are still in Mexico. This is why Dad looked for the black sombrero. In my memory it was magnificent, with silver adorning the black velvet. I've seen a picture, the boy is so proud, grinning, the hat slips down over his eyes. He was just turning five. I was seven.

I open to a page in Notebook Seven. Again, I read about my brother:

Scott asked to learn to read and wrote the four on the left to show he already knows something about it. So I began with letters from the newspaper. He could read the O's. Later refused to listen to Scott as he carried on in bed after Sandra refused to read him a story after he said he didn't want it. Attacked by S for not listening to him, so listened. Couldn't grasp what he was saying and made him repeat it. Stunned when realized he was saying "Ask her to forgive me."

Sandra says he has been stammering. Trying to get a word in and no one listening.

Also interested in Julie whose personality and mind are now fascinating, mercurial. Suspect an intellect with temperament. She stormed because she has read all the three library books she got in the last couple of days – yesterday, I think. I suggested she look at books around house and read to her from book of poems, choosing "The Bridge of Sighs." She demanded

A NECESSARY DISTANCE / *277*

more, instantly grasping idea that poetry is music even when you don't know what it means. Opened Shakespeare to *Romeo and Juliet* and wants me to read it to her. Good Lord!

It was harder for my dad to leave my mother than to leave us, the children, but when he comes home from the trip, he seems to pay attention differently, as if surprised by these two strange beings in his house.

I look again at the opening shots of the film. He wrote the following narration the day after he discovered my brother's stutter. A child's funeral:

```
Close-up of a man's booted feet and the hooves of
two long-horned cows plowing.


Narrator:
The Altiplano rises up to 14,000 feet in the Andes
which may be irrelevant. Perhaps less irrelevant
is the fact that the Incas converted this infer-
tile land into a rich breadbasket, and what has
been done may be done again.


But since that time, children have made this
trip regularly, people like Julio and Felice have
observed it, and the thing that killed the chil-
dren was a hidden hunger, malnutrition.


Shot of young man in suit, panning to young woman
in black coat and hood, dark hair braided and
parted in the middle, full cheeks and looking
into the camera with a frown.
```

278 / JULIE SALVERSON

The sensation to be endured by Julio and his expectant wife is shared throughout the larger portion of the earth. Normally, Julio would have regarded the death as a slip of the charm, on the part of the witch doctor. But Julio had been losing some of the suspicion that goes with the heredity of serfdom.

Close shots of the procession, no narration. We hear the feet on the ground, step by step crunching along.

It's a nice touch, this quiet, like the sound of the wind a few moments ago in the sequence. In 1963 did a film not need to have the frantic pace of today? Or are these men – Dad, Grahame and Gene – giving the viewer time. A moment. Just to listen. To see.

4:51 Julio put on his hat. His wife, sitting on the ground, puts on hers, round bowler. She starts to crochet, or weave something.

Narrator:
Of course, it was wrong to expect a man and woman to experiment with their own flesh and blood. There's nothing like the security of past traditions. And the witch doctors recommended by your friends. All the same, another child was dead.

Cows plowing intercut with the group and coffin approaching the large cross that is waiting.

A NECESSARY DISTANCE / *279*

```
Every human life has a common pattern. We all share
it. And this is what they buried on Altiplano. New
life begun, childhood, youth, marriage, parent-
hood. Striving, achievement, maturity, wisdom,
old age. New life begun again. All the pattern,
the universality of human experience, buried in a
child's coffin on top of the world. Undone.
```

"You won't go far harnessed to the carriage of the past," says my Ukranian friend's mother, Tetiana Rewa. I guess this is a privilege, this tiny window into my father's thoughts as he encounters his children. I'm not sure. But I want this information, if that's what to call it.

I shove back my chair and search the house. I am looking for an old drawing. I pull boxes from the bedroom cupboard, but nothing. Then I find it hidden in plain sight. Hanging in our downstairs hall outside the kitchen is a pencil sketch of a boy's face. Soft bangs fall over eyebrows that frown slightly. The look in the eyes is direct. He is not smiling. He seems, to my inevitably interpreting gaze, accepting. There is no date or signature, but this is my brother at four years old. Or just after his fifth birthday.

"Our lives have painful, precious precarity," writes Maggie Russell. For years I have preoccupied myself with global issues. I thought that was what a book about Dad's trip around the world would address. I was prepared for the Jakarta Method and colonialism. I am broken open by my sweet baby brother.

"Ask her to forgive me."

On Wednesday Dad makes a list of clothes he needs and wonders if he can pay for them. That night, my parents visit the Goldsmith's next door.

Charming long talk with Manny – increasing courage as became evident he agreed with my own conclusions – not absolutely, but generally.

He thought I should not conceal my feelings but have a duty to reveal them to my friends, since I have the experience and they have only concepts. The fact they won't believe me doesn't change my responsibility. Well!

So, I have clashed with Alfie, who is widely connected with publicity seekers from many lands re Front Page Challenge, and have met with sympathy from Manny, a scholar of experience. Must take notes of the reactions of other friends.

There is a call from producer Bob Allen about something he calls in his notes "the Turquner script." (I never find out what it was.) Allen apologizes for taking so long to read it and tells Dad, "It was excellent." My father: "All this means is, no matter how well you work for the drama people, you and your money will wait for months. If I hadn't been away I would have been waiting in surly anger."

Dad drives downtown and delivers the script. He takes the afternoon off to skim through his photos of the world. He copies into his notebook an exchange with his young daughter – me: "Julie: 'Can I go out on the porch?' 'No.' 'I want to pray to God.' 'No.' 'I'll dress warmly.' 'No.' 'But I want to pray to God.' 'You can pray to God somewhere else.' She at once accepted this. Her religious play had failed to strike a chord of weakness and she instantly recognized this fact. Some dialogue!"

Dad delivers the script on Thursday, March 28. Four days after returning home. Another job done.

Night River

Dad visited my playwriting class at Queen's in 2001. I listen to the cassette recording of his voice with relief: finishing this book

A NECESSARY DISTANCE / *281*

doesn't meant finishing with my father. He talks about being a professional scriptwriter. I'm proud of my student's questions: "What's the difference between radio and television? How did you find stories? Did you struggle over the right words?" Some of Dad's replies: "You have to go inside the scene and the characters. The situation is what matters. I didn't agonize over words because I didn't believe in it, I believed in decisions."

I play a clip. *Night River* has always been my favourite of my father's radio dramas. He tells my class that he was interested in 1830s Upper Canada and had found the diary of a Scottish immigrant. The Quakers had sent the farmer a runaway slave to protect. Two slavers arrived and demanded the young man. As they were forcing him out of the yard a gunshot came from an upper window in the farmhouse. A ten-year-old boy was firing. The slavers left and were last seen fleeing down the road to Hamilton.

"The play grew in my mind, and how the slave would take command at the end and make things work on his own terms."

The show opens with haunting music by Morris Surdin and my father's words:

> Wait for the king,
> Night River King.
> Wait for the king
> of the Night River.

The show was directed by Andrew Allan and starred John Drainie as the slave. In those years, only white actors were in the radio company. Dad said he'd wondered how Drainie would manage to play the Black king, but when he heard the voice on radio he was convinced. Probably Drainie felt the challenge himself. How his performance would sound to a Black audience now would depend on each individual listener. Tommy Tweed played the

282 / JULIE SALVERSON

farmer, Billie Mae Richards the boy and Robert Christie the voice of the narrator, the boy grown up. Here is a bit of the opening:

Narrator: I remember him. That strange man unlike any in my world. That was before the road. My dad never wanted the road, *people* came down the road. He didn't want *people* coming down the road.

The boy and the man are in the cemetery, where they go each day to visit the dead mother's grave.

Narrator: Standing and praying. My father would pray, but never kneel. Not even to God.

Boy: Pa, can Ma hear us?

[After some discussion of the boy's confusion as to why God keeps her up in heaven . . .]

Father: When you take responsibility for another person, it stays with you all of your life. I took responsibility for her and she died. Responsibility is a fearful thing. Remember that.

[A bit later . . .]

Boy: Pa, why is it wrong to receive favours?

Father: Because it makes you . . . responsible.

This is the curtain line of the scene. My father tells my class: "The opening scene lays all the seeds for what comes."

A NECESSARY DISTANCE / 283

"Mr. Salverson, did you have a list, you know, a chart with all that you had to put in?"

Pause.

"I think I just wrote it. I knew what I needed. The farmer is horrified by all the things the Black man has to say, but he doesn't want to be responsible. And in the play, at the end, it's the slave who takes responsibility. That's what a king would do. He knows he is a king from his ancestral inheritance from Africa. It's a pro-African piece, if you like."

I turn off the tape recorder. It's something I'd never noticed, and have only just now put together. The show is from the early 1960s. How perfect, I think, this is what happened when he got home. He had a whole new perception of Black men and ancestry and freedom.

I look up *Night River* on Google. It was first produced in 1960. So much for tying Dad's response to the trip into a nice tidy bow. How did he change, how was his life different because of the trip? I have no idea.

Fade to Black

"We wish to thank Colgate-Palmolive Limited, sponsor of *Don Messer's Jubilee*, for relinquishing their program time tonight. *Don Messer's Jubilee* will return at the regular time over most of these stations next week."

The Secret Hunger was part of a new concept, a global assault on hunger launched in 1960. The introduction spoken by Peter Ustinov proposes hunger as being fundamentally connected to poverty, lack of education and war. The documentary aired in May of 1963 in a prime-time Saturday night slot normally occupied by *Don Messer's Jubilee*, one of the most watched shows in Canadian broadcasting history. It matched the old CBC *Stage* in having a viewership second only to *Hockey Night in Canada*, and outranked the imported CBS *Ed Sullivan Show* in numbers. I have been unable to find any reviews or historical commentary on how the show was received. Dad, I'm sure, was busy with the next projects by the time the film was finished.

Here's how it ends:

28:25 Shot of one Indonesian man in hat, holding stick.

Narrator:
One life. The cycle begins again. All man is one, in living and in need.

Cut to Bhagat smoking his long pipe.

One hundred years ago, there were one billion of us.

Shot of Senegalese fisherman on boat.

Today, there are three billion.

Fisherman throws a net out into the sea. Camera dissolves to boy and father in Serengeti, father shooting arrow toward the sky.

Two billion are gripped at the borderline of want by poverty and ignorance. In thirty-five years, there will be six billion people.

Shot of Altiplano man eating from a plate.

A NECESSARY DISTANCE / *285*

For them, the world has declared a new kind of war — on hunger and its causes.

Cross-fade to man walking with plow behind two cows up a hilly path.

Every one of them has heard on the horizon the sound of a struggle.

Shot of man carrying child's coffin with mourners behind, first moments of film.

And has seen the advance patrol. It's a beginning.

Camera stays with mourners and coffin beside the large cross. Guitar.

Fade to black.

Text onscreen: This film was produced by the CBC in co-operation with the FAO for the Visual Information Board of the United Nations.

Then logo: CBC Radio Canada, over the image of Canada with the circles of latitude and longitude on top.

I finish typing out Dad's script on a cool June afternoon with music in the park outside, it is equinox arts festival day. Voices, wind in the trees, some children's screams of excitement.

Going through the film slowly is different than watching it in one sitting. I admire the script's economy, I feel it gathering at the end. I understand what he's doing as he shapes the story, the mix of the personal narratives with the overview, the philosopher in the writer. A kind of elegance.

I learned storytelling from him, not formally, but by being around it all the time as he talked about what he wrote, figured out plots and characters out loud, ran ideas by his young daughter. I'm less nervous than when I first watched the film. I see a kind of naive innocence he has written into the people in these countries; as he makes them recognizable and sympathetic, he also gives them a simplicity. His protagonists are not the Indonesians and Indians and Ghanaians and Senegalese and Peruvians who run the organizations, they are the people who work with their hands to feed their families. I think he makes this choice in order to speak to the way that the rest of us are ordinary in our anxieties, our suspicions and our peasant status in the face of the rulers of the earth. It is not tribal kings who rule us but multinational CEOs who want the status quo, who sew distrust of others to keep their control. My dad brought to this project his own suspicion of those who hold the keys – a suspicion he inherited from his parents.

But the film does not challenge the idea that poverty is caused by lack of education, ignorance and local wars. In this sense, it infantilizes its subjects. There is no getting away from the implication that the First World NGOs are now here to save these people from themselves.

A forty-six-year-old white man of Icelandic/Norwegian heritage travels in Japan, Indonesia, Africa, South America and Mexico. For the first time. What has prepared him for this? Perhaps his mother's insistence on reading world literature, her sharp brain and her sense of justice. These were passed on. But he is also appalled by his inability to react competently to what he is encountering and this leaves him vulnerable. His emotional responses and his ideas of the world do not help him understand the kaleidoscope of

A NECESSARY DISTANCE / *287*

information and impressions. When Dad looked in the mirror at the end of this trip he did not like what he saw.

I have spent months of lockdown in the grip of a posthumous uncomfortable encounter with my father. I have had to confront a truth I've given lip service to for years but now understand more fully. It is not only other people who are complicated – angels and devils, greedy and generous, hurting and helping – it is true of myself and the people I love. But perhaps I knew this all along and it is only made clear by the journals. I knew my family was complicated. Maybe it's their similarity to everyone else's that I resisted. Their ordinariness.

My mother was an angry, generous, willful and frightened woman with great loyalty and great love. My father was stability. He talked about justice. He was gentle, a man of character. He also had a temper. He recognized his own ignorance. He contributed something that matters to the stories and aspirations that make up Canada and what it means to be a citizen. And the stories he told, the scripts he wrote, did not come from nowhere.

My father insisted that Icelanders became Canadians almost as soon as they arrived here in the late 1800s. They rarely looked back. But he was proud of his heritage – the love of stories and reading, the independence of spirit. In his last years he called himself "the old Icelander." All my adult life I flirted with the idea of taking him there, but it never happened.

In the summer of 2023, I get an email. Karen Gummo, a storyteller from Calgary, Alberta, has created a one-woman show about my grandmother. She is going to perform it in Reykjavík. Karen knows more about my ancestral background than I do. She tells me that Laura was the first non-English newcomer to write an immigrant story and that she chose to write in English – also a first – and thus lost much of the Icelandic Canadian and Icelandic audience. Taking the trip now is a no-brainer. It's time.

I am over northern Canada gazing out the Icelandair cabin window at the northern lights when it hits me: I am the first person in my family to return to Iceland since Laura's parents emigrated in 1876. I feel an unexplainable sadness. My dad would have loved this. All it would have taken was for me to buy us tickets.

I wish I knew more about the conversations in my father's home when he was a child. He learned by osmosis and Icelandic stories shaped him. He knew who he was. Dad was raised on Icelandic literature and on his mother's tales of immigration and survival. Both his parents knew poverty and its politics. He had roots. I have roots. Some of them are blood. Some of them take the form of an instant recognition of what is embedded in the stories of fellow artists anywhere in the world. We humans recognize experience in each other. There is more to read of my grandmother's novels, more of her public talks to dig out of the Ottawa archives. There is much I don't yet know. But I have found something for myself and my brother, for my nieces and nephew. A gateway.

My parents meet in Mexico City and reignite their fond and fierce marriage. Then Toronto, the homecoming. My father is distraught when the moment of the wildebeest's death lands on the cutting-room floor. Then he is struck with acute hepatitis, which he blames on Jakarta. He is bedridden for six months. I serve him mashed peas in a bowl. Life goes on and the trip recedes into flickering black-and-white images stored away in a canister in a Toronto archive. Over fifty years later I find his notebooks. Eventually I watch the film.

The Lost Kiss

Come back, Dad. I have more questions.

To travel through my own bloodlines, ancestry and teachers, the whole of what has made me – to begin this journey is to begin a

A NECESSARY DISTANCE / 289

practice. A habit of regularity, returned to day after day, hour after hour. It will take forever.

Your favorite work of poetry was *The Rubáiyát of Omar Khayyam*. You memorized it frontwards and backwards. A reporter once asked you if you had a religion. You answered with this:

Myself when young did eagerly frequent
Doctor and Saint, and heard great Argument
About it and about; but evermore
Came out by the same Door as in I went.

Come, fill the Cup, and in the Fire of Spring
The Winter Garment of Repentance fling:
The Bird of Time has but a little way
To fly – and Lo! the Bird is on the Wing.

Late in life you said, "I had the best time. I worked with the best in my field, had the most beautiful wife, wrote stories that took me into worlds I would never have known." Your letters to me were always signed the same way: "Have fun." It was your benediction. Your blessing.

There is a big binder in the boxes. It has all the little pieces you wrote when you lived at PAL, the Performing Arts Lodges in downtown Toronto, with all those people from your past. Columns you wrote for the newsletter. Inside I find the story of Eleanore, your first love. The story you told us so many times, but never in detail. It seems to me it belongs here. The long view from the old man, I might call it. But your title is best.

290 / JULIE SALVERSON

THE LOST KISS
A memoir by George Salverson

On my eleventh birthday my daddy told me, son, I know you like Kamloops with its big rivers and mountains and orchards and watermelon fields, but I'm transferred to Vancouver – and that is really something you'll not only like, you're gonna *love!*

Love! If he had only known.

My daddy was a magical person – he ran the railroad. He made the trains go. He was part of a big fascinating world in which he had a name that defined his magicianship: he was a *Railroader!* Which was why he could transport his little boy to love.

All Mommy did was write novels, with strange people always coming to see her to ask how it was done, which, over the years would unexpectedly supply a prepared career to her eavesdropping little boy, Georgie.

The boy with the magical father.

Waking in a Pullman Berth, I shove up the blind and see the Fraser Valley sliding, sliding, sliding past. It's green. Such a green greenness. A greenery wonder.

Vancouver in 1928 – Wow: mountains and harbours and ships and ocean and English Bay and, yes, Robert Louis Stevenson was right: the water really is what the little boy rushes in to check – salt! This boy is ready for real magic.

Memory preceding the magic is wiped; it begins with the magic itself up what Mother (a Viking scholar) calls a fjord – Burrard Inlet. Little Georgie wakes in another berth, the top of a bunk bed. First light. Must rise. Mustn't wake somebody below. Too late!

A NECESSARY DISTANCE / *291*

Looking up at my scrambling effort is a grinning girl face. Black hair, dark eyes laughing. I hear a low friendly chocolate chuckle (in later years I would learn the word is "contralto" and would realize how lucky to have an eleven-year-old girlfriend who doesn't squeak).

The Magic Beginning

First impressions: out on the rocky cottage base sloping to the ocean water, sparkling in the morning light.

We are wrapped together in first light.

There are two sets of parents somewhere, but they are not in this first memory.

We two are alone together, two within one experience: the magic morning.

Mountains border what seems a huge river. A splendour of colours.

Out on a floating log, a sea lion watches us complacently.

There's a ship anchored out in the middle of this huge waterway. Why? Miles from Vancouver? Why? Ah, the girl and I know why. We've seen the same silent movies: we saw young Police Detective Jimmy Durante trying to save Americans from drowning in bathtub gin in the essential horror film of all time, *The Wet Parade*. That misplaced ship out in the middle of Burrard Inlet hidden away up this Viking fjord is another kind of Viking, a new kind of pirate, a rum-runner! What a wonderful place of mysteries!

Look: there's a dock. There's a rowboat. We take it, Georgie rows, the girl navigates. We mustn't get too close to the rum-runner. But somehow, we're right alongside. There's a ladder arrangement coming down. We stare up at it. A man in a uniform cap is looking down at us. The rum-runner! He speaks!

"Come on up, kids. I've got tea and cookies."

And there we are in his cabin, answering his polite questions about us, who we are, from where? I'm Georgie from Kamloops. The girl tells him I'm Eleanore Russell from Vancouver. We are careful not to ask him if he's a rum-runner (anyway, we've figured that out for ourselves).

Back in the boat we row onward over the mysterious water and find a sort of waterway side street, and come upon an astounding sight. Ships – more ships of all kinds and sizes. Abandoned. A ship cemetery. It's obviously a place for ghosts, the ghosts of dead sailors, we guess. (Never asked by us, never explained.)

Obviously two sets of parents are there, and various meals and activities, but all is wiped from memory: memory retains only the mystery of two little persons wrapped in one magic day.

We two are returning by night, standing together on a small deck at the back of a cabin cruiser. We are enclosed in experience, joined together by more wonderment. The cruiser murmurs soothingly, the wash stirred up in the ocean water hypnotizes us – it's on fire. The flowing waves are alive with light: as we stare mile after mile into the miracle of the phosphorescent night, hour by hour we are blended into one person by the mystery of this night.

A day, a night that will endure through life.

At Home with Smitten Georgie

In 1928 Little Boy Culture had simple but rigid rules regarding girls. A little boy did not associate with a little girl, or he would be condemned as a sissy. His reputation would be ruined; he would be fair game for ridiculing (sisters were necessarily exempt).

A NECESSARY DISTANCE / *293*

Now we have in 1928 an eleven-year-old boy who is supposed to hate girls forcing himself to say to his mother what he never should say to anyone. He goes into the kitchen where she is cooking (a novel in her brain, Viking vinarterta in her stove) and with a terrible effort blurts, "Can I see Eleanore again?"

A moment of surprised reaction. "Who? Oh!"

Food forgotten, novel forgotten, my mother the novelist, who understands everything about people, is looking at me with warmth (hidden humour) and love.

She's on my side.

"Why not?" she says, and shakes a frying pan.

Georgie eavesdrops a lot.

My mother and father seem to be having an argument, when they don't know little Georgie hears them. Mother: "She's the apple of his eye. He'll be living on streetcars, for God's sake." Father: Laughs. Mother: Indignant. "What's so funny?" Father: "You've got it wrong. The kid's no apple." Mother: "Oh, you insensitive unobservant Railroader!"

I am astounded. Mother insults our Railroader?

And I hear my Railroader say, "That little lady is no apple . . . she's a peach. Leave it to me."

Bike Shop

Suddenly I am with my father in the biggest bicycle store in downtown Vancouver.

"Is this the best you've got?" says my father, *The Railroader.*

"Yes sir," says the clerk, apologetically, "this CCM is the best money can buy anywhere in the world. But it is fifty-five dollars."

My father looks at me: "Okay, son?"

I nod, speechless. *Oh, yeah, Dad – you just gave me Eleanore!*

Moviegoers

We're allowed to go to the movies on Granville Street but forbidden ancient, converted stage theatres on Hastings. Parents can be strange, but both sets make it easy for us to go to every show at the magnificent Orpheum with its (Hello, Mr. Jolson!) talking pictures and amazing Vaudeville.

There's a party at our house and Vaudeville comes right in upon us, a startling lady named Mrs. Baumgartner who laughs and jokes, has everyone laughing, while Eleanore and I are surprised, having seen her on the stage and had no idea it was a real person. Her voice soars above the crowd: "If you burn your ass you gotta sit on the blister!"

Dad looks at us as if just discovering us, says, "You kids don't want all this. Go on upstairs and play."

Years later I reflected on possible interpretations. What we did, we had a pillow fight in which, to my shock, I made her nose bleed. Chuckling chocolates, she held a cloth to her nose and gave me a quote from the last talkie we'd seen, in which someone was accidentally knocked about: "Oh, you're so confectionate."

As close to the wrong interpretation as we ever got.

And what was that Vaudeville actress doing in my house? Well . . . that's how it always was with Mother, you never knew who was coming in the door. She had fans. Book fans. I finally figured (thirty years later) what Mrs. Baumgartner meant by her burning ass: it was she in Vaudeville getting burnt by the arrival of talkies.

A NECESSARY DISTANCE / 295

Shock Treatment

Except for a mysterious older brother only seen by Georgie at big parties thrown by Eleanore's parents, a close commingling developed. We kids, when not together at the movies, were together with our two sets of parents, or just with one set at a time, and the meaning and doing of it all is lost to memory, except the moment little Georgie suffered the Shock Treatment of Conflict with that Little Boy Girl Culture.

Mr. Russell is taking us somewhere, just closing their apartment door. Mrs. Russell gives me one of her looks of kindly amusement. Speaks terrible words.

"Eleanore – kiss George!"

Instant panic. Georgie looks down the long hall, ready to run. Aware of the absurdity of the reaction, looks at Eleanore in a state of total alarm.

Eleanore, the chuckle confined to her dark eyes, shakes her head slightly. She's telling her buddy Georgie he's safe with her, even from her mother's little joke.

Mr. Russell ushers us away from the moment; but never in Georgie's memory. Something had happened.

What?

Living with DeMille

Eleanore's older brother, about nineteen, Georgie sees only in the presence of tipsy flappers. During a party at Eleanore's, Georgie feels uneasy seeing Big Brother sneaking out the door with two Clara Bows and a bottle, probably going upstairs to play. I catch expressions. Eleanore's British father becomes a stiff upper lip. Her mother's face in a moment of fear instantly covered. Eleanore turning away, the laughing eyes no longer laughing.

Georgie says to Mother later, doesn't Eleanore like her own brother? "Nonsense," says Mother, "why should she like the brat, he's not her real brother." What? "No, and her mother is not her mother, but her stepmother. Her father is her father, all right; you can see where the girl gets her good looks and manners. He was an officer in the British Army, some sort of aristocrat. You can see all that in your little friend, and none of it in that so-called brother." Mother seems angry to be talking about this.

Georgie is bewildered. "Then who is her real mother?"

Mommy wants to brush this aside. "Oh, her father was stationed in Egypt. Her mother died there. She was Egyptian. Listen, this is none of our business, so just forget about it, and count yourself lucky to have such a good and lovely little friend. Go and wash up for dinner. Go on, scoot." Like that. Like Mommy is mad for having even opened her mouth. Georgie will go figure forever.

Egypt? To Georgie that exists only in movies by Cecil B. DeMille. There was this silent film, *The Moon of Israel* set in Egypt, and an Egyptian princess is falling in love with an Israeli prince, or whatever. Her face fills the screen for a long time so we can see how much she loves him. Golly, remembering this, I can imagine Eleanore working for Mr. DeMille, being an Egyptian princess.

That beautiful, mysterious face filling the screen (later I will learn to call it close-up, and even later CU. Cut to CU, Eleanore as Egyptian princess. Cut to her POV: Georgie as he watches her, absorbing this magical mystery of her, to which he has been transported by his magical father. Maybe one day she will go into the movies.

Wrong. Georgie goes into the movies. Eleanore disappears.

A NECESSARY DISTANCE / *297*

Losing Vancouver

Daddy gone somewhere. Cigar smoking professor; note taking reporter; painter with an awful gift picture; a touring Arab just like that *Valentino* movie; all passing through for tea and philosophy with Mommy. But that's the same wherever we live. Now something different in the air. Then I learn.

Daddy's been transferred again. To where? Never heard of it. Ontario.

"You'll like it," says Mommy. It has a lake as big as an ocean, and even a mountain they call the Sleeping Giant. Not much as a mountain, but lovely as a giant.

And then I'm at a Pullman window, with Mommy, and down there on the platform is the Egyptian Princess, with her step-mommy, who catches my eye and makes a smiling teary face, a friendly mockery of what she sees in me. I turn away, embarrassed, feel the train jerk, look out the window again, and Eleanore slides.

Like the Fraser Valley. Slides . . . away . . . away . . .

Away forever.

The Long After

I'm in Central School in Port Arthur on Thunder Bay (yep, a sort of mountain across the bay, unimpressive to a British Columbia kid). The teacher says, we have a new student today. "Where are you from, George?" I say "BC." The whole class gives a surprised burst of laughter. They think I came Before Christ.

Years vanish. Mrs. Russell sends pictures of thirteen-year-old Eleanore. She's okay.

More than okay. Wonderful.

More years. Suddenly Mother (no longer Mommy!) is disturbed, leaves town on the first train, then returns looking strange, not wanting to speak. Magician Father digs it out of her. Mrs. Russell came to Minnesota, sent her a message. "What, so you rush to Duluth – what kind of message was that? So you saw her?" "No."

Mrs. Russell is dead. Mother won't say how. Father (no longer Daddy) changes in a weird way. Asks no more questions. Shakes his head when young George (no longer Georgie) says, "What . . . ?" Whatever the hell it is, it's keep your trap shut time.

After hours (days?) young George dares to ask, "What about Eleanore?"

Mother gives me a long look. Then speaks, almost in a whisper.

"Eleanore's father has gone back to the British Army and has taken her away from all of us forever."

And so there's that forever again.

Time.

Mother has just won her second Governor General's Award for excellence in literature and now she's writing another. I don't pay much attention but get impressions. Her new title is "Pleasant Vices." From Shakespeare, she says – all the good titles come from Shakespeare. (Maybe she's right.) It's about a lifestyle she despises. I'm in her office borrowing notepaper and see a title page she has written by hand, with a subtitle: "The Gods are just, and of our Pleasant Vices make instruments to plague us." By it is a clipping from a Vancouver newspaper. The headline catches me.

"Three Die in Ditch."

A NECESSARY DISTANCE / *299*

I read the story. Two are girls. The cause, drunk driving. The third is Eleanore's brother.

TIME.
Strange: I'm no railroader, no magician, but I'm in my mother's profession. I return to the Vancouver scene, with all the investigative research powers of a national radio network. I use them. Nothing. Orpheum is still there, now a sort of monument. I walk (again with her) along Georgia Street, to her dance school (gone) and to her luxurious apartment building (now a parking lot). Nothing. Forever nothing.

TIME
They tell me, you're a writer – you should write. So I'm writing already, I'm writing a goodbye.

I wake in the dark of the lonely morning to something irreparable.

It's seventy-five years ago and I'm there. *We* are there. I climb down the bunk. The low chocolate laugh. We're on the rock, by the sparkling morning water, we're with the sea lion on his log, we're with the rum-runner and his teapot, we're on the Avenue of Forgotten Ships, we're locked together into the phosphorescence of the ocean water night, we're in the hall, your mother is saying "Kiss George," and George is ready to run down the hall, but you don't. Why? Why? Why not? It's gone. It's lost.

It's the end.

The Box
Poet Brian Bartlett has words that help me come to an ending, of sorts: "I think we need to make the effort, as doomed to failure as it is . . . for each thing to be itself, and for us to try to see it being itself

. . . But in the end we only scratch the surface . . . We're like mice gnawing away at some door – a door as hard as rock."

It is a damp, grey day with dirty snow in the park. Toddlers in pink and blue snowsuits are climbing the red steps to the top of the slide, then slipping down laughing. A woman walking a black dog slips on a patch of ice, regains her balance, then wiggles herself in a circle pretending to skate. Two more days left in the year.

It has no end, this unravelling. I pull out the box with the letter my father wrote to his father where he explains why he won't see George Senior anymore. He is exasperated. The old man is in rough shape, but he won't let anyone come in to look after him. There are so many more things to discover.

Under the letter, I find a greeting card to my father from Denise, the Quebecois Catholic fiancée who had owned his heart, but whose unquestioning faith in the end he couldn't accept. They'd parted tearfully at the train station in Toronto after he'd broken it off. It was terrible. I knew that part of the story. But the card is dated just weeks before they were to be married. A few years after my mother died my father pulled out a small box that held Denise's engagement ring. For the rest of his life, he kept it opened beside his computer. Bill and I got engaged the week before my father died, but I didn't get to tell him. I now wear the ring.

The last thing in the box is my own journal from 1983. I was twenty-seven and trying to make sense of political activism, civil disobedience, faith and, as it turns out, my father. My notes from that time are not untypical for a young woman. "I said today I want to cut out everything in me that's like my mother – I'm trying to appear like Dad emotionally but terrified that someone will find out I'm really like Mom. I assume Dad is feeling all these things, suffering all these things. But maybe he isn't. It strikes me I may want to be needed by my father almost as much as I want to *not* be needed by my mom."

A NECESSARY DISTANCE / *301*

One more journal. Mine. August 27, 1981. Notes at the cottage on Silver Lake, near Port Carling. "Dad is talking about his past. Sitting in the dark at the lake, where all the memories come."

The cottage is a tiny boathouse we rented from actress Ruth Springford. She owned the property and lived in the big house up the path. We are sitting on the dock. I am twenty-five, my dad is sixty-five. He watches the smoke from his cigarette.

"I come like water and like wind I go." He is quoting Omar's *Rubáiyát*. My father didn't believe in God or a creator. He took all the responsibility for his choices, his words and his actions.

"I'm supposed to sit here and let the wind blow and forget about everything. Well, that's what I am doing now. Letting it all slowly blow away."

He looks at me for a moment. As if just noticing I am here.

"I know what the future is, Julie. It's this. I made it."

George Salverson announcing the bombing of Pearl Harbor, December 7, 1941.

304 / JULIE SALVERSON

In early 2024, Julie found these photographs of her father's trip in a neglected photo album. The only figures she recognized were her father and cinematographer Grahame Woods. They may be waiting by a plane in Ghana for their equipment to be unloaded. The other photos appear to be at a wedding in the village of Ganvie in what is now Benin. One of the other men may be someone George calls Tevoedjre.

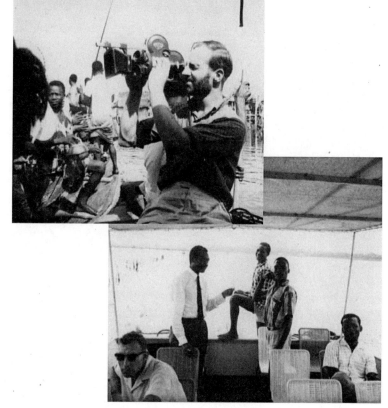

ACKNOWLEDGEMENTS

Noelle Allen for believing in this book from the beginning and being a phenomenal editor and writer's advocate. Ashley Hisson for meticulous work and patience with me! Megan Beadle for heroic copy-editing, all my thanks. And to all at Wolsak and Wynn, thank you for the years of making beautiful books. Marijke Friesen for another stunning cover.

For real help with editing, Vera DeJong in particular. Also Bill Penner and Carolyn Smart.

For reading drafts and helping me see the book it was becoming: Diana Wyatt, Kate Sykes, Lin Bennett, Richard Plant, Ruth Howard.

For loaning me homes and spaces to write: Barbara Hannigan, Mathieu Amalric, Rosemary Jolly.

Apologies to anyone I am forgetting. Seven years to make a book means lots of help of many kinds.

/ 307

SELECTED BIBLIOGRAPHY

Allan, Andrew. *All the Bright Company: Radio Drama Produced by Andrew Allan.* Kingston: Quarry Press and CBC Enterprises, 1987.

Allan, Andrew. *Andrew Allan: A Self-Portrait.* Toronto: Macmillan of Canada, 1974.

Bevins, Vincent. *The Jakarta Method: Washington's Anticommunist Crusade and the Mass Murder Program that Shaped Our World.* New York: PublicAffairs, 2020.

Drainie, Bronwyn. *Living the Part: John Drainie and the Dilemma of Canadian Stardom.* Toronto: Macmillan of Canada, 1988.

Eamon, Ross A. *Channels of Influence: CBC Audience Research and the Canadian Public.* Toronto: University of Toronto Press, 1994.

Frick, N. Alice. *Image in the Mind: CBC Radio Drama 1944 to 1954.* Toronto: Canadian Stage & Arts Publications, 1987.

Manera, Tony. *A Dream Betrayed: The Battle for the CBC.* Toronto: Stoddart, 1996.

Miller, Mary Jane. *Rewind and Search: Conversations with the Makers and Decision-Makers of CBC Television Drama.* Montreal: McGill-Queen's University Press, 1996.

Miller, Mary Jane. *Turn Up the Contrast: CBC Television Drama Since 1952.* Vancouver: University of British Columbia Press/CBC Enterprises, 1987.

O'Connor, Ryan. *The First Green Wave: Pollution Probe and the Origins of Environmental Activism in Ontario.* Vancouver: UBC Press, 2015.

Salverson, Laura Goodman. *Confessions of an Immigrant's Daughter.* Montreal: McGill-Queen's University Press, 2023. First published 1939.

Salverson, Laura Goodman. *The Viking Heart.* Toronto: McClelland and Stewart, 1923.

Julie Salverson is a nonfiction writer, playwright, editor, scholar and theatre animator. She is a fourth-generation Icelandic Canadian writer: her father, George, wrote early CBC radio and television drama and her grandmother Laura won two Governor General's Awards (1937, 1939). Julie's theatre, opera, books and essays embrace the relationship of imagination and foolish witness to risky stories and trauma. She works on atomic culture, community-engaged theatre and the place of the foolish witness in social, political and inter-personal generative relationships. Salverson offers resiliency and peer-support workshops to communities dealing with trauma and has many years of experience teaching and running workshops. Recent publications include *When Words Sing: Seven Canadian Libretti* (Playwrights Canada Press) and *Lines of Flight: An Atomic Memoir* (Wolsak & Wynn). Plays include *Thumbelina* and *The Haunting of Sophie Scholl*. She is Professor Emerita of Drama at Queen's University's DAN School of Drama and Music. https://jsalverson.wordpress.com/

Drawing by George Salverson, found by his daughter after his death. Date unknown.